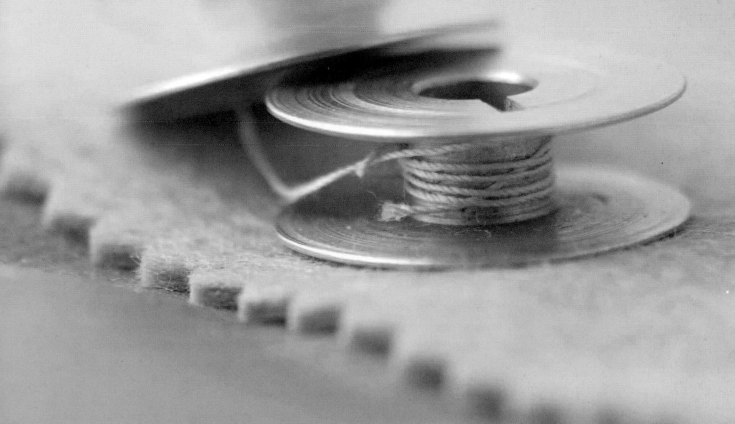

contents

introduction   6

sewing basics   8
basic techniques   24
dressmaking   52
advanced tailoring   116
home furnishings   134
care and repair   238

glossary   246
about the author   252
acknowledgements   252
suppliers   252
index   253
photo credits   256

introduction

If you are of the generation who never learned to sew at school, but whose interest has been stimulated by the 'sewing revival' of recent years (thanks to popular television series, YouTube demos, internet blogs, and exciting new magazines), this is the book you won't want to be without.

Learning to sew will not only save you money, it will also give you an outlet for your creativity, enabling you to create clothes that fit you perfectly, rediscover vintage styles, up-cycle favourite garments that may have seen better days, and furnish your home with fabulous fabrics without spending a fortune.

The Ultimate Sewing Bible is designed to cover all the information you will need to learn to sew, and to provide you with an invaluable source of reference for a range of techniques you will use constantly in your sewing projects. It is divided into seven chapters, each of which covers a specific area of sewing skill.

Sewing Basics covers the very basic details of what sewing equipment is available and its uses, and provides you with absolute confidence for getting started. It also explains how to set up a practical working area, how to store all your materials and equipment safely and conveniently, and how to choose the right sewing machine. The different compositions and construction of fabric are covered in brief, so you can become familiar with their characteristics and uses, although further information on fabrics is also covered in the Dressmaking and Home Furnishings chapters. Basic Techniques covers all of the necessary stitches, seams, and techniques that you will use time and time again, all explained with helpful step-by-step diagrams.

In Dressmaking you will master the various elements that make up a dressmaking project. In no time you will understand patterns, how to alter them to make a garment that fits, and how to make that first brave cut in the fabric. The Tailoring section covers rather more advanced skills, which will enable you to make clothes that are more structured and look extremely professional. The section on Home Furnishings will give you the skills to make everything from a simple napkin to a slipcover for a three-seat sofa.

Once you understand how everything is put together you will be able to make any item you desire using a commercial pattern and you could even develop your own projects from scratch should you wish to. At the end of the book there are some useful reference sections: Care and Repair explains how to look after and launder your projects and the Glossary is a quick reference you can return to again and again for a review of some of the more common terms used in sewing.

If you are new to sewing, start by selecting a very simple project, and use it as an opportunity to get to know your sewing machine and what is and is not possible using fabric and thread. This will give you confidence in your abilities and prepare you to try something a bit more complex, expanding your skills each time you sew. Before long you will be ready to begin using some of the more advanced techniques featured. If you don't have time for a full project, many of the techniques can be adapted to make purchased and ready-made items more 'individual'. Any kind of sewing is good skills practice and will build your knowledge, so don't be afraid to experiment. Remember, the only way to become accomplished is by sewing, sewing and more sewing!

COLLINS & BROWN

ULTIMATE

Marie
Clayton

SEWING

BIBLE

A Complete
Reference with
Step-by-Step
Techniques

sewing
basics

If you are new to sewing or have not done very much, the basics in this chapter will get you on your way. Here you will find indispensable advice on what tools and equipment are essential and what extras will be useful, while handy storage tips will help you set up an organized and inviting work area. This section also includes fundamental information about the different types and widths of fabric that are generally available.

equipment

Top-rate sewing is a combination of skills and materials. You will need a few pieces of special equipment, but most of the items are affordable, portable, and—even better—reusable. Start by purchasing the nuts and bolts: needles and pins, a tape measure, your choice of marking tools, fabric shears, and a seam ripper. Buy the best you can afford and add non-essential items as (or if) you need them.

Marking and measuring

Choosing which marking and measuring tools to use is mainly a matter of personal preference. At times, however, fabric and project types may also be factors.

Chalk pencil
This useful pencil has a chalk centre instead of lead and often incorporates a brush at one end. Marks can then be easily brushed away when they are no longer needed.

Water-erasable marker
Sponging with water or washing removes the marks made with this tool, so it may not be suitable for fabrics that must be dry cleaned or are difficult to wash.

Air-erasable marker
Marks made by this tool will slowly fade over time. The period of time it takes varies depending upon the fabric, so it may not be suitable for use on a project that will take a long time to complete.

Dressmaker's chalk
Solid chalk for marking fabric often comes in a triangular shape for ease of use and to make a range of line thicknesses.

Powdered chalk wheel
This clever utensil makes a fine chalk line on fabric, which can be brushed away. The dispenser can be refilled with different colours of chalk powder.

Pencil
An ordinary pencil is useful for marking paper patterns. A silver marking pencil shows up well on darker fabrics and can be washed off.

Tracing wheel and dressmaker's carbon
This is the quickest way to transfer continuous lines. The dressmaker's carbon is placed between the pattern and the fabric, and the tracing wheel is run along the lines to transfer lines of dots to the fabric.

Marking tips

Always test your marking tool on a scrap of the fabric you are using first to make sure the marks show up and can also be removed safely.

Transfer all the dots and notches from your paper pattern to the fabric.

There is no need to mark seam allowances—the base plate of your sewing machine has engraved lines showing the most commonly used seam widths, which you can use as a guide when stitching.

Flexible curve

Ideal for drawing curved lines, this can also be used to measure around awkward shapes.

Tape measure

A flexible tape measure is useful to take measurements of the body or any three-dimensional item.

Metal ruler

A metal ruler can not only be used as a measure but also as a reliable cutting guide that can withstand a knife blade without being damaged.

Adjustable seam gauge

This is a tremendously useful piece of equipment if you need to mark up a regular seam allowance around shaped pieces.

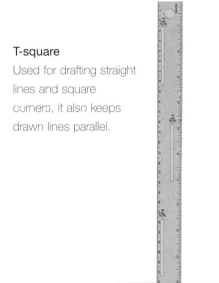

T-square

Used for drafting straight lines and square corners, it also keeps drawn lines parallel.

Plastic ruler

The big advantage of a plastic ruler is that it is transparent, allowing you to see everything as you work. Do not use it as a cutting guide, however, as sharp tools will damage its edge.

Retractable tape measure

Available in a variety of lengths, the most useful kind is marked with both metric and imperial systems. It is handy to carry around and easy to use.

Yardstick

A useful item if you need to measure lengths of fabric or things above your head height.

Calculator

If you plan to make alterations or draft your own patterns, a calculator will be invaluable to get the perfect fit.

Set square

Practical for drawing short, straight lines at right angles to a base line, set squares can be a fixed shape, as this one, or adjustable so you can change the angle of the diagonal side.

Adjustable ruler

This extends to quite a length and is also reasonably stiff, making it handy for measuring areas where a tape measure might buckle, such as windows or beneath furniture.

Cutting equipment

Achieving a clean-cut edge is crucial if you want to achieve professional-looking results. Choose the right cutting tool for the job and make sure your sewing scissors are never used for anything else!

Seam ripper

This special tool is invaluable. It has a sharp prong to push into stitches and a short curved blade to cut them. It can also be used to cut the slit for machine-stitched buttonholes.

Pinking shears

These shears have notched blades that cut in a zigzag line, which is useful to trim raw seam edges to prevent fraying.

Embroidery scissors

The short, shaped blades of embroidery scissors are designed to trim threads. Do not use your fabric shears for this, as it can also eventually blunt the blades.

Cutting tips

Make sure shears used for cutting fabric are particularly sharp and never used to cut paper other than pattern tissue. You don't want blunt blades!

Measure twice, cut once!

Rotary cutter

A cutter with a circular wheel that makes a continuous cut and can slice through several layers of fabric at a time. It is most often used to cut out numerous identical shapes for patchwork.

Small sewing scissors

A smaller pair of scissors is always handy for more delicate cutting work and to reach into difficult corners.

Dressmaker's shears

These have blades at an angle to the handles, so the blade can slide along the work surface when cutting without lifting the fabric much. This allows for more accurate cutting.

Scissors

Keep a spare pair of scissors for cutting paper and any other general cutting work.

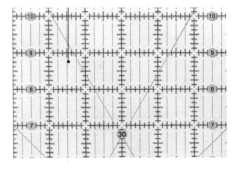

Quilter's rule

This favourite tool of many a quilter is an acrylic ruler marked with a grid of squares. It is useful for cutting small pieces of fabric, such as patchwork.

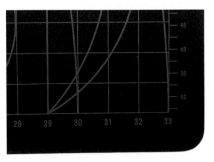

Cutting mat

You will need this for use with a rotary cutter or knife blade to protect your work surface. It is self-healing, so it can be cut into many times without showing a mark.

Hand-stitching equipment

Hand-stitching is an essential part of both dressmaking and many home furnishing projects. High-quality professional items are almost always finished by hand, even if much of the basic sewing has been done by machine.

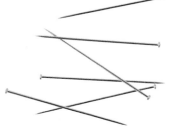

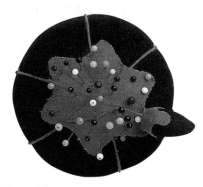

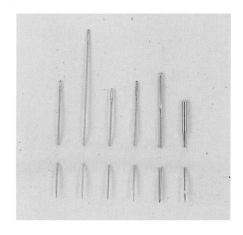

Needles

From left to right: sharps (ordinary sewing needle available in several sizes); darner (long needle for darning and basting); small-eye embroidery (for fine embroidery yarn); large-eyed embroidery (for thicker embroidery yarn); tapestry (blunt with a large eye for canvas fabric and threading ribbon or thin elastic); sewing machine needle (available in a variety of sizes and shapes for different uses).

Pins

Plain steel pins are fine for most tasks and are also available in an extra-fine thickness for delicate fabrics. To keep pins fresh and rust-free, store them in a pincushion or plastic box rather than a tin.

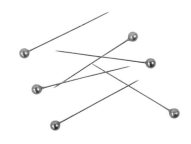

Glass-headed pins

The large, coloured heads of these pins brighten up your sewing and make them easy to spot when you need to remove them. Choose glass heads over plastic, which may melt if caught with an iron.

Pincushion

There is a wide range of pincushions available, so experiment and find what works best for you. A popular choice is the kind with an elastic strap that can be worn on the wrist, literally keeping your pins close at hand.

Basting thread

This fine cotton thread comes in a limited range of colours and is made to break for easy and swift removal of stitches when they are no longer needed. Alternatively, you can use inexpensive, ordinary, or leftover thread from your stash or from another project.

Upholstery needles

The curved tip of these needles allows you to sew through fabric that is stretched around a three-dimensional shape.

Thimble

Many people do not like thimbles, but their fingers sure do! If you do a lot of sewing you will soon get accustomed to the way a thimble feels.

Thread

Thread comes in a range of fibres—both natural and synthetic—and colours. It also comes in different thicknesses for a variety of purposes. Thicker threads are normally used for techniques like topstitching, where the stitches are visible as part of the design.

Needle threader

This priceless tool is a convenient alternative for quick and easy threading of even the smallest needle.

Bodkin

This short, blunt needle can be used to tease out sharp points and corners, and to thread thin elastic.

Pressing equipment

As well as pressing the finished item, you will often need to press your work at regular intervals throughout the sewing process—pressing seams open, for instance. You can use your regular ironing surface and steam iron for this, but there are also a couple of additional items of equipment that you may find useful.

Pressing tips

Always make a note of the care instructions for different types of fabric when you purchase them. Sometimes they can be found on the end of the bolt of cloth or woven into the selvedge.

Use a pressing cloth to avoid marking delicate items or wool.

Gently steam fabrics with a nap (see page 23) on the reverse side.

Steam iron

An ordinary household steam iron is fine, but be careful not to get water on "dry clean only" fabrics, as it may leave marks that are difficult to remove.

Tailor's ham

A rounded, three-dimensional shape, the tailor's ham is useful for pressing curved seams and awkward shapes.

Ironing board

If you are working on a large project or plan to do a lot of sewing, it makes sense to keep an ironing board close to your work space.

Sleeveboard

Put simply, this is a smaller, narrower ironing board that sits on top of the main board or on a tabletop. It is used to press narrow tubes of fabric, such as sleeves.

Special equipment

If you plan to do a lot of sewing of a particular type, you may find that some of these special pieces of equipment will make your work much easier. For home furnishings a long table and clamps are useful, while for dressmaking a dress form and a full-length mirror are critical.

Long table

A long table is invaluable when working with lengths of fabric. A folding paperhanger's table is ideal and can be packed away when not in use.

Clamps

There are several different types of clamps available—you just need to ensure that they will open wide enough to clamp onto your table and hold firmly without digging in too much and causing damage.

Presser block

Often, folds in fabric need to be gently finger-pressed rather than sharply pressed with an iron. A presser block makes the work easier on long lengths.

Full-length mirror

This is essential to check hem lengths and the general fit of garments. It's even better to have two positioned opposite each other but at a slight angle, so you can check the back view when wearing the garment yourself.

Dress forms

Dress forms are available in different sizes, or as adjustable models. Ideally the surface should be able to take a pin, so you can pin sections in place on the dummy before sewing to check the fit and drape.

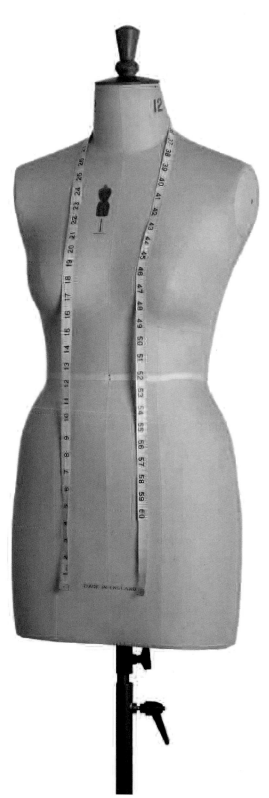

Fabric cutting tips

You can use your dining room or kitchen table, or even a clean floor, for cutting fabric, but be careful not to damage the surface.

If you want to clamp fabric but don't want to invest in special clamps just for one project, try using large office bulldog clips from any office supply or stationery store.

Useful extras

Most sewing projects do take a bit of time from start to finish, and in an ideal world you would have a room where you could leave the machine open, the ironing board up, and the work spread out until you can return to it. Unfortunately, even the most avid sewers often do not have such a space, and if you just want to make the occasional project you will not want to dedicate a whole room to it. However, with clever use of space and the wide range of storage options available, you can make a convenient workplace that can be as temporary or as permanent as you choose.

Table lamp
A flexible lamp that can be positioned to shine where you need extra light is the best option. There are also daylight lamps that are very useful if colour-matching fabrics is particularly important, and for embroidery and other coloured hand-stitching work.

Storage crates
As you build up a good stash of smaller pieces of fabric, you will need somewhere to store your collection. See-through plastic crates with lids are a good option, as they will allow you to see what you have without unpacking, and can be stacked to take up less room.

Closet
Clothes and curtains under construction should ideally be hung up between work sessions to prevent creasing. As a preventative measure, pad the hanger crossbar before draping the fabric across it. Also, try to avoid folding large pieces of fabric if possible, as the weight of the layers can cause a series of creases as well. Large lengths of fabric can be stored on cardboard rolls instead.

Transparent storage case
There are many storage options available for small pieces of miscellaneous sewing equipment. Again, a transparent style is usually best because you can see at a glance what you have. Choose a design with separate compartments or drawers so the different items can be kept apart.

Spool storage
Over time you will build up a stock of different coloured spools of thread. A storage box will keep the spools neat and their ends tangle-free.

Setting up a work space

Have suitable storage on hand so sewing projects and equipment can be stored away tidily when not in use. Alternatively, the unused space under the stairs or in the eaves can often be transformed into a perfect working area; folding doors or screens can stylishly hide all of your sewing clutter away.

You will need electrical outlets nearby for your sewing machine and iron, and adequate lighting is essential.

Make sure both your chair and table are at a suitable working height. You should be able to reach what you are working on without stretching, and your wrists should be level at a height between your waist and chest.

A chair with a straight back and no arms is best to avoid neck or back strain and to allow ease of movement.

Make sure you have all of the equipment you will need close at hand before you begin working. Don't spend too long working in one position! Get up and walk around to stretch your muscles and avoid eyestrain.

Thread rack
If your sewing machine uses larger cones of thread, there are racks available to store your stock in this size.

Bobbin storage
Your sewing machine will probably only come with one or two bobbins, but it is worth buying more so you can keep a stock of the colours you use most frequently already wound and ready to go. A bobbin storage box will keep them neat and tidy.

Sewing machines

The most expensive piece of sewing equipment you will need to purchase is a sewing machine, so it is worth taking the time to be sure you end up with one you enjoy using. Try to borrow one to make your first couple of projects. This will give you some idea of which functions you will actually need and which ones you will not. Try out different machines in the showroom and take full advantage of any professional instruction that may be offered. The instruction book will explain your specific machine, but most share some common features.

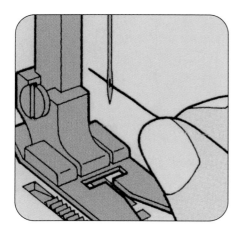

Threading the machine

Turn the hand wheel to position the needle above the plate. Insert the thread through the eye of the needle, in the direction indicated in the manual. Pull the end through, leaving it long enough so you can pull it to the back and secure it under the foot when you begin sewing.

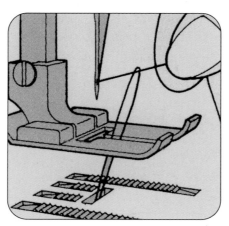

Pulling up the bobbin thread

Check the manual to see which way round to insert the bobbin into its case, pull the end of the thread through the tension spring and leave it hanging free. Put the bobbin in the machine. Make sure the needle is threaded correctly, then turn the hand wheel once. The top thread should catch the bottom thread and pull a loop back up through the plate. Pull gently on the loop to bring the loose end through to the top.

Getting the most from your machine

Sewing machines have a small built-in light that shines down on the plate and creates a bright working area. Replace the bulb immediately if it burns out, as insufficient light increases the risk of eyestrain or accidental injury.

Try to use your machine regularly, even for small tasks, to become fully familiar with it.

Check the manual to see if you need to carry out any regular minor maintenance tasks, such as adding a drop of oil or cleaning the bobbin case. Attention to these points will save on repair bills in the long term.

There are different machine needles for different tasks, just as in hand-sewing. Make sure you select the correct needle for the fabric you are working with.

Thread tension

Both top and bottom thread are held under tension as the machine stitches, and to achieve a perfect seam the tension should be the same on both sides. Modern machines often have automatic tension regulators, but some older machines may need to be adjusted by hand. This is usually done by adjusting the top tension. Most manufacturers recommend leaving the bottom tension alone, though it may be possible to adjust it in extreme cases by turning a screw in the bobbin case. To check that the tension is correct, stitch a seam on a scrap of the fabric you are using.

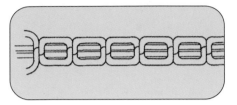  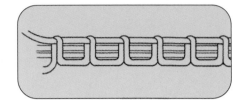

Balanced stitch

If the tension is correct, the line of stitching will look exactly the same on both sides, because the two threads cross over right in the middle of the fabric layers.

Top thread too loose

Here the bottom thread is a straight line and the top thread comes through all the fabric layers to show through on the back. Tighten the top tension with the thread adjustment control to resolve this.

Top thread too tight

Here the top thread is a straight line and the bottom thread is showing through on the back. Loosen the top tension with the thread adjustment control to resolve this.

Machine presser foot

The presser foot on a sewing machine holds the fabric firmly against the plate while the stitch is formed. It can be changed and there are many different types of feet available for different functions. Your sewing machine will come with a couple of basic alternatives and this will be all that you need to begin with, but later you might want to purchase one of the special feet if you are doing a lot of a particular type of work.

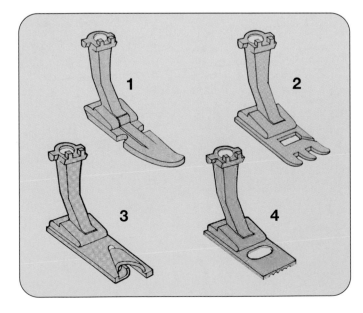

1 Zipper foot

Ideal for putting zippers in neatly. The narrow foot slides down the side of the zipper teeth instead of straddling them. Also useful for inserting piping into a seam.

2 Buttonhole foot

Useful for machine-stitched buttonholes, though many modern machines have an automatic programme to stitch buttonholes using the ordinary presser foot.

3 Hemming foot

This has a special curled piece of metal at the front, which turns under the edge of lightweight and medium fabric to create a double-folded hem as you stitch.

4 Pintuck foot

The ridges on the underside of this foot pull the fabric into a series of small tucks, which can then be stitched in neatly.

Darning/quilting/embroidery/appliqué foot

This has a small round or C-shaped end so very little of the stitching area is obscured. It is often used with the feed dog (the teeth that move the fabric along) disengaged for greater control of stitching direction.

Sergers/overlocks

Commercially sewn items are often finished inside with overlock stitching along the raw seam edges. There are special sewing machines called sergers or overlockers, which use several threads at a time and can stitch the seam, oversew the edge, and trim off any excess fabric, all at the same time. They are excellent and fast at finished seams and many other tasks, but unsuitable for some types of sewing, such as topstitching.

Using multiple threads

Sergers can stitch with several threads at a time, and the number of threads used affects what type of project the machine is most useful for. However, most machines that take a higher number of threads can be set up to use only some of them, making them more versatile.

Two-thread serger

This creates a two-thread overlocked edge, most suitable for lightweight fabrics and lingerie.

Three-thread serger

This creates a seam with some stretch capabilities suitable for any weight of fabric. A three-thread serger can often stitch a rolled hem—the machine rolls the very edge of the fabric to the underside and encloses the edge with thread—as well as sew decorative stitches and handle some special techniques.

Four-thread serger

The four-thread seam is wider and stronger. A four-thread seam is sometimes referred to as a "mock safety" stitch, since it has much of the strength of a seam made with a safety stitch or a separate seam but is not quite as strong. Again, rolled hems and decorative effects can also be achieved.

Five-thread serger

This machine is the most expensive but has many different seam capabilities: three threads are used on the overlocked edge and two are used for the straight seam line. The seam created is the same as on commercially.manufactured items, with an overlocked edge and a chain stitch straight seam. If you are doing production work, this machine eliminates the need to switch between machines for a strong seam finish.

Choosing a serger

A serger will not replace an ordinary sewing machine. If you only want one machine, go for the sewing machine. However, a serger will save you lots of time that you would otherwise spend finishing off raw edges and is useful for creating special effects. It is an excellent buy to complement your other machine if you plan to do a lot of sewing.

With some of the cheaper serger machines you may find that the fabric stretches and puckers as you stitch. Because this is a quite a common problem, be sure to try out several models before you buy.

Some sergers use standard needles, others need special ones—if so, are these easy to find when you need a replacement?

A machine with differential feed will give you more options. You can adjust the feed when working with knits to obtain a good flat seam, or if working with a single layer of woven fabric, you can speed up the feed to create a ruffle. You can also adjust the machine to create a waved-edge effect.

Both the stitch width and the stitch length on a serger can be varied. The width dictates how wide the stitch extends from the finished edge, while the length dictates the number of stitches per centimetre/inch and thus how dense the edging will be.

understanding fabrics

There is such a wide variety of different types of fabric available today, in both natural and synthetic yarns, that they cannot all be featured here. However, there are some factors that are common to ranges of fabric, such as structure—woven, knitted, or non-woven—and available widths. If you are using patterned fabric or one with a pile or nap, you also need to be aware of pattern repeats and the direction of the raised surface, and take these into account when purchasing fabric and planning your project.

Woven fabrics

All woven fabrics are made up of two sets of yarn: the warp and the weft. The warp runs lengthwise in the loom, and is sometimes known as the floating yarn or threads. The weft runs widthwise at right angles to the warp, and is sometimes called the filling yarn, filler, or woof. Woven fabrics can be created with different patterns by using different sequences of warp and weft yarns. The selvedge is the border that runs lengthwise down both edges of a length of woven fabric. Since it is often woven more tightly than the main fabric to stop it fraying, the selvedge may pucker when the fabric is cleaned; therefore, it is generally discarded for sewing projects. The lengthwise and widthwise directions—or grains—of a woven fabric are firm, so fabric has very little give in these directions. However, if pulled diagonally—or on the bias—the fabric will stretch. True bias is at a 45-degree angle to the selvedge.

Knitted fabrics

All knitted fabrics are constructed using one set of yarn running in the same direction. This is possible because the yarn looping around itself holds knit fabrics together. Some knits have their yarn running along the length of the fabric, others have their yarn running across the width of the fabric. The columns of stitches that run the length of a knitted fabric are called wales, and the stitches running across form rows. Because of its construction, knitted fabric has some give in every direction, making it ideal for form-fitting garments. It is used less often for furnishings.

Non-woven fabrics

This category includes fabrics such as felt, interfacing, lace, and net. Machine-made felt is made of compressed wool or acrylic fibre; it does not fray and can be moulded to a shape. Handmade felt is made from pure wool fleece, which is laid out in a design and then rubbed with warm soapy water so the fibres mesh together into a solid mass. Handmade needle felt is also made of wool fleece, which is stabbed repeatedly with a special needle until the fibres mat together into a solid mass. Knitted fabrics can also be felted by being washed at high temperatures and then tumble dried; this process is also known as fulling.

Interfacing is a compressed synthetic fabric used as a backing to the main project fabric, particularly in dressmaking and tailoring, to give extra body, shaping, and support.

Lace and net are made of yarns that are knotted into intricate patterns, and can either be machine or handmade.

Standard fabric widths

Fabrics are available in standard widths, but different types of fabrics have different standards. For instance, printed cotton used for dressmaking is usually 90 cm (36 in), 115 cm (45 in), or sometimes 137 cm (54 in) wide, but voiles for curtains may be 300 cm (120 in) wide, while pure silk may only be 45 cm (18 in). Some manufacturers weave in metric and some in imperial, so conversions may not be exact. For instance, a fabric woven on a 36-inch loom may be labelled as being 90 cm wide, but will actually be slightly wider. In the U.K., the conversion from imperial to metric has also meant some variety in the standards: a fabric that is woven on a 54-inch loom will actually be 137 cm wide, but the nearest round number for a metric loom is 140 cm, which is actually 55 in. For this reason it is important to measure the width yourself before purchasing if it is critical to your project.

Standard fabric widths	
45 cm (18 in)	137 cm (54 in)
90 cm (36 in)	140 cm (55 in)
112 cm (44 in)	150 cm (60 in)
115 cm (45 in)	300 cm (120 in)

Fabric buying tips

Check the fabric width yourself before purchasing if it is critical to your project. Metric/imperial conversions are not always exact and some speciality fabrics may come in unusual widths.

Remember to purchase an extra amount for matching if you are using a fabric with a pattern, pile, or nap. To figure out how much extra you will need, see page 23.

Buy thread and fabric at the same time; it is easier to match the colour with the fabric at hand.

Pattern repeats

If you are using patterned fabrics and will be joining pieces together, you will need to match up the motifs in the design across the seam, particularly if you are making something like curtains or bedcovers requiring several widths of fabric. In most patterned fabrics, whether woven or printed, the same motif or design will be repeated again and again down the length and across the width of the fabric; the distance between these is called the repeat. The pattern repeat measure may be given on the bolt of fabric, or you can measure it yourself: either measure from the tip of one motif to the corresponding tip of the next along the length, or if it is a circular motif use an easily identifiable point in the design instead.

If the pattern repeat is quite small, you will probably be able to match the design without additional fabric, but if it is large you will need to think in multiples of the repeat. To do this, measure the length you need, divide this by the repeat, round the resulting figure up to the next full number, then multiply this by the repeat again to get the length you need in complete pattern repeats. For instance, if you are making curtains with a drop of 230 cm (92 in) and have worked out that you need 4 widths, with no repeat you would simply need length of drop x number of widths = 920 cm (368 in) of fabric. However, say your pattern repeat is 35 cm (14 in). First divide the drop by the repeat to get the number of repeats: 230 divided by 35 = 6.57; round up to the nearest number, which in this case is 7, then multiply the repeat by this number, so 35 x 7 = 245 cm (644 in). Therefore each drop needs to be 245 cm (98 in) and for your four widths you would need 980 cm (392 in) of fabric. As you can see, the repeat can make quite a difference! For how to handle pattern repeats when laying out paper patterns for dressmaking, see page 59.

Nap and pile

These types of fabric have a raised surface. Depending on which way the light falls on the fabric or in which direction it is smoothed, the fabric will look lighter or darker. This means that the nap or pile should run in the same direction on each part of a garment or furnishing project, or it will look as if it has been made with two different colours of fabric. (Of course, this could also be utilized as part of the design.) With napped fabrics the short fibres have been brushed in one direction, while the pile on a fabric is created by raised threads or loops on the surface. Patterns may give special cutting layouts to allow for nap or pile, and may specify an extra amount of fabric.

basic techniques

The basic skills in this chapter are here to help you. Keep referring to them until you are confident that you have mastered them. The hand and machine stitches you will use time and again are all explained in detail, and this section also contains instructions for some decorative stitches, types of seams, and different methods of finishing off edges.

stitches and seams

Stitches are formed by passing a needle and thread through one or more layers of fabric, either to decorate or to join pieces together. Some stitching is designed to be on show, other types are supposed to be invisible. Stitching is a basic skill needed for all types of sewn projects.

Handsewn stitches

Although many projects can be made almost entirely on the sewing machine, there will almost certainly be some hand stitching required. The basic handsewn stitches are very easy to do.

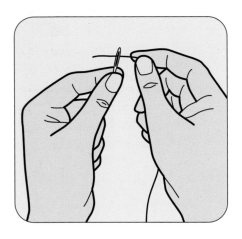

▲ **Threading the needle**

Cut the thread with sharp scissors; it's much harder to thread with a ragged end. Hold the needle in the left hand and the thread in the right hand between thumb and index finger. Pass the end of the thread through the eye of the needle and with the same motion pass the needle into the right hand and use the left hand to pull the thread through and down.

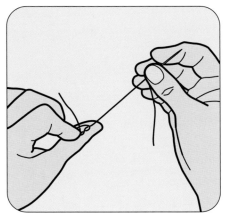

▲ **Quick knotting**

The most common method to secure a length of thread before you begin stitching is to make a knot at the end. Hold the threaded needle in your right hand, pressing against the eye so the thread cannot slip out. Take the other end of the thread in your left hand and use your right hand to bring the thread right around the tip of the index finger to cross over the thread end. Use your left thumb to roll the loop off your finger into a knot.

Thread tips

Always sew with a thread no more than approximately 60 cm (24 in) in length, as a longer thread will weaken and tangle as it is repeatedly pulled through the fabric.

Most hand sewing will be done with a single thread, but for added security you may wish to use a double thread to sew on buttons or other fasteners.

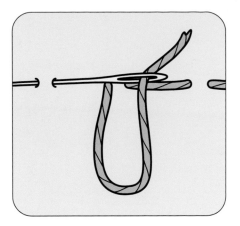

▲ Tacking or basting

This is a technique used to temporarily hold layers of fabric together for fitting or to prevent slipping as seams are stitched. It is traditionally done with large, single-thread stitches and is removed after the final sewing has been completed. Knot one end of the thread and work a long running stitch through all the layers of fabric.

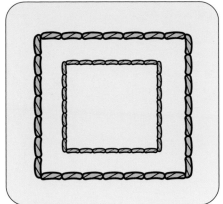

▲ Backstitch

A row of small, evenly-spaced hand stitches ideal for securing seams and mending. Take the needle in and out of the fabric, then begin the next stitch a short distance behind the point where the thread emerged, and out again the same distance ahead. For each subsequent stitch, the needle enters the fabric at the end of the previous stitch so the stitches run end to end like machine stitching.

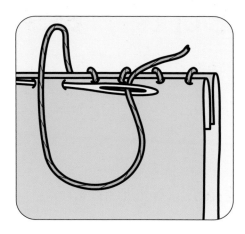

▲ Slipstitch

A stitch usually used to join folded edges, which should be almost invisible. Lay the pieces one on top of the other, folded edge to folded edge, and bring the needle through the folded edge of the bottom piece from the back so the knotted end is secured inside the fold. Take a tiny stitch through the edge of the top fold, then go back into the top layer of the bottom piece of fabric and slide the needle a little way along inside the fold to come out again on the edge. Continue in this way until the seam is complete.

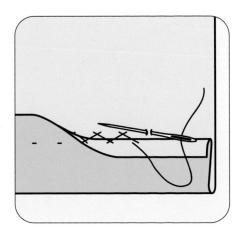

◀ Herringbone hemming

This is worked from left to right in a series of diagonal stitches up and down, crossing slightly at top and bottom. Secure the thread end in the folded hem, then take a long diagonal stitch and catch a few threads of the single layer of fabric in a tiny backstitch. Go back diagonally in the opposite direction and take a backstitch through the folded layer, but not through to the front surface. Repeat along the hem. There should only be a tiny stitch showing on the right side of the fabric. It is useful for heavy or stretch fabrics, as the stitches are more flexible than in hemming and will give slightly.

Stitching tips

Herringbone hemming is ideal to use on children's clothing as it is not easy to pull down and will withstand the rough and tumble of life.

Use contrasting thread for any stitches that will later be removed, so they are easy to spot and can be distinguished from seam stitching.

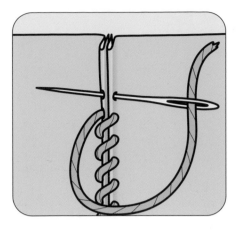

▲ Oversewing

Also known as overcasting or overstitching. A row of diagonal hand stitching done over raw edges, particularly of a seam, to prevent fraying or ravelling. For a neater finish, fold the raw edges before overcasting them together. It can also be done by machine, and some sewing machines even have a special setting.

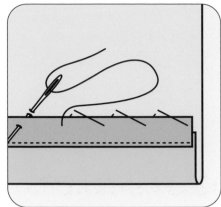

▲ Slant hemming

Also known as slipstitch hemming, this is worked from right to left to join a fold to a flat piece of fabric. Secure the end of the thread in the fold on the wrong side. Take a tiny, inconspicuous stitch in the single layer of fabric through just a few threads, then make a stitch through the fold about 6 mm (¼ in) long. Repeat along the length of the hem.

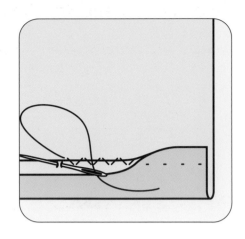

▲ Blind hemming

Hemming stitch worked under the flap of a hem or behind a facing. Roll the edge of the hem or facing back at the stitching point, and pick up one thread from the single layer of fabric, then another diagonally above from the underside of the hem or facing. Don't pull the stitches tight, or a pucker will show on the right side of the fabric.

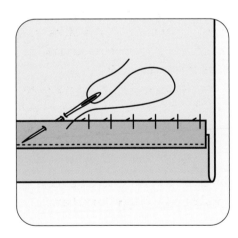

▲ Vertical hemming

A hand-sewing stitch used for all types of hems to secure a folded edge to a flat piece of fabric. Secure the end of the thread inside the fold on the wrong side. Take a tiny, inconspicuous stitch in the single layer of fabric, then take the needle diagonally up through the folded edge. Continue in this way, spacing the stitches about 6mm (¼ in) apart.

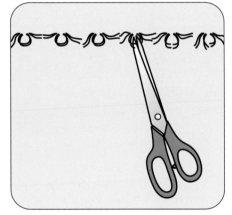

▲ Tailor's tacks

Used to transfer symbols from pattern to fabric. Using a double thread, take the needle through the symbol and both pieces of fabric, leaving a long tail. Make a small backstitch leaving a large loop. Bring the needle to the front, leaving another long tail; cut the thread. Cut loops and detach the pattern. Separate the layers of fabric and snip the tacks between them leaving tufts of thread as a marker.

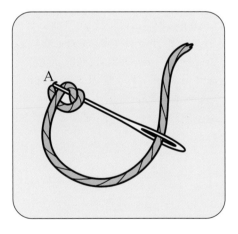

▲ Finishing off

Used at the end of a row of stitching or when the thread has run out. Take a small stitch on the wrong side of the fabric, wrap the thread several times around the point of the needle, then pull the needle through the wrapped threads to form a knot close to the surface of the fabric.

Decorative hand stitches

Given the current trend for embellishing, it is useful to be able to work a few simple embroidery stitches. As you learn more, these can also be combined to make more complex stitches.

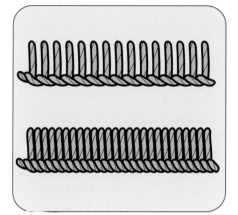

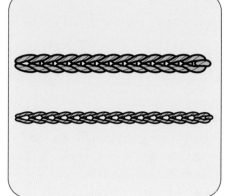

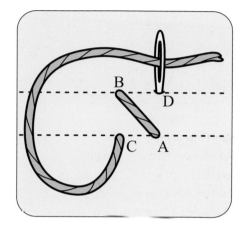

▲ **Blanket/buttonhole stitch**

Primarily a border stitch to finish off raw edges, but can also be used as a decorative feature. The needle goes into the fabric at an even distance from the edge each time, coming out on the edge, and the thread is carried round the point of the needle at each stitch. Blanket stitch is worked with the vertical stitches set apart from each other. Buttonhole stitch is exactly the same technique but the vertical stitches abut each other.

▲ **Chain stitch**

Chain stitch is commonly used to create lines. It has many variations, including lazy daisy stitch, in which the stitches are worked in a circle to create a flower. Take the needle in and out of the fabric at the same point, leaving a loop of thread. Bring the needle back up through the loop and pull the loop tight, then take the needle back though the fabric at the same point, leaving a loop to form the next stitch. Repeat.

▲ **Cross stitch**

This basic embroidery stitch is found all over the world and is a simple x shape that is useful to fill areas or create geometric designs. It is also known as Berlin stitch, sampler stitch, and point de marque, and has a host of variations. It can be worked by making a diagonal stitch, then coming down vertically underneath the fabric to work the second diagonal, in which case the reverse shows a series of parallel lines. In two-sided cross stitch, alternate diagonal stitches are worked before going back over the line to complete the missing stitches, so both sides of the fabric show the x shape.

Creative stitching

The simplest embroidery stitches can be combined to make more complex patterns. Try running a double line of a particular stitch, then weaving a contrasting colour between the two.

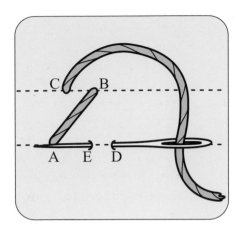

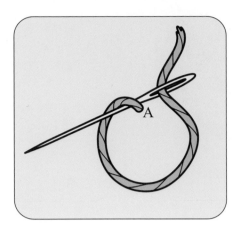

▲ Herringbone stitch

A basic embroidery stitch with many alternative names. Worked from left to right, it is a series of diagonal up-and-down stitches that cross slightly at the top and bottom. Take a small horizontal stitch from right to left, then take a long diagonal stitch from left to right. Take another small horizontal stitch at the lower level from right to left, and another long diagonal stitch in the opposite direction from left to right.

▲ French knots

The French knot is very versatile. It can be worked on its own as a detail, grouped closely together to form a textured area such as a flower centre; worked in a row as a border; or scattered across an area as a filling stitch. Come up through the fabric and wrap the thread around the needle counterclockwise twice. Push the wraps together and slide to the end of the needle, then insert the needle close to where it came out and pull through to form a knot.

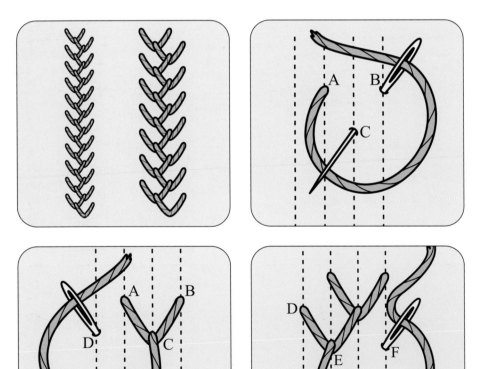

◀ Feather stitch

Feather stitch was a popular decoration on English smocks. It is worked downward, making V-shaped stitches that alternate from side to side to create a feathery line. It is also known as plumage stitch and briar stitch. Come up through the fabric and then down through it again horizontally to the right a short distance away, leaving a loose loop on the surface. Come up in the centre of the loop and slightly below, catching the loop and pulling it down to form a V. Repeat, working left this time.

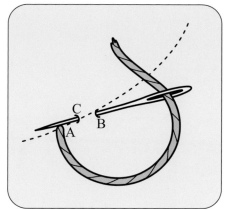

◀ **Stem stitch**

One of the basic embroidery stitches, used to outline motifs and to create the stems of leaves and flowers. It is worked along a line with the stitches slightly diagonal and the beginning of one stitch slightly overlapping the end of the previous one. When worked correctly, there should be a neat row of backstitch on the reverse. Keep the stitches even and be sure to keep the thread below the needle as you work.

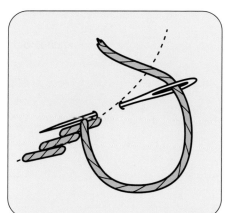

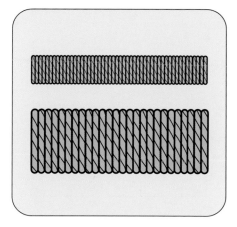

▶ **Satin stitch**

One of the basic embroidery stitches, used as a filling stitch and as the basis for a wide variety of more complex stitches. Satin stitch is made up of a series straight stitches worked very closely together to create a smooth surface with no fabric showing beneath. For best results, stretch the fabric on a hoop or frame to keep it taut as you work. It is also sometimes known as damask stitch.

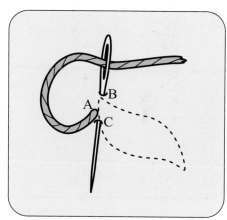

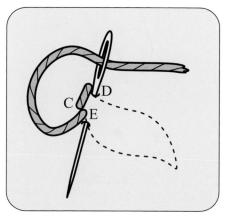

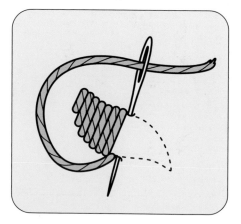

Embellishments

Many sewn items can be quickly and easily customized by stitching on purchased embellishments, such as buttons or sequins.

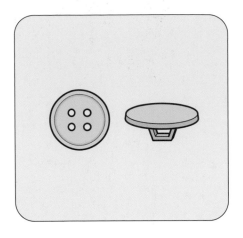

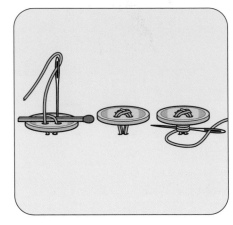

1 ▲ **Buttons**
Some buttons have a loop or shank on the back, which you sew through to attach the button. It also holds the button above the surface of the fabric to allow for the thickness of the upper fabric layer. Other buttons must be stitched through the holes provided and may require a thread shank.

2 To make a thread shank, place a matchstick or toothpick on top of the button and sew over it. Remove the stick, lift the button, and wind the thread around the extra length of thread between the button and the garment. Bring the needle to the underside of the garment and fasten with several small stitches.

▶ **Sequins**
Small pieces of mirrored material made of metal or plastic, usually round, with a central hole for stitching or threading. Sequins come in a range of shapes and sizes and may be flat or faceted. There are two methods of stitching them on: method one is quick and simple but the thread shows and the edge of the sequin may cut the thread in time; method two is slower but looks better and is more secure in the long run.

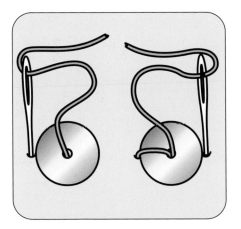

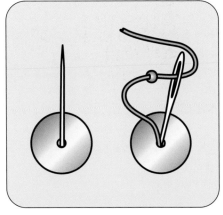

1 Using thread to match the colour of the sequin, come up through the centre hole with your needle and thread, over one side of the sequin and back down into the fabric. Repeat on the opposite side so the two stitches run straight across the sequin.

2 Using thread to match the colour of the sequin, come up through the centre hole with your needle, then thread on a tiny clear glass bead—the smallest size that the needle will go through, but bigger than the hole in the sequin. Take the thread around the bead and back down through the hole in the sequin.

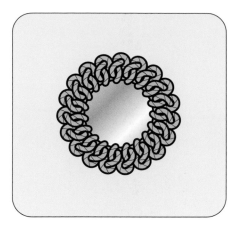

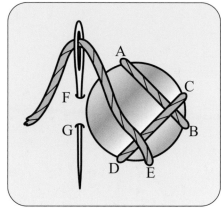

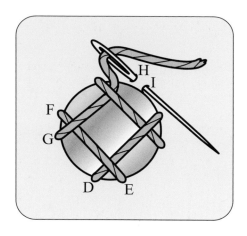

▲ **Shisha mirrors**

Shisha mirrors are small pieces of reflective mica used in embroidery. They are attached to fabric with a special stitch, which covers the edges entirely and leaves a round mirror showing.

1 Working over the mirror, make four stitches to create a diamond-shaped grid.

2 When you take the last stitch, slide the needle under the end of the first one for symmetry.

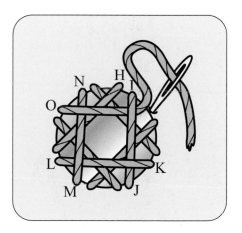

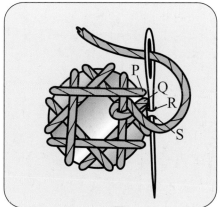

3 Work four more stitches over the first four in the same way, but at a 90° angle.

4 Come up through the fabric again, right next to where the needle went in. Take the needle under and back over the intersection of the vertical and diagonal stitches, then down into the fabric again at the edge of the mirror a little further round. Repeat, weaving around the crossed threads, until you have worked all around to cover the edge of the mirror.

Sequins and beads come in lots of different shapes and sizes and are ideal to add a flash of glitter to your sewing projects.

Handsewn loops and tacks

Loops and tacks are used as part of fasteners, as removable markers, or to reinforce the end of a seam or pleat.

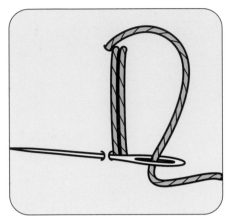

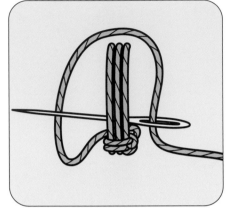

1 ▲ **Thread loop**
Secure the end of the thread on the wrong side of the fabric at one end of the loop. On the right side, take three or four stitches close together the length you want the loop to be. Take a couple of small stitches under the other end of the loop to secure.

2 Without taking the needle through the fabric at any time, work buttonhole stitches very close together over all the threads of the long stitches. Use the tip of the needle to ease the stitches together tightly as you work.

3 The finished thread loop should be firm and neat from end to end. Small thread loops can be used as the loop for a hook, and longer ones made with heavy-duty thread can be used as belt loops.

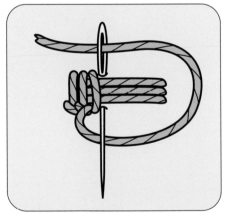

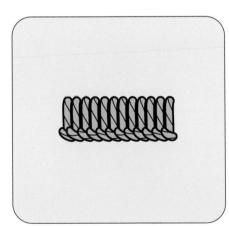

1 ▲ **Bar tack**
Secure the end of the thread on the wrong side of the fabric at one end of the bar tack. On the right side of the fabric, take three or four stitches very close together the length that you want the bar tack to be.

2 Work buttonhole stitches very close together over the threads of the long stitches, picking up several threads of the fabric underneath at the same time. Make sure the stitches are right up tight together as you work.

3 Bar tacks can be used to reinforce any area that may come under strain and can be made to any length. Very small bar tacks are worked across both lines of stitching at one end of a buttonhole to reinforce it, usually without the added buttonhole stitch.

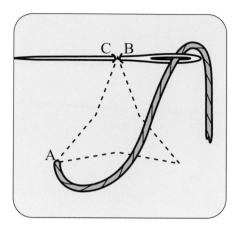

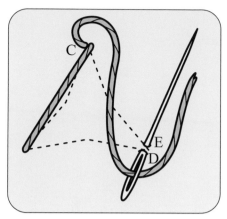

1 ▲ Crow's foot
Secure the end of the thread on the wrong side of the fabric and bring the thread to the right side at the bottom left corner of the triangle. Take a tiny stitch across the top point of the triangle, from right to left, then go across to the bottom right corner and take another tiny stitch from bottom to top across the point.

2 Going back to your starting point at bottom left of triangle, take a tiny stitch from top to bottom under the first stitch made and within the triangular shape. Take a tiny stitch across the top point of the triangle again, from right to left just below the previous one, then go across to the bottom right corner and take another tiny stitch from bottom to top across the point, just to the left of the previous one.

3 Carry on working in this way until the entire triangle is covered. Crow's foot tacks are used in the same way as arrowhead tacks.

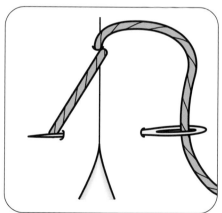

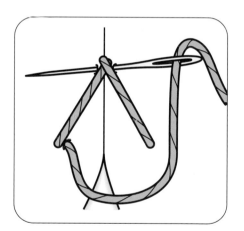

1 ▲ Arrowhead tack
Secure the end of the thread on the wrong side of the fabric and bring the thread to the right side at the bottom left corner of the arrowhead tack. Take a tiny stitch across the top point of the arrowhead triangle, from right to left, then take the needle back into the fabric at the bottom right corner.

2 Bring the needle back out of the fabric just to the right of your starting point at bottom left of the arrowhead, then take a tiny stitch at the top again, just below the stitch made last time and within the triangular shape. Take the needle back into the fabric at the bottom right corner, slightly to the left of where you came out last time.

3 Carry on working in this way until the entire triangle is covered. Arrowhead tacks are used on tailored garments to reinforce the ends of pockets and pleats.

Stitches for curtain making

Curtain making has its own special stitches, used to attach flat layers of fabric together, add fixings, and secure pleats or linings.

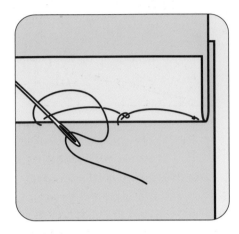

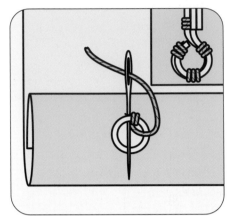

▲ **Professional tip**

Attaching the different layers of a curtain together so they move as one piece of fabric will dramatically improve the drape of your curtains and make the finished result look much more professional.

▲ **Locking-in stitch**

Fold the top layer of fabric back along a straight line from top to bottom of the curtain, starting around 15 cm (6 in) from one edge. Secure the end of the thread where it will not be seen on the face of the curtain. Take a tiny stitch through the fold, then take a stitch in the bottom flat fabric, picking up just a few threads. Repeat around 15 cm (6 in) away to make a long, loose stitch, taking the needle behind the thread each time to lock the stitch in place. Use this method to attach the interlining (if any) to the main fabric and again to attach the lining to the interlining.

▲ **Couching stitch**

Couching is used to attach small curtain fixings that may be required. Place the item flat against the fabric. Using double thread, secure the end of the thread then take several stitches over the item close together at one point. Take the thread under the item and repeat a short distance away, if required. Rings can be anchored at only one point, but hooks should have several fixing points around the bottom ring and along the straight section below the hook.

▼ **Stabbing stitch**

With pleated headings, several layers of fabric need to be pulled together and secured. Secure the end of the thread on the wrong side, then pull the fabric into the required pleat and take a couple of very small stitches straight through, working through all the layers at one point. The stitch should be as inconspicuous as possible and the pleat should fan out gently above and below it.

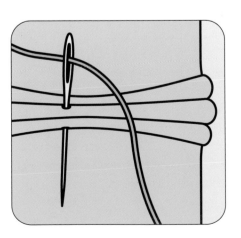

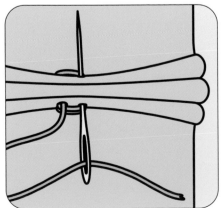

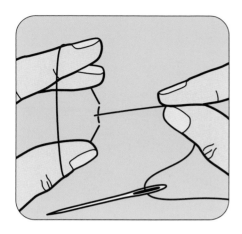

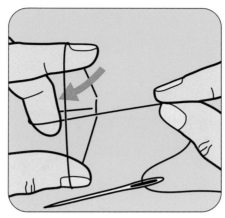

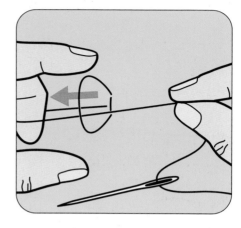

1 ▲ **Chain-stitch thread**
Use this technique to link curtain and lining. Secure the thread on the inside of the curtain at the top of the hem. Take a small stitch, then take another small stitch but do not pull the thread right through; leave a large loop on the right side. Hold this loop open between thumb and finger of the left hand and hold the stitching thread with your other hand.

2 Use the third finger of your left hand to reach through the loop, hook the stitching thread, and pull it through to form a new loop.

3 Let go of the original loop, keeping hold of the new one, and pull the stitching thread gently to tighten it around the thread near the surface of the fabric. Repeat steps 2 and 3 until the chain is around 5 cm (2 in) long. Pass the needle through the last loop to lock the chain, then take a small stitch in the hem on the reverse of the lining and fasten off. Catch the two layers of fabric together at intervals in this way.

Machine stitching

These basic machine stitches will be used throughout all sewing projects. Practice them on different weights and types of fabric.

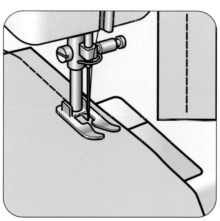

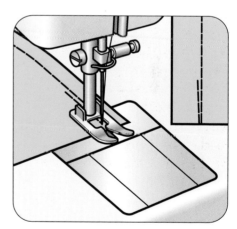

▲ **Straight stitch**
A row of simple, straight stitches spaced slightly apart. Straight stitch can be used to join seams and to finish the edges of seams on knit fabrics. For most seams, the stitch length on the machine should be set to around 2 or 3.

▲ **Backstitch**
The reverse stitch on the sewing machine, used to reinforce the stitching at the beginning and end of a seam. Start off around 12 mm (½ in) from the beginning of the seam and reverse stitch back to the edge, then start stitching forward as normal. At the end, finish by reversing back along the stitching line for 12 mm (½ in).

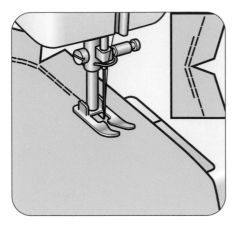

▲ Staystitching

A line of straight stitching within the seam allowance and through only a single thickness of fabric. It is used to hold stretch fabrics or curved lines, such as a neckline, in their original shape and prevent them from stretching as the garment is fitted.

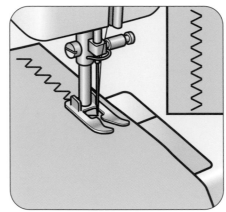

▲ Zigzag

Most modern sewing machines have an automatic zigzag function. Zigzag stitching can be adjusted as normal stitching can: the stitch width controls the width of the zigzag band and the stitch length controls how tightly together the stitches fall. Zigzag stitch is used to finish raw edges and for seams that need some give, such as knit fabrics.

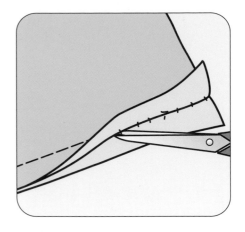

▲ Machine tacking

Also known as machine basting. Like hand tacking, this is used to join fabrics temporarily. Set the stitch length to the longest possible, loosen the tension, and do not backstitch the seam at either end. To make the stitching easier to remove at the end, you can snip through a stitch every 5 cm (2 in) or so.

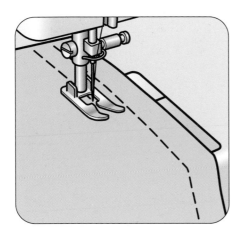

▲ Gathering stitch

Gathering using a machine stitch gives a more even result. Set the stitch length at its longest and loosen the tension slightly. Stitch once just inside the seamline, then again in a parallel line a very short distance away.

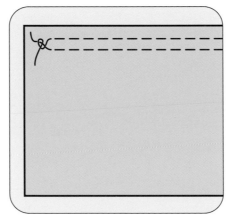

Tie the two top threads together on the right side of the fabric at one end, then tie the two bobbin threads together on the wrong side at the same end.

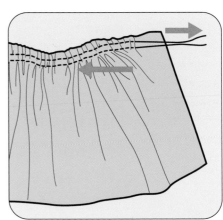

Pull both bobbin threads together at the untied end to gather up the fabric, easing the fabric along gently as you go. Adjust the gathers evenly along the required length, then fasten off the bobbin threads.

Machine seams

The type of seam you choose for a project will be determined by the fabric, but also partly by the effect you want to achieve. For instance, flat fell seams were originally designed to give a strong join on heavy-duty fabric subject to a lot of wear, but are now often used purely for effect.

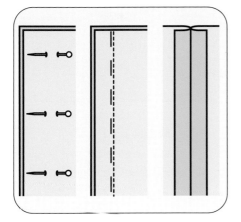

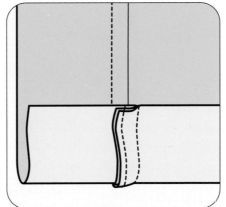

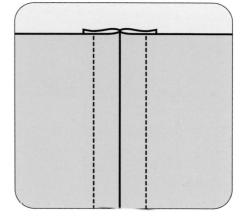

▲ **Flat seam**

Pin the pieces of fabric right sides together. You can either mark the seamline or use the guides engraved on the sewing machine footplate to achieve an even seam allowance. For complex seams or slippery fabrics, it may be safer to tack the pieces together by hand before stitching. Sew the seam on the machine using a simple straight stitch with a short run of backstitching at each end to secure. Finally, remove the tacking threads and press the seam, either opened out flat or to one side, as instructed.

▲ **Single topstitched seam**

This is a seam with an extra row of topstitching made on the right side. Although decorative, it can be functional; it can hold the seam allowance in place and prevent fraying. Press the seam allowance to one side. Use either a matching or a contrasting thread and stitch with a small- to medium-length stitch.

▲ **Double topstitched seam**

A double topstitched seam has a row of topstitching on either side of the seam. Press the seam allowance flat on the wrong side, then topstitch down both sides on the right side, making sure that the topstitched seams are an equal distance from the seamline.

Seam finishing

Finishing the raw edges of the seams inside an item is just as important as the finishing touches to the outside. See page 42 for suggested techniques.

Finished seams not only give a garment a more professional look, they also prolong its life. Always sew knitted fabrics with a ballpoint needle, as this will tend to slide between the fibres and not through them.

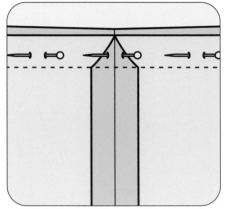

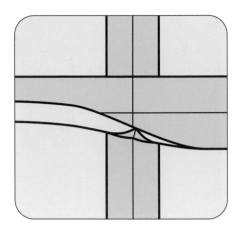

1 ▲ **Intersecting seams**
Start by matching the seamlines on the two sections exactly, so they will run straight across the new seam at a right angle. To reduce the bulk of the extra thicknesses of fabric at the intersection, cut the seam allowances of the original seams into a point on both sides.

2 Pin on the seamlines to hold the sections in line, then pin or tack the rest of the new seam. Sew the new seam with a flat seam.

3 Press the new seam open. On the right side, the four seams should form a perfect cross shape with right angle lines.

Turning the corner

To achieve a neat turn in a seam, stitch to the point at which you need to turn. Leaving the needle down in the fabric, lift the presser foot, swivel the work around to the new direction, lower the presser foot, then start stitching again.

Trimming excess fabric from the corner before you turn the item right side out will give a sharper point. See page 43 for clipping techniques.

Knitted fabrics have more stretch than woven ones and seams need to have some give so the thread does not break. Use a zigzag stitch with a narrow stitch width and a medium length to sew the seam, or use an overlocker.

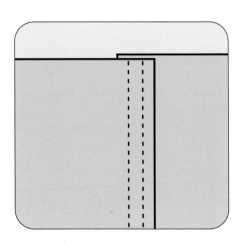

▲ **Lapped seam**
This type of seam can be used on interfacing and interlining to reduce bulk, and also for fabrics that do not fray, such as leather. For interfacing and interlining, simply lap the edges over one another with the seamlines meeting in the centre, and stitch together along the seamline. For other materials such as leather, trim off the seam allowance along the edge of the upper piece, line up the newly cut edge with the seamline on the lower piece, and stitch together with a double row of straight stitch.

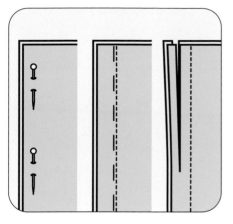

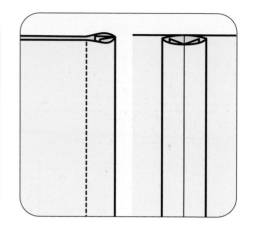

1 ▲ French seam

With WRONG SIDES together, stitch the seam only 12 mm (½ in) from the edge. Trim the seam allowance to a scant 3 mm (⅛ in) and press open.

2a Fold the fabric right sides together along the stitching line you have just made. Pin and stitch a second seam on the seam line, enclosing the raw edges of the fabric.

2b From the wrong side, press the seam to one side, or you can press it flat. A French seam is ideal for sheer fabrics as it conceals the raw edges of the seam.

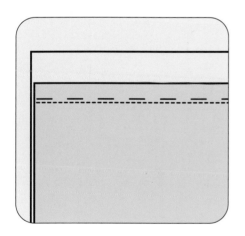

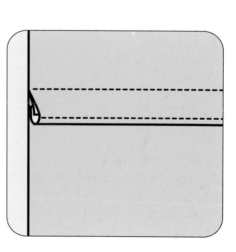

1 ▲ Flat fell seam

With WRONG SIDES together, stitch the seam only 12 mm (½ in) from the edge. Trim the seam allowance on one side only to a scant 3 mm (⅛ in) and press open.

2a Turn under 6 mm (¼ in) along the edge of the top untrimmed seam allowance and tack in place on the right side of the garment over the trimmed edge.

2b Stitch the seam again close to the fold, through the top seam allowance and the garment.

Seam finishes

Stitching or otherwise securing the raw edges of the seam allowance will give your seams a more professional look. It will also prolong the life of garments by protecting the edge of the seam during everyday wear. The different seam finishes below are noted with suggestions as to where they can be best used.

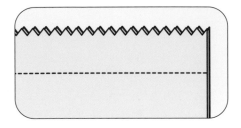

▲ Pinked seam

Stitch the seam, trim both the raw edges with pinking shears, then either press open or to one side. Use for most seams as long as the fabric does not fray.

▲ Double-stitched

Stitch the seam, press, then make a second line of stitching right next to the first within the seam allowance. Use for seams subject to strain.

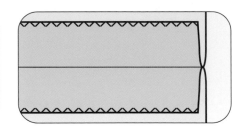

▲ Zigzag stitched

Press open then zigzag stitch along each raw edge. If the seam is pressed to one side, zigzag both raw edges together. For most seams, and fabrics that may fray.

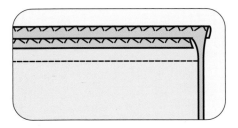

▲ Turned and zigzagged

Turn under a very narrow hem along each raw edge and zigzag along the fold. Use for lightweight fabrics or fabrics that tend to fray.

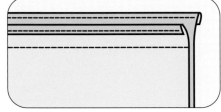

▲ Edge stitched

Turn under a very narrow hem along each raw edge and straight stitch along the fold. Use for light to medium-weight fabrics only.

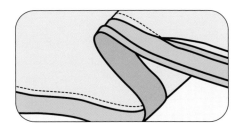

▲ Bias bound

Enclose the raw edge in a strip of bias binding and stitch through the binding close to the edge. If the seam must be pressed open, work both edges separately. If it is pressed closed both seams can be enclosed in the same strip of binding. Can be used for most seams, but particularly those on heavyweight fabrics that may fray.

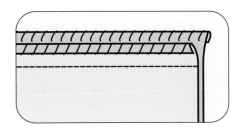

▲ Hand oversewn

Turn under a very narrow hem along each raw edge and oversew evenly by hand along the edge. Best for heavier fabrics.

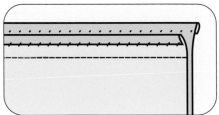

▲ Hand hemmed

Turn under a very narrow double hem along each raw edge and hem. Good for delicate fabrics.

Clipping corners

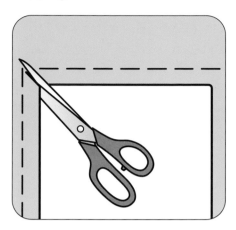

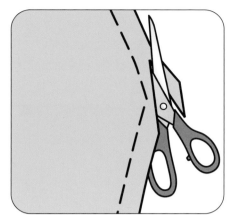

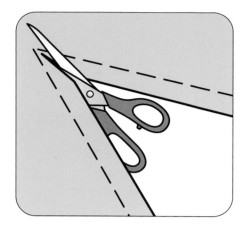

▲ Right angle
Using a pair of small, very sharp scissors, clip into the seam allowance, being careful not to cut through the stitching.

▲ Obtuse angle
Using a pair of sharp scissors with a long blade, clip off the corner within the seam allowance, being careful not to cut through the stitching.

▲ Acute angle
Using a pair of small, sharp scissors, clip into the point within the seam allowance, being careful not to cut through the stitching.

Clipping curves

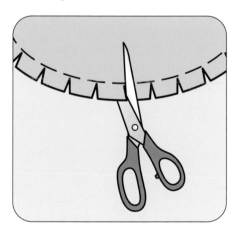

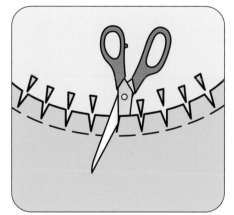

▲ Inward or concave curves
Make little clips or snips in the seam allowance just up to, but not through, the line of stitching, so the seam will lie flat.

▲ Outward or convex curves
Cut wedge-shaped notches from the seam allowance to eliminate excess fullness.

Clipping tips

Use sharp pointed scissors to clip corners or notches—embroidery scissors are ideal.

Be very careful not to cut through the stitching—it is better to stop too short than to get too close.

If you are sewing more than two layers of fabric together you can grade the seam by trimming the seam allowances back to different widths. This will prevent a bulky edge showing on the right side.

edges

Whatever you want to sew, the chances are you will end up with an edge that needs to be finished in some way. Hemming may seem like the obvious choice, but there are plenty of other options available to make your project look that little bit more unique or more professional.

Binding and borders

Making your own edgings gives you a much greater choice of fabric as well as the option of coordinating with other items. Binding is a narrow band of fabric that encloses a raw edge. Borders are wider and may either enclose the edge or be added to it. Both can be made in matching or contrasting fabrics.

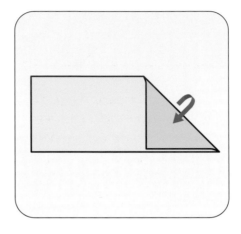

1 ▲ **Making bias binding**
Fold the crosswise grain of the fabric to the lengthwise grain. The easiest way is to make sure the end of the length is straight on the grain then fold it down to line up with the selvedge.

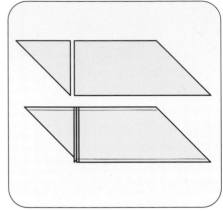

2 Cut along the fold line, then take the triangle of fabric you have just removed and stitch it to the other end of the piece to make the parallelogram shape shown above.

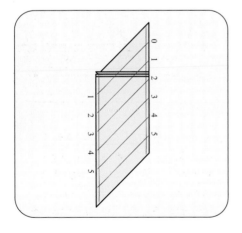

3 Mark a series of lines parallel with the diagonal edge, set apart by twice the width of the binding. Number the bands 1, 2, 3, etc. down the left-hand edge with an air-erasable marker. On the right-hand edge, mark the lines as shown, which will offset the numbers.

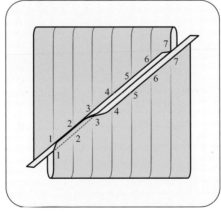

4 With right sides together, bring the edges round and match the numbers so 2 lines up with 2, 3 with 3, and so on. 1 and the last number will not match with anything. Stitch the seam with a 12 mm (1 in) seam allowance, to create a tube of fabric. Press the seam open.

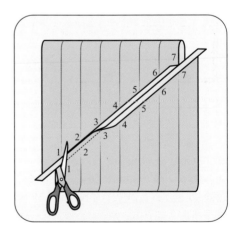

5 Cut along the marked line, which now runs around the tube in a continuous spiral. Fold both edges of the strip towards the middle and press in position, being careful not to stretch the bias binding as you work. A bias binding maker will make this process easier.

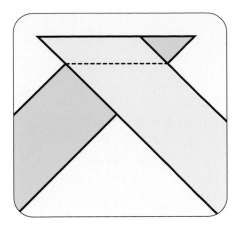

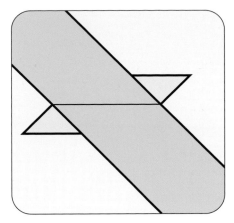

1 ▲ **Joining bias strips**
If you need to join two strips of bias binding, do it before you fold the edges over. Pin the strips right sides together. (They will run at right angles to each other.) Stitch together, leaving a 2.5 cm (1 in) seam allowance.

2 Press the seam open. Remember that if the bias strip has a pattern, you should try to match it on the seamline, not on the cut edges. Trim off the protruding points, and fold over the edges as in step 5 opposite.

Tips for edging

Bias binding is very easy to make, especially if you use a bias-binding maker, which turns under both edges ready to be ironed in place.

When adding borders, try to use fabric that is the same weight as the main fabric for the best result.

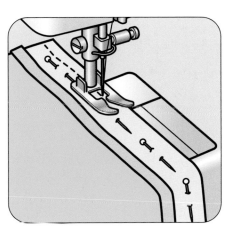

1 ▲ **Binding a straight edge**
Open out the fold along one edge of the bias binding and place it right side together on the edge to be bound, with raw edges matching. Pin in place, being careful not to stretch either edge.

2 Straight stitch along the fold line of the bias binding, removing the pins as you work.

3 Fold the binding around the raw edges to the wrong side. If you don't want the binding to show, fold on the stitching line. If you want a narrow border of binding, fold on the centre line of the binding.

4 Stitch along the folded edge on the wrong side, either hemming by hand if you don't want the stitches to show or with the machine.

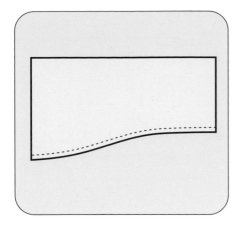

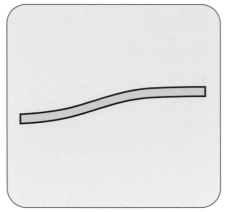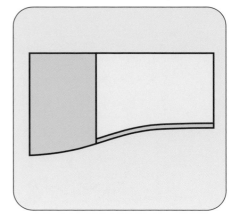

1 ▲ **Curved borders**
Make a template of the curve you want in heavy paper and use it to cut both the edge of the main piece and the lining. Measure a strip along the bottom edge the width the border is to be, plus 3 cm (1¼ in) for seam allowances—12 mm (½ in) on the top edge and 18 mm (¾ in) on the bottom edge. Cut the strip off the template.

2 Use the strip to cut a length of curved border, preferably in one piece. Press under the 12 mm (½ in) seam allowance along the top edge. Place the border over the main piece, lining up the bottom raw edges and pin the two together. Topstitch along the top edge of the border just below the folded edge.

3 Repeat step 2 for the lining. Then place the lining and main fabric right sides together and stitch along the bottom raw edge to join, leaving an 18 mm (¾ in) seam allowance. Clip the curves where required to make the fabric lie flat and press the seam towards the lining so it does not show through the main fabric.

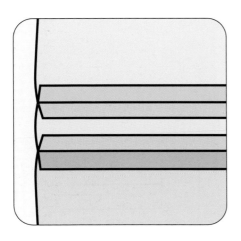

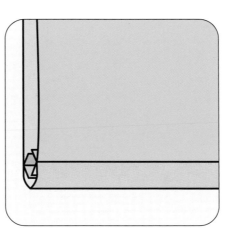

1 ▲ **Inserted borders**
Cut a strip of fabric the width you want the border to be at the front, plus 3 cm (1¼ in) for the back, plus 3 cm (1¼ in) for seam allowances. With right sides together, pin and stitch one edge of the border to the main fabric, with a seam allowance of 18 mm (¾ in).

2 With right sides together, pin and stitch the other edge of the border to the lining fabric the same way. Press both seams open, then measure the width needed for the border and press a fold along that point.

Tips for borders

Borders can not only be used decoratively, but also to extend something that is too short—such as curtains that have shrunk or are being moved to a longer window.

The technique shown for a curved border above can also be used to add a border to any edge that is not in a perfectly straight line.

1 ▲ **Mitred binding**
Make bias strips four times the finished width you want the border to be, and long enough to go all around the edge. Press the strips in half along the length.

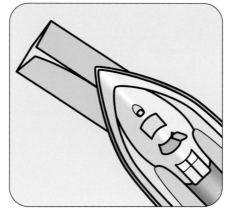

2 Open the strip out again and fold the two long edges to meet at the fold in the middle. Press in place all along the length, being careful not to stretch the strip as you work.

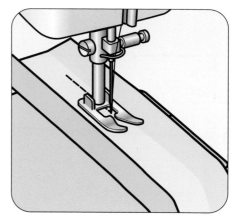

3 Pin strip and item right sides together and stitch along the fold, beginning the width of the seam allowance from the top and stopping the same distance from the bottom.

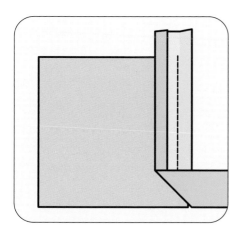

4 Cut the threads and remove the piece from the machine. Fold the strip to the right at the bottom, to make a diagonal fold across the corner.

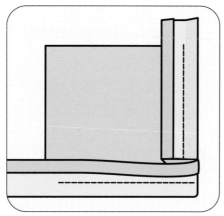

5 Fold the strip back to the left, so the fold line runs level with the edge of the side just stitched, aligning raw edges at the bottom. Pin and stitch as step 3.

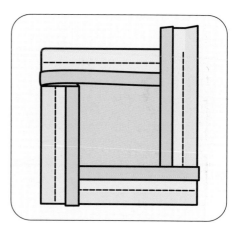

6 Repeat step 5 for the other two sides. Fold the last binding strip as step 4 at the final corner and tuck under the first strip. Stitch up to the seam allowance.

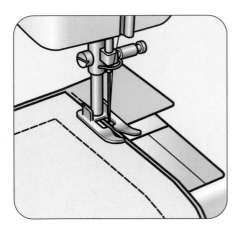

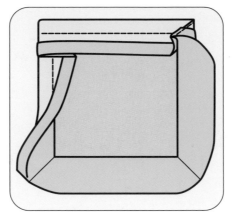

7 Turn over and stitch across the first and last binding strips close to the edge of the piece. Trim off the excess fabric quite close to the seamline you have just made.

8 Turn back and fold the binding over to the wrong side, enclosing the raw edges. A mitred join will appear at each corner.

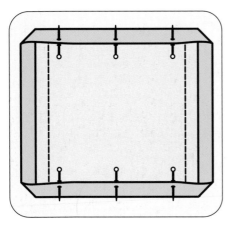

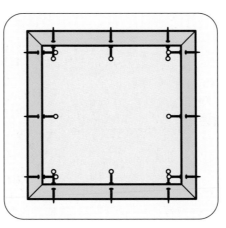

9 Turn back to the wrong side again and turn up the top and bottom edges so the fold on each lines up with the seamline. Pin in place.

10 Fold over the two sides so the fold on each lines up with the seamline. At the corners, fold the excess fabric into a mitre. Pin and slipstitch around and along the mitres.

Piping and cording

Piping is a strip of flat, folded fabric inserted into a seam for decoration. Cording is piping with a cord inside the fold, giving it a more rounded appearance. Cord for piping comes in a range of thicknesses, and both cording and piping can be made with matching or contrasting fabrics and colours.

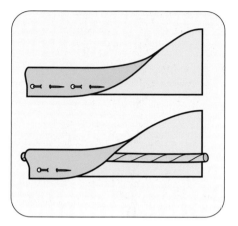

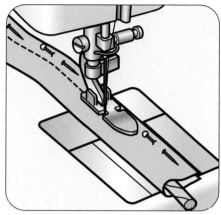

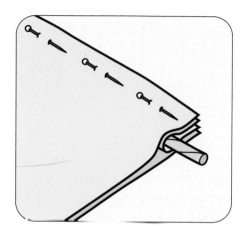

1 ▲ **Piping and cording**
For piping, make a strip of bias binding twice the width you want the piping to be, plus 3 cm (1¼ in) for the seam allowances. For cording, it should be three times the width of the cord, plus the seam allowances.

2 Fold the strip in half, wrong sides together and raw edges aligned. For cording, insert the cord into the fold and stitch along the strip as close to the cord as possible.

3 On the seam that is to be piped or corded, place the fabrics right sides together with the piping or cording in between and all raw edges aligned. Pin or tack together.

Piping and cording tips

Piping gives a soft, rounded finish, while cording is firmer and gives a more sculptured look.

For a quick corded effect, or to add cording to a finished item, just stitch a length of decorative purchased cording around the seam.

Piping does not have to be inserted into a straight edge seam—interesting three-dimensional effects can be obtained by stitching it into flat fabric.

Piping and cording are not just for soft furnishings—they can also be used to define edges in dressmaking.

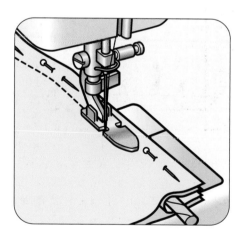

4 Use a zipper foot on your machine for cording; for piping you can just use the ordinary foot. Stitch along the seamline, being careful not to catch the cord in the seam as you work.

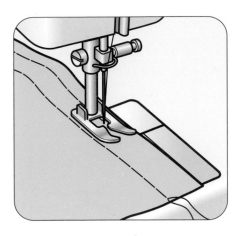

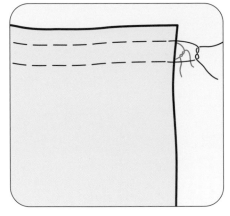

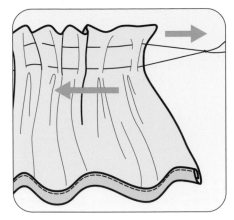

1 ▲ **Frills and ruffles**
Cut a strip of fabric the width of the frill or ruffle, plus 3 cm (1¼ in) for the seam allowances. Run a double line of gathering stitch (see page 38) along the top edge, one on the seam line, and one within the seam allowance.

2 Take the two threads on the right side at each end of the stitching and knot them together. Repeat for the two threads at each end on the wrong side. Fold over the ungathered raw edge twice and hem or topstitch along the length.

3 Holding the bobbin threads in one hand, ease the fabric along into gathers with the other hand. When the frill is the length you need, adjust the gathers evenly then knot the threads at each end so they don't slip.

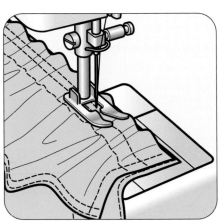

4 Pin the gathered edge to the edge of the flat piece to which it is to be attached, matching edges. Stitch with straight stitch between the two lines of gathering stitch so the gathers are even. Remove any threads on the right side.

pressing

Pressing is essential to achieve neat seams and a professional finish. You use only the tip of the iron and work quite lightly. Do not press over bulky areas, such as zippers and pockets.

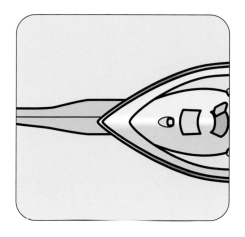

▲ Flat seams

Remove any pins and tacking, and with the wrong side facing upward, open out the seam. Run the tip of the iron along the seam to press it flat.

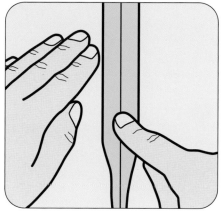

▲ Fingerpressing

Place the piece on a hard surface, wrong side upward, and run your finger along the seam to press flat. This technique is not suitable for fabrics that will stretch or fray easily.

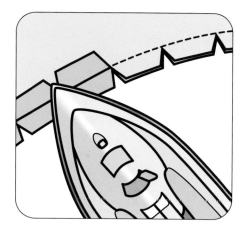

▲ Clipped seams

Place the piece flat on the ironing board, wrong side upward, and the seam allowances lying together. Use the point of the iron to press back the top layer of the seam allowance.

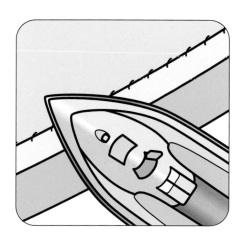

▲ Hems

Press hems from the fold towards the stitching, with wrong side uppermost, to avoid the edge showing on the right side.

Pressing chart

Heat	Fabric
Low	Acetate, shiny surfaces
Low to moderate	Blends, nylon, pile/nap, polyester, rayon, silk
Moderate	Acrylic, blends, wool
Moderate to high	Cotton
High	Linen

dressmaking

Most garments are made up of standard components so if you learn how to construct these you will be able to make almost anything. Here we start with the basics—understanding a pattern, laying and cutting out and constructing darts and facings. There is also a short section on the types of fabric suitable for dressmaking.

fabrics for dressmaking

Whatever you plan to make, you will need some kind of fabric. Today there is such a wide selection of fibre types, weaves, patterns, and colours that it may all seem quite bewildering. Colour and pattern are your personal choice, but certain types of fabrics are more suitable for some uses than others.

Linen and cotton

Linen and cotton are both natural yarns. Linen is made from the cellulose fibre obtained from the flax plant; its natural colour is off-white or pale tan, and due to its wax content it has a natural lustre. Cotton is a natural vegetable yarn made from the soft white fibrous material found around the seeds of the tropical and subtropical cotton plant. Cotton is almost pure cellulose, and in its raw, undyed form it is a light to dark cream, although it may also be brown or green. Cotton is often classified by its geographical region of origin, hence Egyptian cotton, Indian cotton. Cotton and linen can both be washed easily.

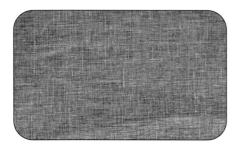

▲ Linen

Linen can be woven in various weights, from very light weights suitable for handkerchiefs or scarves to heavier weights for suit fabrics. Pure linen is cool and comfortable to wear but creases very easily. Its distinctive crumpled look has often been very fashionable, but it can also be blended with other fibres to reduce the possibility of creasing.

▲ Cotton/linen woven stripes

Cotton and linen blends are quite common. Stripes are always in fashion and woven stripes come in many different combinations and widths. Seersucker has lines of bunched threads that create alternate stripes of puckered and smooth finishes. The stripes on seersucker always run lengthwise in the direction of the warp and they are often blue and white: the puckered stripes are coloured and the flat ones white. Seersucker is often used for women's blouses, casual shirts, and children's clothing.

▲ Printed cotton

Cotton fabric is often printed with an all-over design, and there are countless different patterns available. Small floral prints on a contrasting background colour are very popular and are commonly used for dresses, aprons, and quilts. Printed cotton may be made of mercerized yarn, which has been subjected to a wet finishing process to make it stronger and more lustrous, and also allows the dyes to take better for brighter, deeper colours. Glazed cotton fabric has a glossy, polished finish.

Wool fabrics

Wool is the fibre or fabric made from the fleece of sheep or lambs—lambswool is softer and finer. However, the term is also often applied to other animal hair fibres, including the hair of the camel, alpaca, llama, and vicuna. Some types of wool can be washed, but most should be dry-cleaned—always check the care instructions before laundering an item.

▲ Denim

A rugged, durable twill cotton fabric that is most popular in indigo blue, but also available in other colours. Denim is mainly used for casualwear, particularly for jeans. Denim shrinks considerably when first washed, but most commercial clothing is made of pre-shrunk fabric. Stretch denim has added Lycra®.

▲ Wool tweed

Tweed is a term broadly applied to a range of sturdy fabrics in coarser grades of wool, usually with colour effects created by stock-dyed wools. The most popular weaves for tweeds are plain, twill, and variations of twill, such as herringbone.

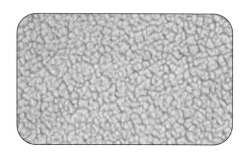

▲ Wool fleece

A fabric made primarily of wool that is knitted and then brushed to compact the cloth, trap air, and raise the fibres. The surface is then sheared to create a smooth, even finish. Fleece is soft, easy to sew, does not fray, and water-repellent. It is warm yet lightweight and ideal for outerwear.

Wash and wear

Always check the laundering instructions on the fabric bolt when you purchase your fabric.

Choose thread to match the composition of the fabric you will be using.

▲ Wool gabardine

A tightly woven, smooth, durable, twill-weave fabric with either a lustrous or a dull finish. It comes in various weights and generally wears extremely well, although it is inclined to develop a surface shine with wear. Wool gabardine is popular as a fabric for tailored suits and it is also used for coats, raincoats, and uniforms. Gabardine is also made in spun rayon, cotton, or various blends.

▲ Fine jersey knit

A soft, slightly elastic knit fabric mainly used for shirts and dresses. It is ideal for form-fitting designs as it clings to a shape but still drapes well where it falls. Jersey can be made in cotton, wool, or silk.

Silks and fine fabrics

Silk is a natural filament fibre produced by the silkworm in the construction of its cocoon. Most silk is collected from cultivated worms and comes from Asia, primarily China. Silk is one of the finest textiles; it is soft, has a brilliant sheen, and is extremely strong and absorbent. The silkworm moth was originally a native of China, and for about 30 centuries the gathering and weaving of silk was a secret process, known only to the Chinese. Some silk can be laundered by hand, but most types should be dry-cleaned.

▲ **Dupion**

This is made with yarn from the cocoon of two silk worms that have nested together. The double strand is not separated, so the yarn is uneven and irregular, with a large diameter in places. The fabric is plain-weave, very irregular and shows many slubs. Since the interest comes from the texture, this fabric is usually available in solid colours only.

▲ **Silk voile**

Silk can be woven in very light weights that are almost transparent. Organza frequently has a silvery sheen and creases quite effortlessly, but is easy to iron. It is used for evening wear, scarves, and to line items that need to be stiffened without added weight. Silk chiffon is an extremely light, thin and very sheer fabric commonly used for scarves and evening dresses.

▲ **Satin**

A fabric with a lustrous surface on one side, produced by a twill-weave in which with the weft threads are almost hidden, and dull surface on the other. Satin is made in many colours, weights, qualities, and degrees of stiffness; a low-grade silk or cotton filling is often used in cheaper cloths. It is used mainly for lingerie and evening wear.

▲ **Fine hand-printed silk**

Silk takes dye very well and can be hand-printed or even painted to achieve unusual effects and original designs. Finely woven silk with a very smooth surface is the best choice for these techniques, since the coarser silks rely on their surface texture for interest.

Tips for working with silk

To avoid puckered seams when sewing silk, place a layer of lightweight tissue above and below the seam before sewing, Stitch through the tissue, then tear it away afterwards.

Use sharp pins when working with fine fabrics and pin within the seam allowance.

Silk is extremely strong, but repeated exposure to sunlight will weaken the fibre. Avoid using it for curtains or home furnishings exposed to sun.

Fancy fabrics

There are hundreds of unusual man-made fabrics available, offering many different effects. Some of them are difficult to sew and may required special handling. Many of them also need specific techniques when they are cleaned, so be sure to check the care labelling when you purchase. However, since these unusual fabrics are most often used for special occasion garments, rather than items for everyday wear, out-of-the-ordinary cleaning needs should not prove too much of a problem.

▲ **Lurex®**

This is the registered brand name for a range of high-quality metallic yarn and for the fabrics that have been woven from such yarns. Lurex® can have a backing fabric or may be woven without one. It does fray very easily and can be quite difficult to sew.

▲ **Lamé**

A brocade-type fabric woven with metallic threads, usually either silver or gold. Lamé is often used in evening and dress wear and for theatre and dance costumes. Lamé comes in different varieties, depending upon the fibre content of the yarns used.

▲ **Sequinned fabrics**

These fabrics have sequins stitched at regular intervals, usually on a sheer woven backing fabric. They are not ideal for garments that require a good deal of structural stitching, such as darts or pleats. Take care not to cut through sequins when working.

dressmaking

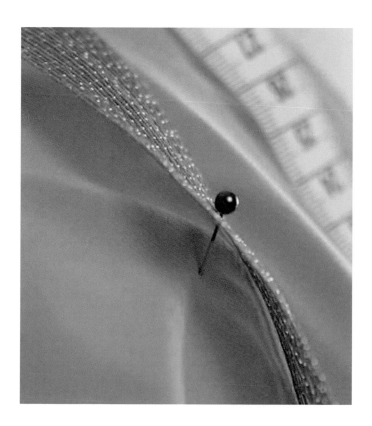

▲ **Fur fabric**

A man-made fabric with a long "fur" pile, that may be coloured in imitation of an animal's pelt. Fun fur is similar but is made in bright colours and is more obviously artificial. Imitation fur is usually made of acrylic, although other fibres can also be used. It is often made into throws, outerwear, or used as a lining or trim on coats or hats.

patterns

Commercial paper patterns in a selection of set sizes have been available since 1863. Previously clothes were made to measure or a sewer could buy a basic guide pattern that came in one size and had to be reduced or enlarged to the size required. Some experienced stitchers can make clothes without a pattern—and for simple shapes they may not be necessary—but for most of us it helps to have a guide to follow and instructions on the order of work.

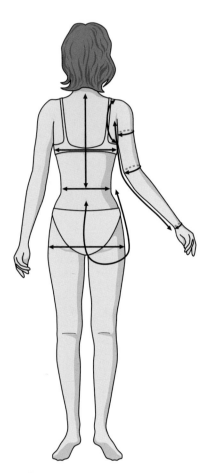
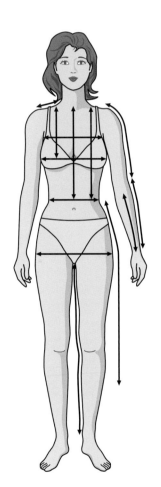

Body measurements

Take your measurements carefully! It may help to have the assistance of a second person to take a few of them, to be sure of accuracy. Wear form-fitting underwear that is not too tight or constricting. Record all your measurements on a chart; it will save time for future projects. You will need the following set of measurements to cover all options:

Chest circumference – under the arms with the tape straight across the back.

Bust circumference – around the fullest part of the bust, keeping the tape level at the back

Hip circumference – measure around the largest part of your bottom/thighs.

Waist circumference – measure the waist at the natural waistline, which should be the smallest part of the torso. To find it easily when taking other measurements, pin a 6 mm (¼ in) wide length of tape or elastic loosely around your waist.

Shoulder length – from neck to shoulder tip. Find your shoulder tip by raising your arm to a horizontal position and feeling for the hollow/pit between the shoulder and arm bones.

Shoulder to bustline – from the shoulder seam to the tip of the bust.

Neck to waistline – measure from the base of the neck at centre front to the bottom of the tape at the waist.

Shoulder to waistline – measure from the shoulder seam to the bottom of the tape at the waist.

Overarm to elbow – measure with the arm slightly bent, from the tip of the shoulder to where the arm bends.

Elbow to wrist – measure with the arm slightly bent, from where the arm bends to the wrist bone.

Skirt/dress length – measure from the bottom of waist tape to the desired hem length.

Inside leg – from the crotch to the ankle.

Back length – put on a thin necklace, or drape a piece of string around your neck. Measure from the place where the necklace falls on the back of your neck to the lower edge of the waist tape.

Bicep – measure the greatest circumference of your upper arm at the top and just above the elbow.

Underarm – from the armpit to the wrist bone.

Wrist circumference – around the wrist over the wrist bone.

Crotch depth – measure from the top of the waist tape at the front, through the legs to the top of the tape at the back.

Understanding paper patterns

Commercial pattern companies issue new collections regularly and the patterns are available in a range of body proportions and standard sizes. For information on how to select the right pattern for you, see page 64. For information on how to alter parts of a pattern for a better fit, see pages 65–68. Remember, any alterations to the pieces should be made before you lay out the pattern on the fabric!

Pattern tips

If a pattern is multi-size, there may be several different cutting lines marked. Identify which one you need to follow on all pieces and highlight it with a marker pen so you do not cut out the wrong size.

Do your layout for cutting on a large flat surface, such as a dining table or even on a clean floor.

If either the fabric or the pattern pieces are very creased, press them with a cool iron before you begin to make pinning them together easier.

Pattern layout

The pattern envelope and/or the instruction sheet inside will have suggested cutting layouts for different widths of fabric and sometimes also for different garment sizes. When you are laying the pattern out on the fabric, be aware that some pieces may need to be placed printed side up and others printed side down to fit the layout. This is indicated by different shading on the pattern shapes on the cutting layout. It will not make any difference to the final fabric pieces because generally you are cutting through a double layer of fabric, so you are cutting two mirror-image pieces at the same time. Some pieces need to have one side placed to the folded edge of the fabric, so you are cutting half the shape, which will unfold to make one large fabric piece. The side to be placed on a fold will be marked on the pattern—do not cut along the fold! A few pattern pieces may need to be placed on a single thickness of fabric; if so, this will also be indicated on the layout.

Pattern symbols

 Grain line – place on straight grain of fabric parallel to the selvedge

 **Foldline** – place on fold of fabric

Centre line – centre marking of front or back of garment

 **Notches and dots** – location marks for matching key points across different pattern pieces

 **Cutting line** – indicates where to cut and is usually a heavy solid line. There may be several types of lines if the pattern is multi-size

Adjustment line – double lines indicating where you can lengthen or shorten sections of a garment

 Dart line – triangular or diamond-shaped lines indicating edges to be joined to shape the garment

Laying out pattern pieces on patterned fabric

Some patterned fabrics may need careful placement so the patterns match across pieces or look attractive on the garment. When matching across seams, fold one piece along the seamline, line the fold up along the other seamline matching the motifs, and slant hem the seam before the final stitching to be sure it will not slip as you sew.

Matching patterns across pieces

If you are working with large patterns it will be very obvious if the motifs do not match across the seams. The notches indicate where pieces will match together, so you can use these to line up the motifs as well. Line up a notch with an easy-to-recognize section of the pattern, then match the notch on the corresponding piece with the same part of the motif. Remember to match on the seamline, NOT the cutting line.

Patterned fabrics

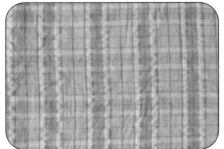

▲ **Floral patterns**

Many floral patterns are one-way designs, meaning that they have an obvious top and bottom. You must lay out all the pattern pieces so the pattern runs in the same direction. Make sure that large motifs fall above the bustline instead of over it, at approximately the same height front and back, and at the same level on the sleeves. Ideally, they should also match at the seams. When choosing a design, avoid ones with lots of seams within the bodice and the skirt; simple shapes are best.

▲ **Even checks or plaid**

Even checks are repeated identically in both the crosswise and lengthwise direction, allowing you to match up the lines exactly if you fold the fabric on the diagonal. A bold lengthwise line in the design should be placed to fall at the centre back and front of the garment. Crosswise lines should be at the same level across the bodice and sleeves.

▲ **Uneven checks or plaid**

With uneven checks, the stripes are not repeated symmetrically. The design may be asymmetrical lengthwise, or widthwise, or in both directions. If only the widthwise stripes are asymmetrical, fold the fabric lengthwise with selvedges together and lengthwise stripes matching precisely before laying out the pattern pieces. The centre of a check or bold lengthwise stripe should fall at centre front and back, and all the pattern pieces should run in the same direction. If only the lengthwise stripes are asymmetrical, choose a design with a centre seam or opening at front and back, or you will not be able to match the design at both side seams. If stripes are uneven in both directions, you will only be able to match all the stripes if the fabric does not have a right and a wrong side and the pattern has a centre line seam or opening. Lay out all the pattern pieces on a single layer of fabric and cut. Then reverse all the pattern pieces and cut them out again, making sure the same stripes fall in the same places each time.

▲ **Even stripes**

Even stripes are repeated symmetrically in width and colour; if you fold the fabric lengthwise the stripes in each half match. Line up stripes across seams by placing relevant notches on the same stripe. If the garment is cut on the bias, use a design with a centre seam or opening at front and back so the stripes can meet here, or it will be impossible to match side seams.

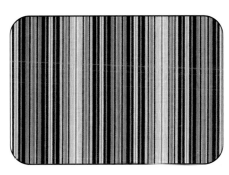

▲ **Uneven stripes**

In a fabric with uneven stripes, a group of several stripes will be repeated across the width of the fabric, but the two halves of the group will not mirror each other. Wherever you fold the fabric lengthwise, you will never be able to match up the stripes in the two halves. As with any one-way design, make sure you place all the pattern pieces running the same way in the cutting layout.

Fabrics with a nap or pile

When laying out a pattern pieces on this type of fabric, all of the pattern pieces should be pointing the same way. To find the direction of the nap or pile, lay the fabric flat and smooth your hand over it; in the direction that the nap or pile is pointing the surface will feel smooth.

Pinning and cutting

Handle paper patterns carefully as they are made from very thin tissue that is quite delicate and easily torn. If you do tear the tissue, just repair it with transparent tape, so you can still see the markings. If you plan to use the same pattern several times, it may be worth mounting or copying it onto slightly heavier paper or making a fabric toile (see page 72).

Using the pattern

1 Identify which pieces of the pattern you will need. Most commercial patterns have one or more alternate options, so you may not need every piece for the garment you are making. Cut the pieces out roughly from the background tissue so you can position them on the fabric as required.

2 If the paper is very creased, press gently with a cool iron. Pin each piece to the fabric, following the cutting guide layout. Check all the pattern markings as you work to be sure you do not make any mistakes. They can be easily corrected at this stage, but after cutting it will be too late!

3 Use sharp dressmaker's shears to cut out the pieces, keeping the fabric as flush to the surface as possible and following the cutting line for the size you are making. Cut with long, smooth strokes; do not close the shears right to the tip each time, as this will lead to a series of irregular edges in the line.

4 Mark notches on the edge of the cutting line by cutting around them as you work. This will save having to mark them separately later. Some will be single and some double—this is just to differentiate between them so you can be sure you are matching the right ones.

5 Double or triple notches can be cut as one unit; there is no need to cut separate triangles. You can cut the notches outward rather than inward—a safer option for fabric that tends to fray and for seams that may be under strain, as it leaves the seam allowance intact and therefore stronger.

6 There is usually no need to mark the seam allowance, but there is a special tool with a slide and ruler that can be set to the correct width, allowing you to mark an even distance from the raw edge. Alternatively, you can use the lines on the base plate of your machine to guide you as you sew.

More pattern tips

Lay out all pattern pieces printed side up unless instructed otherwise in the cutting guide layout.

When the cutting guide shows a double thickness of fabric, fold the fabric with right sides together.

When the cutting guide shows a single thickness, place the pattern piece printed side up and the fabric right side up. However, if the right and left sides are being cut separately, remember to turn the pattern over to cut the second piece of fabric.

Check twice, cut once! Be absolutely sure that everything is correct before you make that first cut.

If you want to extend the life of your pattern, make a version in brown parcel wrapping paper. Pin the tissue pattern to a single layer of brown paper and cut around it as if it were the fabric—although in this case you will cut along the fold line as well. Transfer all the markings to the wrapping paper using dressmaker's carbon and/or a tracing wheel.

Marking from patterns

The pattern pieces will have a variety of markings that will need to be transferred to the fabric in some way. There are several ways of doing this and the one you choose will depend partly on personal preference and partly on the type of fabric. Remember to check marker pens on a scrap piece of fabric to be sure the mark will show—and can be removed later.

Water- or air-erasable marker

These are very useful to mark straight lines. Just fold the pattern back along the line as a guide and draw the line on the fabric using a ruler to keep it straight. To remove the marks, follow the manufacturer's instructions.

Tailor's chalk

Since this traditional type of marker is available in many colours, choose one that will show up on your fabric. Fold the pattern back along the line and draw along the folded edge. The chalk marks can be brushed away when they are no longer needed.

Tailor's tacks

These are ideal if the marks need to be transferred through two layers of fabric and for single point marks like dots. Make a double stitch through the pattern and all layers of the fabric, leaving a loose loop of thread.

Snip the loop and remove the pattern. Carefully separate the layers of fabric a little and snip through the threads between the two layers, leaving a few in each piece to mark the point.

Tracing wheel

Note that dressmaker's carbon is indelible, so you want to make the marks on the wrong side of the fabric. Fold a piece of carbon with the carbon side inward, placing the bottom layer under the fabric and the top layer between the fabric and the pattern. Run the tracing wheel along the lines marked on the pattern, holding it firmly and pressing down gently. This method is ideal for curved lines, but will make lines of holes in the paper pattern, which will weaken it.

Body shapes/proportions

When you make your own clothes you will want them to be stylish. Study current trends, but don't follow fashion blindly! Some trends fall out of favour quickly. Also, the advantage of making your own clothes is that you can create styles that suit both your individual taste and figure.

Body types

Commercial patterns come in different body types as well as different sizes. Before you even consider the size required you should decide which body type you need:

Babies, toddlers, or children – for infants and young children, generally sized by height

Girls'/Girls' Plus – for growing girls with undeveloped figures

Junior – for the young preteen figure

Petite – for a fully developed but shorter figure

Misses – for a fully developed figure of average height

Women – for a larger, more fully mature female figure

Unisex – for figures that fit between female and male size ranges

Boys/Teen-Boys – for undeveloped male figures

Men – for fully mature male figures

Pattern books give size ranges, but they may differ slightly depending on the manufacturer.

Choosing your size

Patterns are designed with ease, which is an extra amount added to the body measurement to allow the clothes to hang and be worn comfortably. Some manufacturers allow more ease than others, so you may find that one brand of pattern fits you better than another. This does not mean you cannot use the other patterns, but you may need to buy a different size or adjust the fit.

Design notes

When choosing your style and fabric, make the most of your best points and minimize those that are not so good.

Big bust – avoid halter tops as the bust will not have enough support. Scoop necks are more flattering, while wrap tops will accentuate the waist instead.

Boyish figure – deep V-necks will break up the upper body. Tailored jackets and coats will fit around the waistline and flare out over the hips, giving more shape to the torso. Wide belts create a waist.

Tips for choosing your pattern size

Generally you will take the same size in a pattern as you do in ready-made garments.

Select your pattern by bust measurement and make any adjustments necessary in other areas.

If the bust is larger than the chest measurement by more than 10 cm (4 in), buy the pattern one size smaller than the bust and enlarge through the bust. It is important that the pattern fits at the shoulders and armholes, and this area should be changed as little as possible.

Another option for the larger bust is to buy two patterns, one to fit the bust and one a size smaller. Use the front part of the bodice of the larger pattern and the smaller pattern for all the other pieces. You will have to enlarge the darts at the waist, shoulders, and underarm so the sections will fit together. For skirts and trousers, buy patterns by hip measurement.

Hourglass – choosing a design with a slashed neckline will balance the width of the lower half of your body. With skirts, go for A-line, rather than a pencil shape or one that clings around the hips. Trousers should have a wider leg; try a boot cut or slight flare. Long line, tailored tops are also flattering.

Short legs – choosing a empire-line or high-waisted top or dress will disguise the proportion of leg to body. High-waisted trousers or skirts are also a good option, as dropped waists or cropped tops or trousers can make your legs look even shorter.

Alterations

However carefully you choose your pattern size, there are often some minor alterations that are required to achieve a perfect fit. Each pattern piece has key points where you can enlarge or reduce it safely.

Where to measure

There are certain crucial points that must be right for the garment to fit correctly. Check these against your own measurements before you begin and make any corrections to the pattern pieces required following the instructions on the following pages.

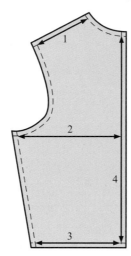

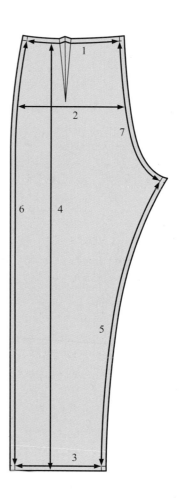

Bodice front

1. Shoulder 2. Bust 3. Waist
4. Neck to waist
5. Neck to dart point on bust

Bodice back

1. Shoulder 2. Underarm to centre back
3. Waist 4. Neck to waist

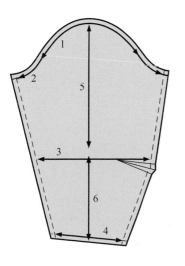

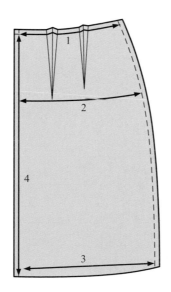

Trousers

1. Waist
2. Hips
3. Ankle hem
4. Waist to hem
5. Inside leg
6. Side seam length
7. Crotch

Sleeve

1. Sleeve cap to balance marks
2. Sleeve cap to underarm
3. Elbow 4. Wrist 5. Shoulder to elbow
6. Elbow to wrist

Skirt

1. Waist 2. Hips
3. Hem 4. Waist to hem

Altering the pattern

You can enlarge a section of the pattern by cutting and inserting an extra strip of paper, or reduce it by creasing and pinning a fold. For more complex shapes, cut and overlap the edges.

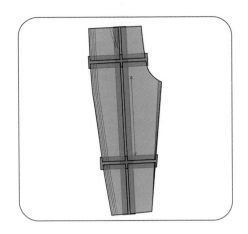

◀ **Increasing or reducing the width or length of any pattern piece**

To increase width, cut from the top to the bottom, avoiding any construction markings. Move the pieces apart as required, cut a strip of paper a little larger than the width of the gaps, and tape into place. To reduce, fold a pleat in the same place and tape in position. To increase or reduce length, adjust as described above at the lengthen or shorten lines marked on the pattern piece.

Reducing bodice fullness

▶ **Front**

On the front piece, cut approximately one quarter of the way up the pattern from the waist in a line almost parallel to the centre front. Then cut a diagonal line that misses the tip of the bust dart and ends just above the bottom curve of the armhole. Overlap the pieces of the pattern and tape in place. If you have reduced by a lot, you may need to add an extra strip of paper at the side seam to straighten it.

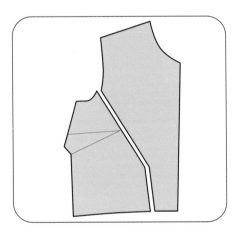

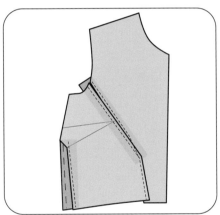

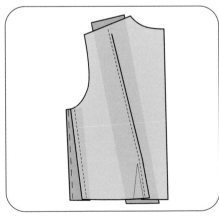

◀ **Back**

On the back piece, start the cut in the same way as on the front, but change the diagonal line to a shallower angle ending about halfway along the shoulder seam. Overlap the pieces of the pattern and tape in place. If you have reduced by a lot, you may need to add an extra strip of paper at the side seam to straighten it.

Alteration tips

When taping extra paper into a pattern, use transparent tape so the original markings can still be seen.

Construction markings must be transferred to any new areas inserted.

When making a pattern piece smaller, remember that the width of the tuck should only be half the amount you want to reduce by.

When lengthening a piece, keep the grainline straight across the join.

Don't forget to adjust any separate facing pieces so that they match.

Increasing bodice fullness

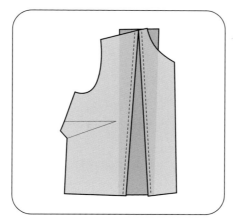

1 To alter the width on the front piece, cut straight up from the waist to the shoulder seam, avoiding any construction elements such as darts. Move the pieces apart as required, cut a strip of paper a little larger than the width of the gap, and tape into place.

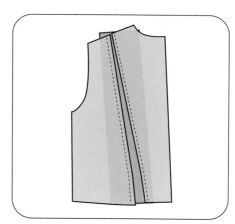

2 To alter the width to match on the back piece, cut on a slight diagonal from the waist to the shoulder seam. Move the pieces apart as required, cut a strip of paper a little larger than the width of the gap, and tape into place.

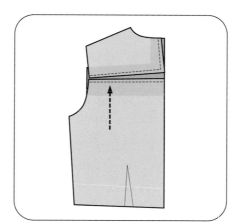

3 To alter the length above the bust on the front and back pieces, cut straight across from the centre line to between the shoulder and underarm seam. You may need to add an extra strip of paper at the top of the centre line to straighten it. Alternatively, if you need more length beneath the bust, cut across halfway between the bottom of the armhole and waist. Move the pieces apart, cut a strip of paper a little larger than the width of the gap, and tape into place.

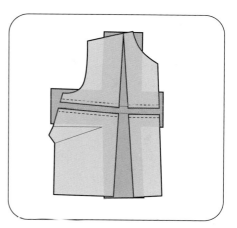

4 To alter both width and length on the front piece, first cut straight up from the waist to the shoulder seam, avoiding any construction elements such as darts. Then cut straight across from the centre line to between the shoulder and the underarm seam. Alternatively, cut across halfway between the bottom of the armhole and the waist, as needed. Move the pieces apart as required, cut a width of paper a little larger than the width of the gaps and tape into place.

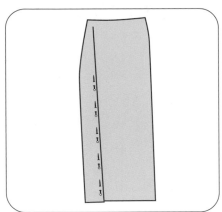

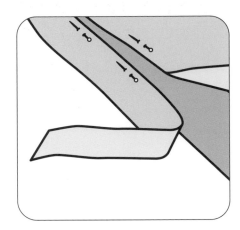

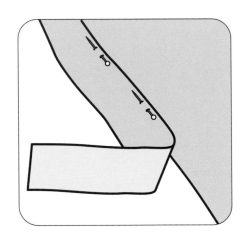

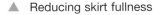

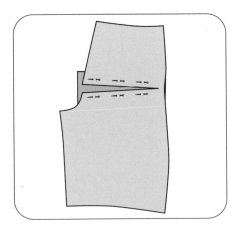

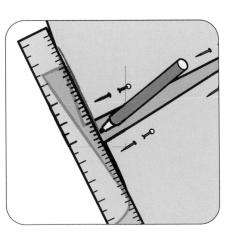

▲ Increasing sleeve cap size

You may want to do this either to allow for a bigger upper arm or to make a gathered sleeve top in place of a more tailored one. Cut a slit in the pattern from the centre balance line at the top towards the bottom as far as necessary. Move the sides apart as required, cut a width of paper a little larger than the width of the vent, and pin or tape into place. At the bottom of the vent, crease the excess paper so that it lies flat.

▲ Reducing skirt fullness

Cut from the hem to around the hipline, avoiding any construction markings. Overlap the pieces of the pattern and tape in place; at the top of the vent, crease the excess paper so it lies flat.

▲ Increasing skirt fullness

Cut from the hem to around the hipline, avoiding any construction markings. Move the sides apart as required, cut a strip of paper a little larger than the width of the vent, and tape into place.

◀ Increasing crotch depth

Cut from the centre line at the crotch above where it curves, right across to almost reach the seamline on the side, avoiding any construction markings at the waist. Move the sides apart as required, cut a width of paper little larger than the width of the vent, and tape into place. Trim any excess paper at the centre line to get a smooth line.

basic garment elements

Most garments are made up of set components that can be slightly different shapes or put together in a slightly different way to change the design. A sleeve, for instance, can be long or short; set in or raglan; have a fitted, gathered, or pleated head—but to make all these the construction techniques are more or less the same, with only minor modifications. This means that once you understand basic construction methods you will quickly be able to work out how to make almost anything. The following pages take you through all the basic elements that you may need to make a whole range of garments.

Facings

A facing is a second layer of the main fabric that is used to finish the garment's edges at places such as the neckline, front and back openings, or sleeve cuffs. It both strengthens the edge and provides a neat finish.

Interfacing

This is a third layer of fabric often used between the main piece and its facing to provide extra support or body.

Darts

Darts are short triangular or diamond-shaped folds or tucks positioned at strategic places to shape the garment to the body.

Tucks

These are stitched folds of fabric used to provide fullness or decoration. Additionally, in children's clothing they are sometimes used to hold extra fabric out of the way until it is let down to accommodate the child's growth.

Pleats

Pleats are folds in fabric designed to provide fullness. They are often made at the waistline for a more generous hem. They may be unstitched or stitched for a short way at the top.

Collars

Collars finish off a neckline and come in a variety of styles. Stand-up and fold-down collars alike are made of a double layer of fabric, sometimes stiffened with interfacing, and inserted into the neckline with a facing to hide the raw edges.

Sleeves

Set-in sleeves are inserted into an armhole opening in the side of the garment, while raglan sleeves have a diagonal seam running from the underarm to the neckline, so part of the sleeve also forms the bodice.

Cuffs

These finish off sleeve ends. Styles range from a simple ruffle to a fully tailored button cuff.

Plackets

A sleeve placket is the finished vertical opening at the cuff of a sleeve. It creates a wider opening when the cuff is unfastened. There are several different ways of constructing a sleeve placket.

Waistband

The waistband in its simplest form is a folded strip of fabric used to finish the waistline edge, but it can be wide or narrow, stiffened or unstiffened, and fastened in a host of ways.

Pockets

The two basic types of pocket are the patch pocket, which is a separate piece of fabric stitched to the outside of a garment, and the inset pocket, which is hidden inside the garment and comes in many variations.

Hems

The hem finishes off the bottom edge of any sewn item. Although its construction is very simple, there are many different ways of achieving a neat result.

Linings

Lining a garment hides the construction seams inside and also provides additional structure and support.

Fasteners

Fasteners are an essential part of most garments, since openings wide enough to go over the body need to be held closed when the garment is worn.

Facings and interfacings

A facing can be cut as a separate piece of fabric, stitched in place and folded under, or be cut as part of the main piece and folded back. In most cases the facing will be the same fabric as the main piece, but it can be made in a lighter fabric to reduce bulk, or in a contrasting colour as a design feature. Interfacing is sometimes added between the main piece and the facing to provide bulk, and can be ironed on or stitched in place. Armhole facings are made in the same way as the separate facing shown for a neckline.

One-piece facing

This can be constructed with ordinary or iron-on interfacing, but here we show the iron-on version.

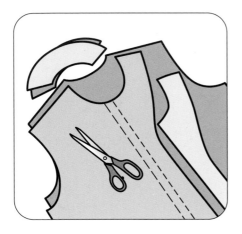

1 Cut out the required pieces of iron-on interfacing and the main fabric pieces. Transfer markings and tack the fold line on the section to be interfaced.

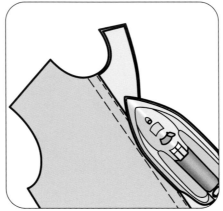

2 Iron the interfacing onto the wrong side of the appropriate sections of the main fabric. Follow the manufacturer's instructions and make sure the iron is set to the correct temperature.

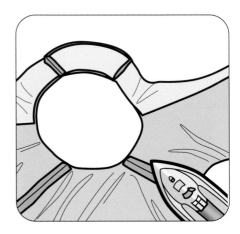

3 Stitch the pieces together and press seams open. Turn the interfaced pieces back along the fold line, right sides together with the garment. Tack and stitch the curved neckline edge.

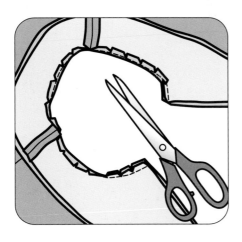

4 Fold under the raw edges of the interfaced pieces and stitch in place. Trim corners and clip the seam allowance at the neckline, being careful not to cut through the stitching.

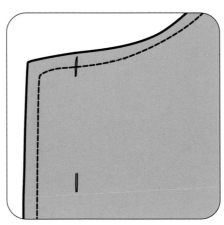

5 Turn the entire interfaced piece to the wrong side, easing any puckers along the seamline. Press in place, or topstitch along the folded edge if this will add to the design.

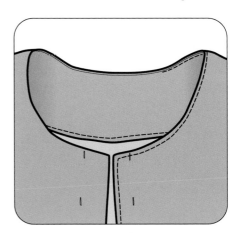

6 The completed facing is in place. It neatens the edge of the neckline, covering all of the raw edges and adding extra strength around the opening.

Separate facing

A separate facing is a separate piece of fabric, rather than an extension folded over as in the one-piece facing shown opposite. It is usually cut from exactly the same fabric as the rest of the garment. However, the facing shown here is indicated in a slightly different colour just so that it can be seen more clearly in the illustrations.

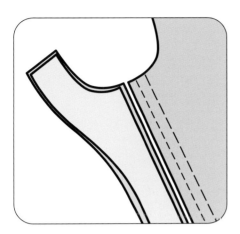

1 Cut out the facing and main pieces. Add a layer of interfacing, if required, and tack in position on the facing piece.

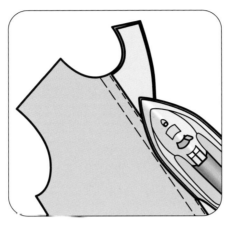

2 Stitch the facing and interfacing to the main piece along the long straight seam at the front leading edge. Trim the interfacing close to the seamline along this edge. To complete, follow steps 3–6 for the one-piece facing on page 70.

Easing curves

To ease the curve on a facing, clip the seam allowance at a slight angle, then staystitch the edge. If you are using a very delicate or a very heavy-weight fabric, work herring-bone stitch (see page 30) along the edge after stay-stitching, to prevent the edges from fraying.

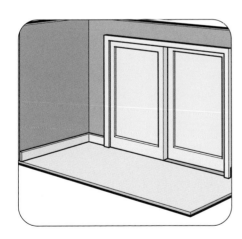

1 ▲ **V-neckline facing**
This is both a binding and a facing, done with a wide strip of fabric cut on the bias (see page 20), which creates a neckband. Cut out the main fabric pieces and a bias facing strip. Tack along the neckline edge at the seamline. Staystitch the point of the V for about 18 mm (¾ in) in each direction.

2 Stitch the shoulder seams of the garment. With right sides together, tack the band around the neckline, leaving the last 5 cm (2 in) unstitched. Ease seam at the back of the neck so that it lies flat.

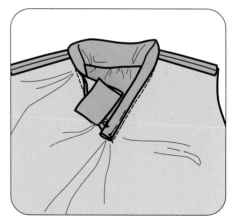

3 Stitch around the neckline, again leaving the last 5 cm (2 in) free. Turn the neckband through to the inside. On the wrong side, begin at the stitched end of the band and turn the raw edge under twice. Tack in place for the first 7.5 cm (3 in).

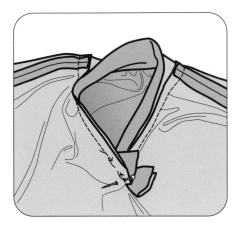

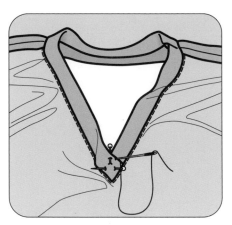

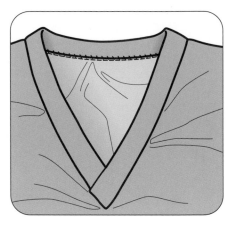

4 Match the raw edge of the free end of the neckband to the neckline, enclosing the folded and tacked end. Stitch the last part of the neckband right down to the point of the V, catching the other end in the seam as you sew.

5 Work round the remainder of the neckband, turning under a double seam and hemming in place along the line of the seam. At the point of the V, fold under the last end of the band in line with the seam and hem in position.

6 The finished neckline has a band around it, overlapping at the front in a sharp V-shape.

Using a toile

If you plan to use the same pattern many times, it is worthwhile making a toile, a pattern made from inexpensive cotton fabric instead of paper. Make all your alterations to the paper pattern, then cut all the pieces from thin cotton fabric and transfer all of the markings. You can roughly stitch the toile together to check the fit and make any necessary changes. Use the toile just as you would a paper pattern.

Darts

Darts are used to add fullness to allow for the curves of the body at the bust, waist, hips, and shoulders. They are almost always stitched into the flat pieces of fabric before they are joined together into a garment. Vertical darts at waist and shoulder are pressed toward the centre line of the garment. Horizontal darts, such as those at the bust, are usually pressed downward.

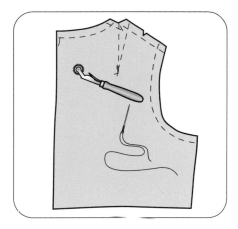

1 ▲ **Straight dart**
Mark the dots indicating the line of the dart, or mark the entire stitching line if the dart has a curved stitching line, or if you prefer to do so.

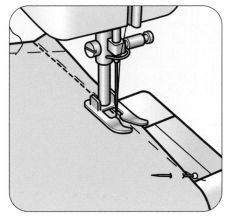

2 Fold the fabric in half, right sides together, along the centre line of the dart. Stitch from the seamline to the point of the dart, taking a couple of stitches beyond the point. Do not backstitch.

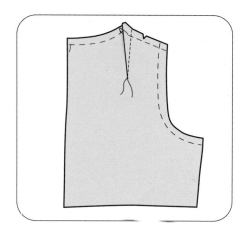

3 Finish with long ends, tie them together, then snip short.

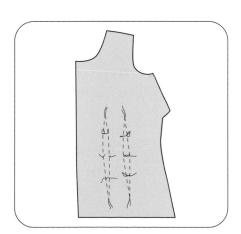

1 ▲ **Double-pointed dart**
Work as for the straight dart for steps 1 and 2 only. When stitching, work from the middle to the point in each direction.

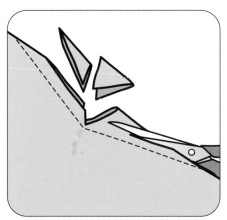

2 If the double-pointed dart is very deep, it may need to be cut so the fabric lies smoothly. Remove a triangle of fabric at the centre and trim the ends fairly close to the seam. Be careful not to cut through any stitching.

3 After cutting you can press the dart flat, working on one end at a time.

Tucks and pleats

Tucks and pleats are basically folds in fabric. Tucks can be very decorative and regular or irregular, and are generally stitched completely from one end to the other. Pleats are usually much more regular and are stitched in place only at the top, so the remainder of the pleat falls in a straight, pressed line right to the bottom of the piece.

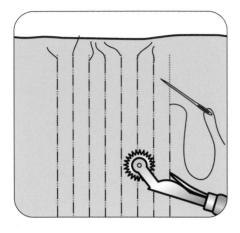

1 ▲ Tucks
Tucks can be made horizontally, vertically, or diagonally across the fabric. Transfer the parallel lines of the tuck from the pattern to the fabric.

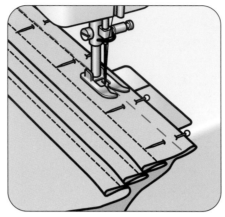

2 Working on only one tuck at a time, fold over the first guideline to line up with the second, then stitch in place. Repeat for the remaining guidelines.

Tucking tips

Tucking on striped or checked fabric can create attractive effects and colour variations.

Work on one tuck at a time to make sure the line is straight.

You can use the guides on the machine footplate to get the lines of tucks even.

When making pleats in fabric that does not hold a sharp crease, press the pleat and stitch along the fold using a matching thread.

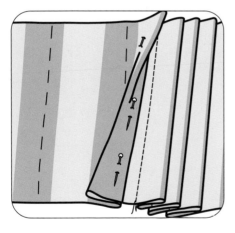

1 ▲ Tucking striped fabric
Using a fabric with wide stripes, create tucks within the width of alternate stripes, leaving a very narrow band of the other colour along the edge.

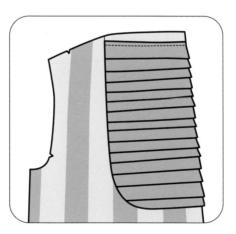

2 Here the yoke set in a bodice has been tucked before being cut. This has created an area of textured plain fabric within the main striped area of the garment.

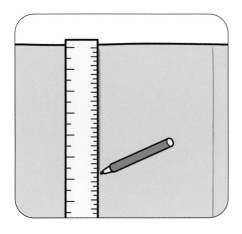

1 ▲ Knife pleats

These are a series of pleats of the same width and running in the same direction. Using an erasable marker, draw parallel lines on the wrong side of the fabric to mark the fold lines and the placement lines that the fold will line up with.

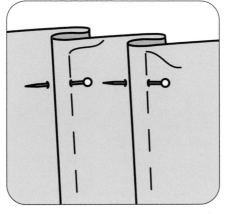

2 Fold the fabric along the marked fold line, lining up the fold with the placement line. Pin and tack each fold in place from top to bottom. At the top of the pleat, pin the fold in position then stitch in place just inside the seam allowance.

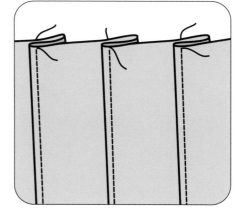

3 If required, topstitch along the first few inches of the pleat to hold it firmly in place. Press the pleats from top to bottom before removing the tacking. For soft folded pleats, press after removing the tacking.

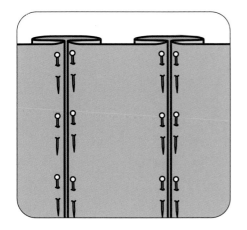

1 ▲ Inverted box pleats

These are two pleats that turn towards each other. Mark the pleats as for step 1 of knife pleats, but on the right side of the fabric. On the right side, fold the two pleats to meet each other in the centre, pin in place and then press.

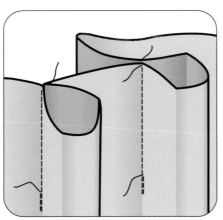

2 Remove the pins. Working from the back, and keeping the folds of the pleats touching, tack the pressed folds together for about 15 cm (6 in) to 20 cm (8 in) or the length you desire. Machine stitch down the length of the tacking, backstitching at the end to secure. Press the pleat into position. Repeat for all the box pleats.

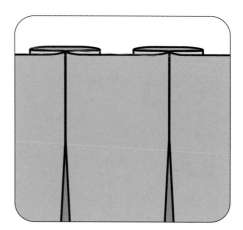

3 The stitching of the pleats will not show on the front (right side). As an alternative treatment, the underlay fabric behind the pleat can be a different fabric: tack the two folds of the pleat together like a seam, press open, lay a strip of the other fabric underneath, and stitch the raw edges together on each side.

Collars

Most collars share the same basic construction technique and are made of a double layer of fabric, usually with a layer of interfacing between them, which stops the shape of the seam allowance showing through to the front of the collar. A man's shirt has an extra band of fabric between collar and shirt, called the stand, which allows for the wearing of a tie.

Collar-making tips

Topstitching around the collar will add an extra touch of style and will also stop the edges rolling.

A Peter Pan collar is made in exactly the same way as the simple collar, but the edges of the collar are rounded, not pointed.

Combining a simple collar with a stand piece creates a smart shirt collar.

A mandarin collar is a sophisticated way to finish a neck opening with no facing.

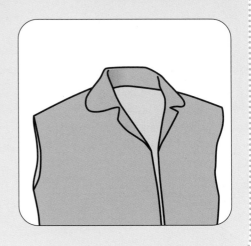

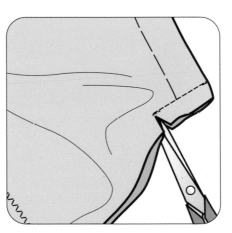

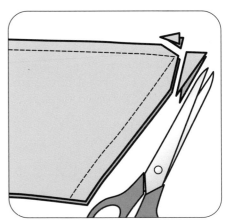

1 ▲ **Simple collar**
Make up the main pieces of the garment as instructed. Add the interfacing to the wrong side of one piece of the collar, either by ironing on or by tacking it in place.

2 If the garment has lapels, fold and stitch the seam to finish this section. To make the points sharp and neat, clip them as shown.

3 Tack and stitch the two collar pieces, right sides together. Trim and layer the edges if the interfacing is stitched, then clip the corners. Turn right side out and press.

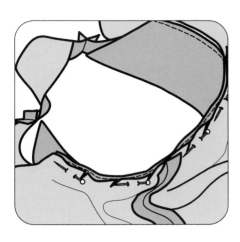

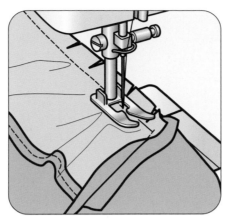

4 Pin the collar to the raw edge of the neckline, right sides together, with the interfaced side of the collar to the garment and notches matched carefully. Tack in place.

5 Pin and tack the back collar facing in position over the collar, right sides together. Stitch the neckline seam through all layers. Turn the facing to the inside and press.

Making a point

To make a really sharp point, clip the corners (see step 3 on opposite page) and turn the collar right side out. Use the sharp end of a pin to tease out the fabric. Work carefully to avoid pulling the stitching or damaging the fibres.

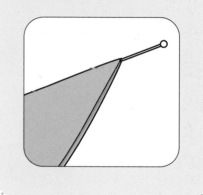

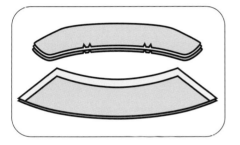

▲ Shirt collar with stand

1 Make up the main pieces of the garment. Add interfacing to the wrong side of one collar piece and to one piece of the stand. Tack and stitch the two collar pieces, right sides together. Trim and clip the corners, then turn right side out and press.

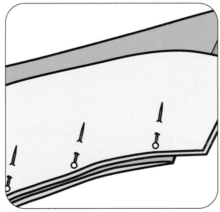

2 Pin and tack the pieces of the stand to either side of the collar, right sides together, to enclose the raw edge of the collar seam. Match the interfaced side of the stand to the interfaced side of the collar.

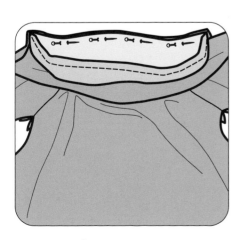

3 Stitch the stand to the collar, working through all thicknesses. Trim, grade and notch the curved section of the seam. With right sides together, pin and tack the stand to the neck edge, matching notches carefully.

4 Stitch the stand to the neckline. Turn the stand over the raw edges of the neckline, fold under the seam allowance along the bottom edge and slipstitch in place along the seamline to hide any raw edges.

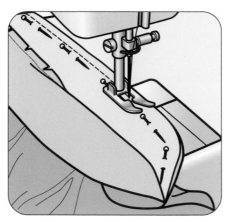

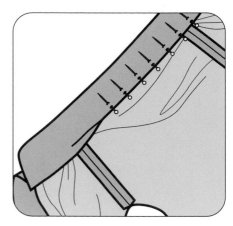

1 ▲ **Mandarin collar**
Make up the main sections of the garment and the collar pieces as described in steps 1 and 3 on page 76.

2 Stitch the collar to the raw edge of the neckline, right sides together, with the interfaced side of the collar to the garment. Match raw edges and notches.

3 Turn the collar over the raw edges of the neckline, fold under the seam allowance along the bottom edge, and pin in place.

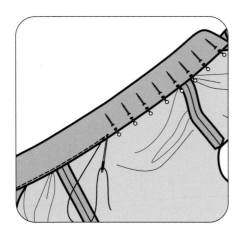

4 Slipstitch the folded edge of the collar in place along the seamline to hide any raw edges.

Sleeves

Set-in sleeves can be styled in a variety of ways—long, short, puffed, gathered, pleated, just about anything, really. Raglan sleeves offer much less variety, but are very simple to make.

Sleeves are generally made in the same fabric as the main garment, but can be made in a contrasting or lighter fabric as part of the overall design.

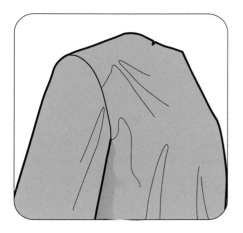

Gathered set-in sleeve

This type of sleeve has gathering over the cap, where the sleeve fits into the top of the armhole.

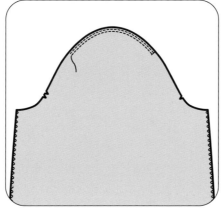

1 Make up the main sections of the garment. Transfer all markings to the sleeve pieces, then run a double line of gathering stitches between the dots at the sleeve cap. Zigzag the raw edges of the underarm seam.

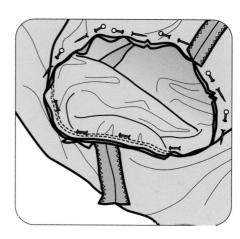

2 Stitch the underarm seam and press open. Turn the garment inside out and with right sides together, pin the sleeve into the armhole, matching seams and notches. Pull up the gathering threads to fit the cap into the armhole top.

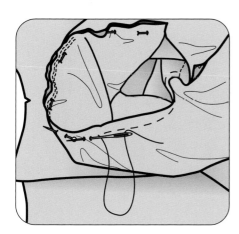

3 Tack the sleeve into the garment, making sure that the gathers over the top of the sleeve are even or the sleeve will look unbalanced. Stitch the sleeve into position.

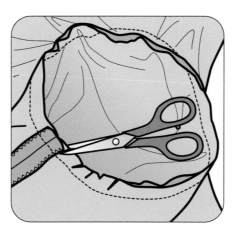

4 Clip the curve on either side of the underarm seam, being very careful not to cut through the stitching. Finish the raw seam edges of the armhole, either with zigzag stitching or binding.

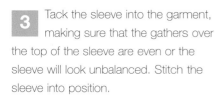

Sleeve-making tips

If the fabric you are using frays easily, double stitch the seam and enclose the raw edges with bias binding.

Pleated sleeves are usually fuller than gathered ones and look better in heavier fabric.

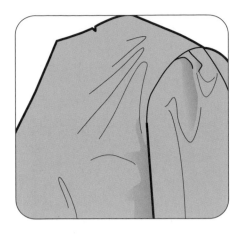

▲ **Pleated set-in sleeve**

This is similar to the gathered sleeve, but has pleats instead of gathers.

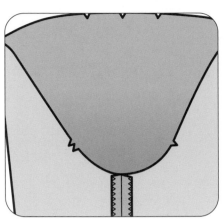

1 Make up the main sections of the garment. Transfer all markings to the sleeve pieces, then zigzag the raw edges of the underarm seam. Stitch the underarm seam and press open.

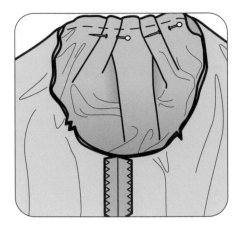

2 Turn the garment inside out and with right sides together, pin the sleeve into the armhole, matching seams and notches. Match the markings and pin pleats in position. Fit the cap into the top of the armhole. Finish as for gathered set-in sleeve.

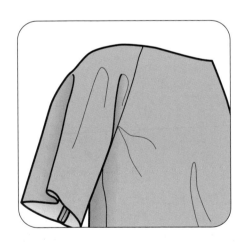

▲ **Raglan sleeve**

With this sleeve the seam runs from under the arm diagonally across to the neckline, so a section of the sleeve also forms part of the front and back of the garment.

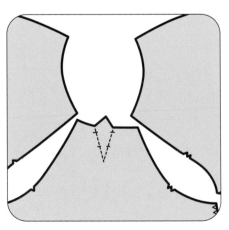

1 Transfer all markings to the front, back, and sleeve pieces. Zigzag the raw side edges of all the pieces.

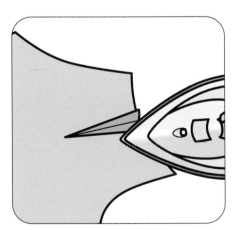

2 Some raglan sleeves have a dart at the cap for a better fit over the shoulder. Stitch the sleeve cap dart on each sleeve, then slash it open and press flat.

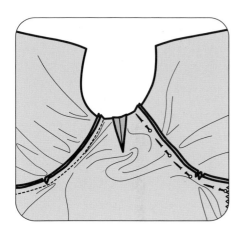

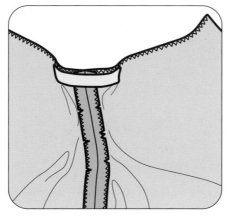

3 Pin and tack the sleeve to the front and the back, matching notches. Stitch together, then clip curves and press seams open.

4 Pin and tack the sleeve seams, then stitch the sleeve/underarm seam. You can place a 10 cm (4 in) length of tape across the seam to reinforce it.

Raglan sleeves

Sports garments and casual wear often have a raglan sleeve because it gives a looser fit, making movement easier, without being baggy.

For a sporty look, try making both the raglan sleeves in a contrasting colour to the fabric used for the back and front of the top.

Cuffs and plackets

A cuff is the finishing touch to the end of a sleeve and there are many different looks that can be achieved. If the cuff fastens tightly around the wrist the sleeve will need a finished opening, called a placket, that creates a wider aperture when the cuff is unfastened.

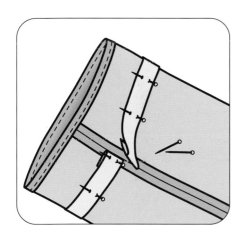

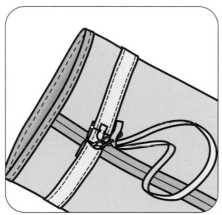

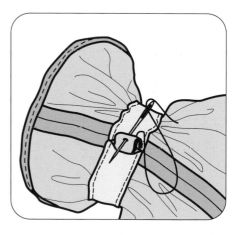

1 ▲ **Gathered and ruffled cuff**
Turn under and hem the bottom edge of the sleeve. Measure the depth of the desired ruffle from the edge and pin a length of seam tape on the wrong side, above the line just measured. Turn the ends of the tape under at the seam to neaten and pin in place.

2 Stitch the tape to the sleeve end along both long edges only, to create a casing for the elastic. Measure a piece of elastic to go around the wrist, then attach a safety pin to one end and guide the elastic through the casing.

3 When the elastic is fully threaded through the casing, pull the two ends together and overlap them by approximately 6 mm (¼ in). Stitch the ends together securely and close the casing opening with slip stitch.

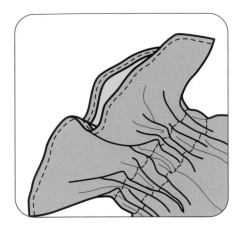

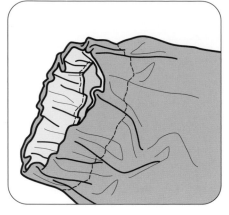

A casing with elastic is a quick and neat way of achieving this look. On translucent fabrics, however, the casing would show through. You can get the same effect by stitching rows of shirring elastic on the wrong side.

For a simpler gathered cuff, stitch the tape or a binding strip right sides together on the raw edge of the sleeve with short ends in line with the underarm seam. Stitch in place, turn to the inside, and stitch the other long side. Then proceed as for the ruffle cuff.

Hemmed placket

This is not a true placket but gives the same effect. Slash the seam allowance to the seamline at the marked notches on the sleeve end. Turn over the section between the notches to make a double hem and stitch in place. Add the cuff in the normal way—the hemmed section of the sleeve will fold neatly when the cuff is fastened.

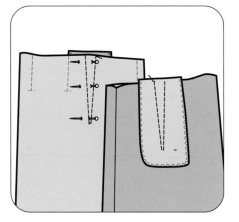

1 ▲ Faced placket
Transfer markings to the sleeve and the placket piece and zigzag round the two long and one short edges of the placket. Pin the placket to the sleeve, right sides together. Stitch along the marked line of the V shape, then slash down the centre of the V with a pair of very sharp, small scissors, being careful not to cut through the stitching.

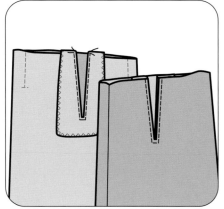

2 Turn the placket piece to the inside through the slash and press into position. Edge stitch along the fold to hold it neatly in position.

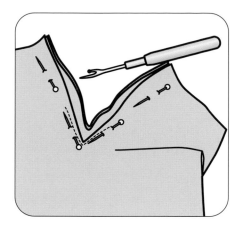

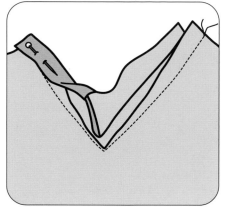

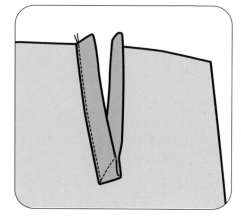

1 ▲ Bias placket

Cut a bias strip for the placket piece and transfer markings to the sleeve. Staystitch the last 5 cm (2 in) at the end of the V shaped opening, with a small horizontal stitch at the very point. With sharp scissors, slash the opening to the point of the V. With right sides together, pin and tack the bias strip to the edges of the opening.

2 Stitch the seam from end to end around the opening. Turn the bias placket strip to the inside, enclosing the raw edges of the seam just made. Turn under a hem of 6 mm (¼ in) along the free raw edge of the bias strip, then pin it in place along the seamline you have just made.

3 Hem along the edge to secure the bias strip in position. Stitch a diagonal line across the folded end of the placket, which will hold it flat against the sleeve and prevent it turning outwards. Press the under section of the bias strip against the sleeve and tack across the end to hold it in place until the cuff is added.

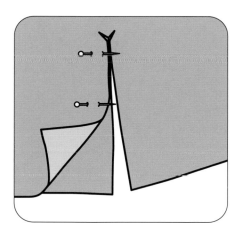

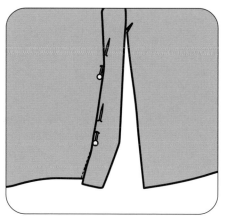

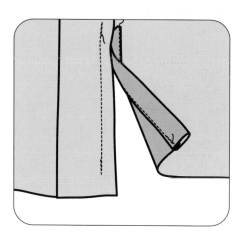

1 ▲ Tailored placket

Cut and transfer any markings to the sleeve and the two placket pieces. Cut a V shape in the sleeve end for the placket opening and pin the smaller underlap placket piece with the right side of the placket piece facing the wrong side of the sleeve. Stitch the underlap piece to the sleeve.

2 Turn under the seam allowance on the free long side of the underlap piece and press in place. Turn the piece through to the right side of the sleeve, enclosing the raw edges of the seam made earlier, and pin. Edge stitch along the edge of the pressed fold, holding the piece in place.

3 Place the right side of the overlap placket piece to the wrong side of the remaining slashed edge. Stitch in position, then stitch across the short end through all thicknesses, including the top of the underlap.

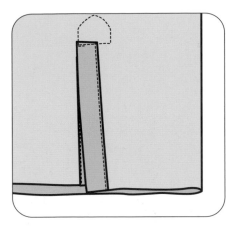

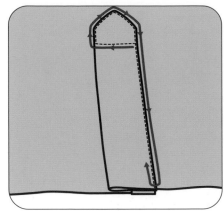

4 Turn under the seam allowance of the overlap. Press and tack in position. Fold it over the seamline and pin in place. Edge stitch along the pressed fold to the top of the opening, then stitch across, up, and around to form the pointed end of the placket, making sure not to catch the underlap as you work. To finish and secure all the layers, stitch downward and follow the seam.

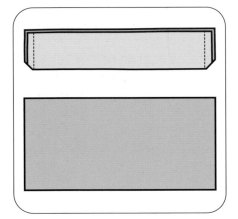

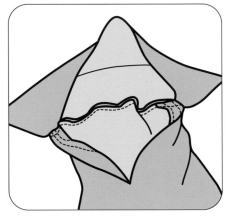

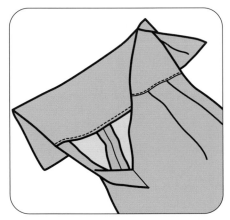

1 ▲ **Attaching cuffs**
Cuffs can be single width (as shown in step 2, right) or double width and folded back (as in step 3, right); both are attached in the same way. Transfer markings, interface the wrong side of the cuff, and stitch the two cuff pieces right sides together. Trim seams and corners.

2 Pin the interfaced side of the cuff to the sleeve end, right sides together, and matching raw edges and notches. Ease in any fullness according to the instructions for this in the pattern. Tack and then stitch the seam.

3 Turn the seam allowance of the other raw edge to the inside and press. Turn the cuff over to enclose the raw edges of the seam and bring the folded edge to the seamline. Pin and slipstitch in place, or edge stitch along the fold on the machine.

Waistbands

There are many variations on the waistband. It can be wide or narrow, have an overlap or not, be stiffened to stand on its own, or act as a casing for elastic or a drawstring. Detailed instructions to achieve the variations will be included in your pattern, but most of the construction basics will remain the same.

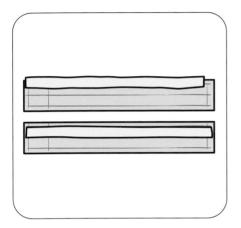

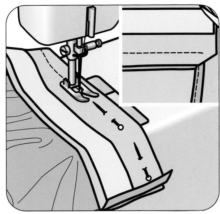

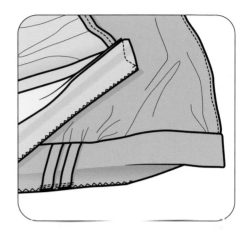

1 ▲ **Simple waistband**
Transfer markings to the waistband sections. Add iron-on or sewn interfacing to the wrong side of one half of the waistband. Press the centre fold down the length of the waistband, right sides together.

2 Pin or tack the waistband to the waistline of the garment with right sides together, notches matched, and the non-interfaced half next to the garment. Stitch the waistband seam, then stitch across the short ends of the waistband. Clip corners and trim seams.

3 Finish the raw edge of the waistband, either with zigzag stitching or turning under and pressing. Turn the waistband right side out and pin or tack the inside layer in place. Topstitch just above the seamline on the right side.

4 If you want to add belt loops to hang the skirt up, use short lengths of seam tape or ribbon. Fold in half and catch the raw ends inside the seam when you work the topstitching.

Tips for perfect waistbands

When working with medium- or lightweight fabrics you can finish the waistband inside by turning under the seam allowance and tacking, then top-stitching just above the seam on the right side.

If you are using thick fabric, grading the seams will help to reduce bulk and make the waistband smoother.

To make sure an elastic waistband gathers evenly, you can stretch it out flat with the elastic inside, then zigzag down the middle of the waistband to hold all of the layers together.

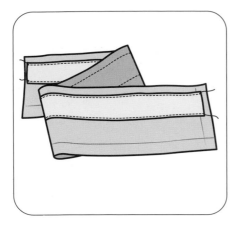

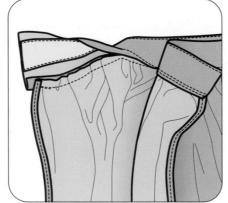

1 ▲ **Stiffened waistband**
Make the waistband as you would the simple waistband, but tack a length of grosgrain (petersham) ribbon to one side instead of the interfacing strip. Machine-stitch along one long edge to hold it firmly in position.

2 With right sides together, stitch the waistband to the waistline of the garment. Then turn the long raw edge under and press. Turn the waistband right side out, fold in the short ends and slipstitch in place. Topstitch on the right side.

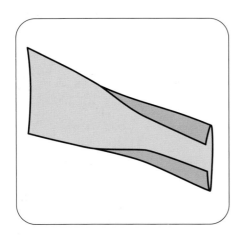

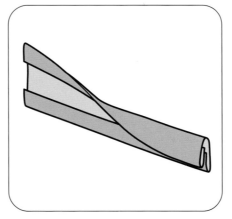

1 ▲ **Belt loops**
Cut a strip of fabric on the straight grain 3 cm (1¼ in) wide by the width of the waistband or belt plus 3 cm (1¼ in) for each loop.

2 Press a strip 6 mm (¼ in) wide to the wrong side along each long edge, then press the whole belt loop in half lengthwise.

3 Edge stitch along both long edges, working as close to the fold line as possible. Do not backstitch at ether end of the stitching.

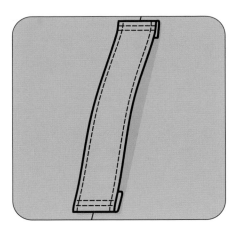

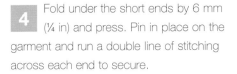

4 Fold under the short ends by 6 mm (¼ in) and press. Pin in place on the garment and run a double line of stitching across each end to secure.

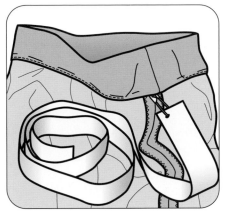

1 ▲ **Elastic waistband with folded casing**

Measure the width of the waistband plus 6 mm (¼ in) and turn over the waist edge of the garment to the inside. Turn under the raw edge by 6 mm (¼ in). Topstitch along the bottom edge to create a casing, leaving a gap unstitched. Thread the waist elastic through the gap.

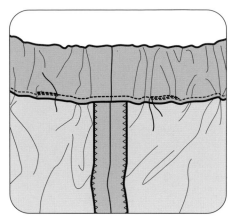

2 Pull the two ends of the elastic clear of the fabric and pin together. Make sure the strip of elastic is not twisted along its length, then stitch the two ends together firmly, either by slipstitching along the double layer edges, or by machine stitching a square on the overlapping section. Close the gap in the edge by topstitching across it to match the original topstitching.

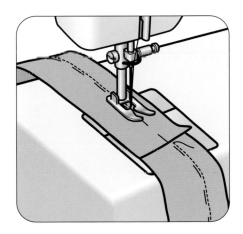

1 ▲ **Gathered waistband with separate elasticized casing**

Stitch the short ends of the waistband casing together, leaving a gap in the seam on one side, to thread the elastic through in step 4 (see overleaf). Press the centre fold down the length of the waistband casing strip, wrong sides together. Stitch the long edges together.

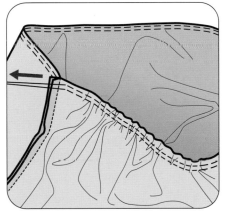

2 Run a double line of gathering threads around the waistline of the garment, within the seamline. Pull up the threads to gather the fabric evenly around the waist, to the length of the waistband.

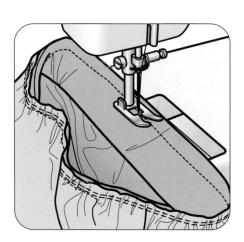

3 Pin then stitch the waistband casing to the waistline of the garment with right sides together, matching notches and seams and easing the gathers evenly. The vertical gap to insert the elastic should fall on the side of the casing facing you at this stage.

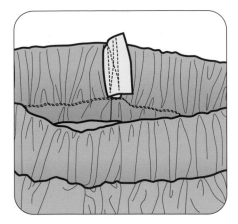

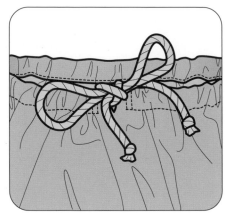

4 Thread the elastic through the vertical gap in the waistband seam. Overlap the two ends of elastic and stitch together to secure. Slide the remaining elastic inside the opening, then stitch it closed.

5 For a drawstring instead of elastic, make sure the vertical gap in the casing seam falls to the inside when stitching the casing to the garment. This insures that it falls on the outside when the waistband is finished. Thread the drawstring and tie in a bow.

 Pocket-making tips

Patch pockets can be decorated with motifs or appliqué, and can be made in a contrasting fabric.

Try making the pocket in two layers with a contrasting fabric beneath to achieve an outline around the sides and bottom.

When making a welted pocket, precise cutting and marking is vital for a clean, tailored look.

Pockets

The most important thing about pockets is that they should be strong enough to withstand normal wear and tear. They are usually made of the same material as the garment, but may be lined with a lighter fabric to lessen bulk. Patch pockets are added to the outside face of a garment and may be lined or unlined.

Alternatively, pockets can be attached to the waist and side seams and sit inside the garment. On jackets and some tailored garments the pocket is concealed inside, and only a welt band trimming the opening can be seen on the outer surface.

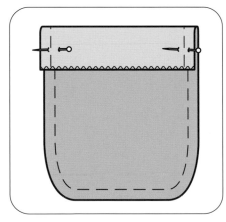

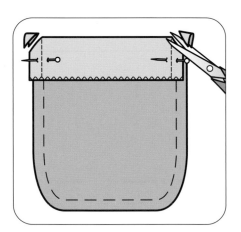

1 ▲ **Basic patch pocket**
Mark the pocket on the garment using a removable marking method, and transfer markings to the wrong side of the pocket piece. Tack the seamline of the pocket and zigzag the top raw edge.

2 Fold over the top edge of the pocket. Make sure the right sides are together and the notches match. Pin in place.

3 Stitch across the ends of the folded section from the top fold to the zigzag stitching only. Clip across the top corners.

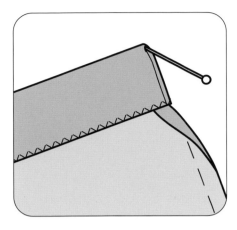

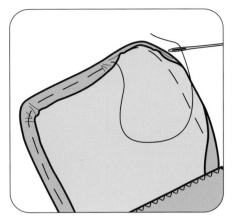

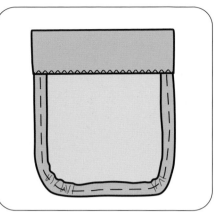

4 Turn the top section right side out and ease the corners to a sharp point; you can use a pin to gently ease it out, but be careful not to pull a thread.

5 Turn the raw edge to the wrong side along the marked line and press. Tack in place. Ease any curves into a smooth line as you go.

6 The finished patch pocket is now ready to be applied to the garment.

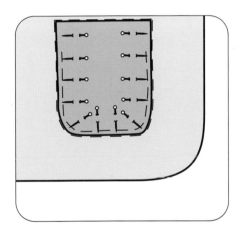

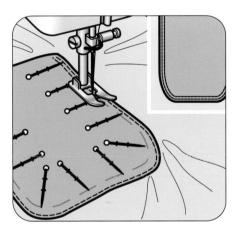

7 Pin the pocket on the garment, following the marked outline. Place the pins at right angles away from the seam so you can stitch without having to remove them.

8 Check you are happy with the pocket position, as it can easily be altered at this stage. If so, stitch in place with a double line of stitching.

False pocket

To make a false pocket or to cover a plain slit pocket, cut two pieces in the shape of a pocket flap. With right sides together, pin and stitch all sides except the top edge. Clip the corners and turn right side out. Press and, if desired, topstitch the edges. Position the right side of the flap upside-down on the garment, fold over to cover the raw edge, and pin in place. Topstitch the flap to the garment.

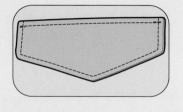

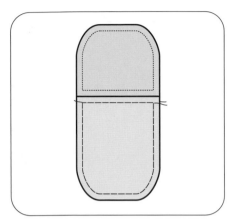

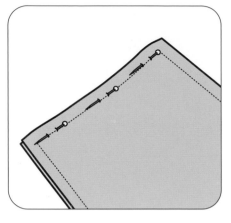

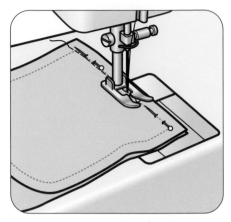

1 ▲ **Lined patch pocket**
The lining here is shown in a contrasting colour, but it can also be a lighter piece of fabric in the same colour. The fold of the pocket is part of the main piece, so the lining does not show on the surface of the garment at all.

2 Mark the position of the pocket on the garment as in step 1 of the basic patch pocket. Mark the seam allowances on both the lining and pocket pieces by tacking along the lines.

3 With right sides together, pin and stitch the lining to the pocket piece along the top straight edge.

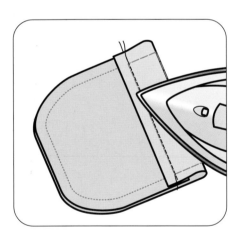

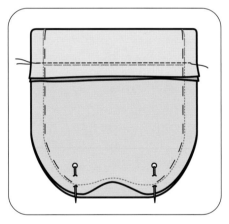

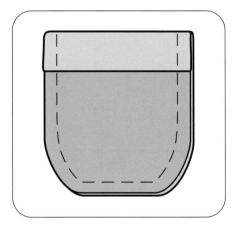

4 Press the seam allowance toward the main part of the pocket and press along the fold line at the top edge with right sides together.

5 Pin and stitch around the sides and bottom of the pocket, leaving a gap at the bottom to turn it to the right side. Turn the pocket right side out and press.

6 Tack around the sides and bottom, to avoid the lining rolling around at the seam and showing on the front surface. Attach the pocket as in steps 7–8 of the basic patch pocket.
For a self-lined patch pocket, work as above, except for step 3. Since the lining is just an extension of the main piece, there is no need to seam them together as shown in this step.

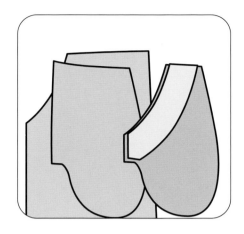

1 ▲ Front hip pocket
Cut out the pieces and transfer all markings to the garment and pocket pieces. Iron or stitch a band of interfacing to the edge of the wrong side of the front pocket piece.

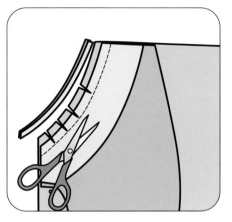

2 With right sides together, stitch the pocket front to the front section of the garment along the curved opening edge. Grade and clip the seam allowances.

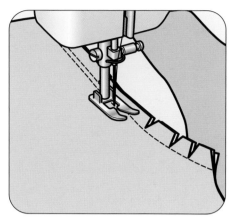

3 Staystitch the inside seam allowance along the clipped seam edge to reinforce the curved opening edge. This line of stitching will show as a line of topstitching on the inside edge of the finished pocket.

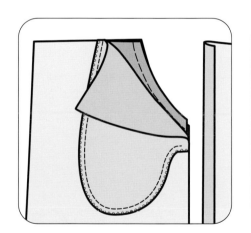

4 Zigzag along the raw side and bottom edge of the pocket back. Tack and stitch the pocket front to the pocket back along the curved seam.

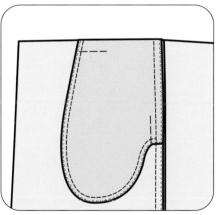

5 Pin and stitch the garment side seam, and zigzag along the seam allowances. Press to one side so the pocket lies flat against the garment front. Tack in position along the waist edge.

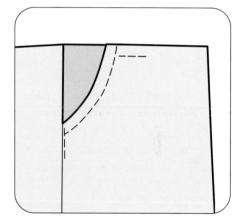

6 From the right side, the back of the pocket looks like a continuation of the main garment and the front of the pocket does not show. The pocket should lie smoothly along the hipline.

Side-seam pockets

There are several versions of the side-seam pocket that may be used in a pattern. Sometimes the pocket is part of the main garment piece, as shown below, or it may be attached to the edge, as shown bottom.

All-in-one side-seam pockets can be used successfully on medium- and lightweight fabrics, but are not a good idea for heavyweight fabric. For extra strength, run a line of backstitching where they join the side seam.

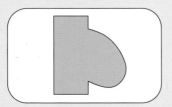

A self-facing side-seam pocket is more suitable for heavy fabrics, as the pocket inside can be cut from a lighter weight fabric. The facing strip in the main garment fabric keeps the line of the garment smooth.

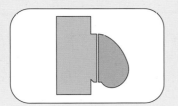

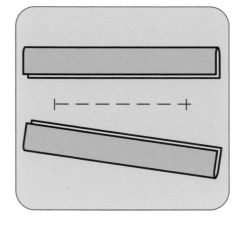

1 ▲ **Welted pocket**
The welt strip finishes the pocket edge, both strengthening the opening and adding a tailored look. Mark and tack the pocket position on the garment. Fold both welt pieces in half lengthways, wrong sides together, and press.

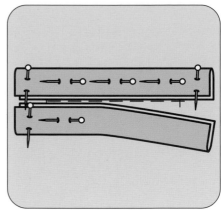

2 Pin the raw edge of one folded welt piece along the top of the tacked line on the right side of the garment, with the raw edges to the line. Repeat with the second welt, pinning it below the tacking.

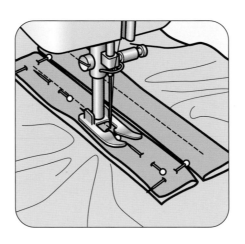

3 Stitch both welt pieces in place along the long edges. DO NOT stitch across the short ends.

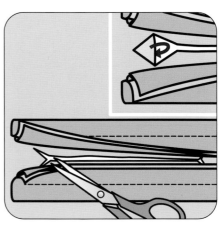

4 Slash the pocket opening from the right side, leaving the last 12 mm (¼ in) uncut. Clip into the corners from the end of the cut. Turn back the triangle at each end of the slash. Tack and stitch on the wrong side.

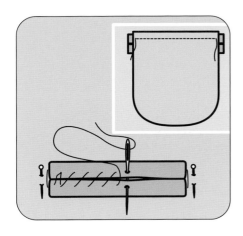

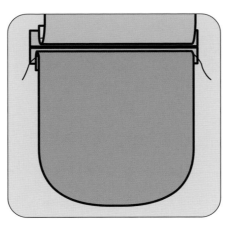

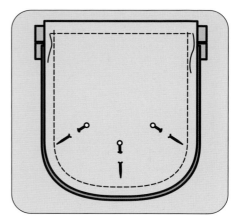

5 Turn the welts to the wrong side through the slit. Tack the folded lips together on the right side to reinforce them until the garment has been completed. On the wrong side, pin and stitch the top edge of the pocket piece to the raw edge of the top welt, making sure you do not catch the garment in the stitching.

6 Stitch the second pocket piece to the bottom welt in the same way. Fold down the top pocket piece and press.

7 Pin the two pocket pieces together and stitch along the edge all round. Zigzag along the raw edges to finish them. Remove tacking.

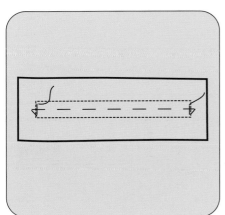

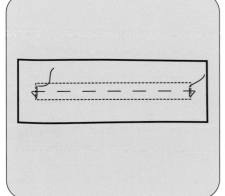

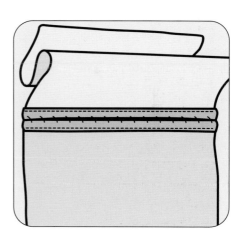

1 ▲ **Bound pocket**
Mark the pocket position on the garment piece and tack stitching lines on the pocket binding strip. With right sides together, tack and stitch the pocket binding strip to the garment around the four tacked guidelines.

2 Slash through the pocket slit on the garment piece as detailed in step 4 of the welted pocket.

3 Turn the pocket binding strip through the opening to the wrong side of the garment. Press then tack the folded edges of the strip closed. Stitch a pocket piece to each long raw edge of the pocket binding strip.

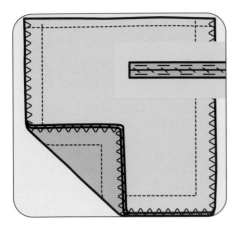

4 Pin and stitch the pocket pieces together along the raw edges, then zigzag along the raw edges to finish them. Remove the tacking. The completed pocket is hidden behind the slit.

More pocket-making tips

Reinforce pockets in children's garments, or those that may receive a great deal of wear and tear, with a double layer of stitching round the bottom.

If a garment is lined, an inset pocket should fall between the garment and the lining.

To help a patch pocket keep its shape, cut a piece of lightweight iron-on interfacing, using the pocket pattern but without a seam allowance or top edge facing, and iron it to the wrong side before you start constructing the pocket.

Hems

The hems detailed here are suitable for both dressmaking and home furnishing projects. A hem can be hand or machine stitched; the choice depends on both the weight of the fabric and the style of the garment. Hemming is usually invisible, but may be used as a design element.

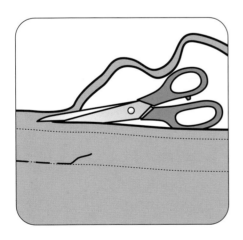

1 ▲ **Simple hand-stitched hem**
Measure the hem, then fold and press the bottom of the hem to mark it. Fold over the raw edge again and press. Tack the fold lines to mark them and trim the raw edge to 6 mm (¼ in) from the second fold.

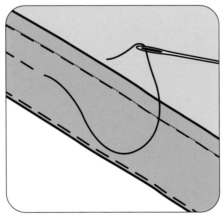

2 Fold up the hem along the line, matching the position of all of the seams as far as possible. You may need to ease the hem if the garment is flared. Tack around the hem through the centre of the fold.

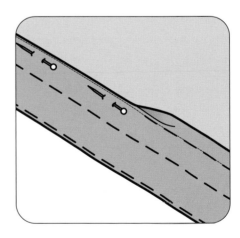

3 Turn under the top fold along the marked line and pin the hem in place. The hem is now ready to stitch.

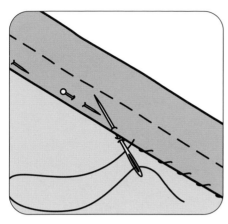

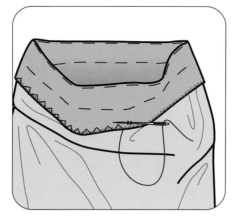

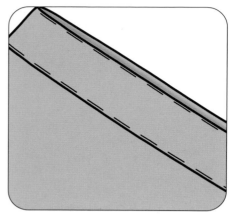

4 Lay the garment wrong side up on a flat surface. Hem along the fold, as described on pages 27 and 28. Remove the pins as you work, and any tacking when you have finished.

1 ▲ **Simple turn-up cuff**
With the leg of the trousers wrong side out, fold and tack three parallel lines to mark the bottom edge of the turn-up, the top edge of the turn-up, and the hemline. Zigzag the raw edge, turn up the centre fold, and press. Herringbone stitch to secure the zigzagged raw edge.

2 Turn the trouser leg right side out. Turn up the bottom fold to meet the line marking the top of the turn-up and press gently. Take a couple of blind hemming stitches (see page 28) at the side seams to secure the turn-up in position. Remove tacking.

Hand-sewn hems

Try out some of the different types of hand-sewn hem to see which one will work best on your project.

Bound hem – made with either bias or straight binding. The binding is machine stitched to the raw edge of the marked hem, then turned up and pressed. It can either be hemmed or machine stitched in place.

Zigzagged hem – the raw edge is zigzag stitched and turned up and the hem held in place with herringbone stitch.

Edge-stitched hem – the raw edge is turned under and edge stitched. The hem is turned up and pressed and stitched into position with ordinary hemming stitch.

Fusible hem – the hem is folded up and held in place with a strip of fusible hem tape. This can be suitable for light-weight fabrics and for emergency repairs, but the tape does tend to come loose after a while.

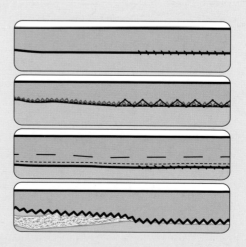

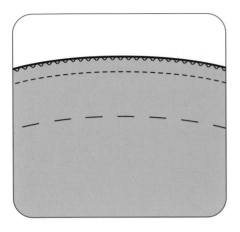
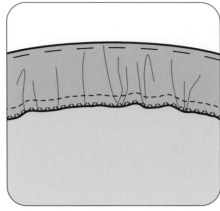
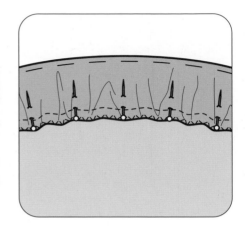

1 ▲ **Curved hem**
Mark and cut the hem into a smooth, even line. Zigzag the raw edge and tack along the fold line. Run a line of gathering stitches 6 mm (¼ in) from the zigzag stitching.

2 Turn up the hem along the tacked fold line. Tack the hem in position all around, close to the folded edge.

3 Matching the seams, pin the hem in place, pulling up the gathering thread to spread the fullness of the fabric evenly along the length.

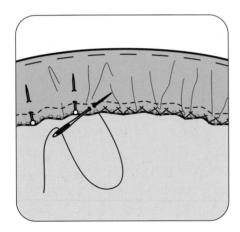

4 Herringbone stitch the hem in position from the wrong side. Remove any pins as you work and the tacking at the end. Press the fold of the hem to finish.

Tips for hemming

Although pinning is often sufficient to hold a hem until it is stitched, tacking it in place will ensure accuracy and a straight line.

If there is not enough fabric to turn under a full hem, the edge can be bound or faced instead.

Twin topstitching can look very smart on a hem. It can be worked with two separate parallel rows of topstitching or by using a twin needle.

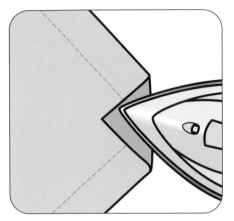

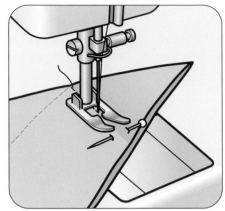

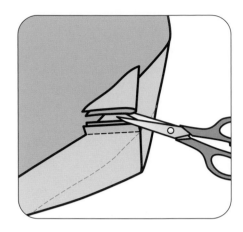

1 ▲ Mitred hem
At the corner of the piece turn up the seam allowance and press along the hemline in both directions. Open the hem flat and turn up the corner triangle, aligning the pressed lines. Press the diagonal line to make a crease.

2 Open the corner and fold it the other way diagonally, with right sides together so the raw edges and the hemline creases meet. Pin in place and stitch along the diagonal creased line made in step 1.

3 Trim off the excess triangular piece of seam allowance from the corner and press the seam open. Repeat on all corners of the piece to be mitred.

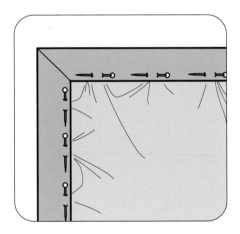

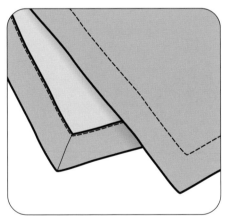

4 Turn the corners right side out. Turn under the raw edges on each side of the hem and pin in place. Stitch the hem.

5 The finished item should have neat corners on both sides. This method is not only used on home furnishings, such as tablecloths and place mats, but is also useful for jacket fronts and skirt slits.

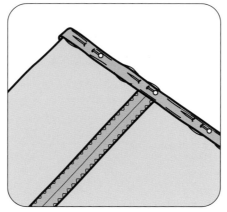

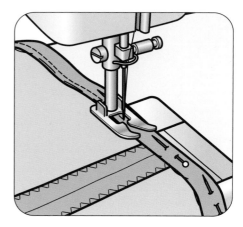

1 ▲ **Simple machine-stitched hem**

Measure, mark, and tack two fold lines, one 6 mm (¼ in) from the raw edge and the other another 12 mm (½ in) in from the first. Turn the first fold under and press.

2 Turn under the second fold and press. Pin or tack the double layer of fabric in position, matching seam positions.

3 On the wrong side of the fabric, edge stitch along the fold line, removing pins as you work. Remove any tacking and press.

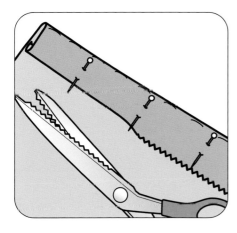

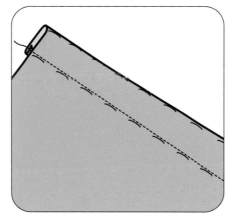

1 ▲ **Top-stitched hem**

Measure and mark the hem and tack along the fold line. Trim along the raw edge with pinking shears. Turn the hem under along the fold line and pin in place, matching seams. Tack in place and remove any pins.

2 From the right side, topstitch all around the hem. Use the guidelines marked on the footplate of the machine to keep the stitching line the same distance from the folded edge on all sides. Remove any tacking and press.

Chiffon hem

To make a chiffon hem, machine-stitch 3 mm (⅛ in) in from the raw edge all round the hem on the right side. Press the fabric under along the stitching line, so the raw edge is pointing upward on the wrong side. On the right side, machine-stitch 3 mm (⅛ in) in from the edge of the fold all round again. Press under along the new stitching line, so the raw edge on the wrong side is now enclosed. If the seam doesn't want to lie flat, tug gently on the seam you just made to ease it. On the right side, topstitch as close as possible to the edge of the hem all round to hold all the folds in place.

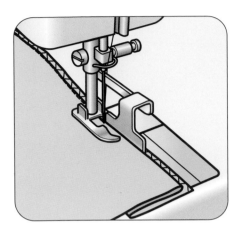

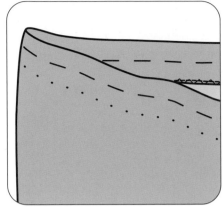

1 ▲ **Machine-stitched blind hem**
Mark the hem and zigzag along the raw edge. Fold under the hem and tack in place 6 mm (¼ in) from the zigzagging. Fold the hem back towards the right side, so you can work along this fold and the zigzagged edge. Using the blind-stitch the hem with zigzag or blind hemming stitch.

2 The tip of each pointed stitch should just catch the fabric on the edge of the fold so on the right side the stitches are tiny and almost invisible. The special foot you need for this technique is available for most modern machines.

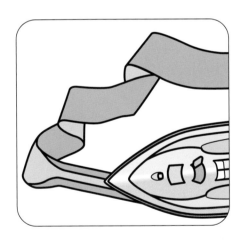

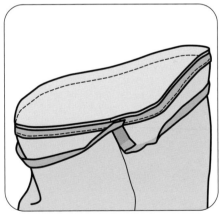

1 ▲ **Faced hem**
Mark the hemline on the raw edge of the piece. Cut a strip of facing 2.5 cm (1 in) wide and the length of the hem plus the seam allowances. Fold under 6 mm (¼ in) along both long raw edges and press in place.

2 Fold under the short ends. Match one short end to a garment seam, and with right sides together, pin one long folded edge to the garment along the marked hemline. Stitch the seam, removing pins as you work. Overlap the other folded short end over the first, and finish stitching.

3 Turn the facing to the wrong side and press in place. Pin the facing to the garment, making sure that the other raw edge is still folded on all sides. Hem along the top folded edge of the facing by hand. Press and remove any tacking or loose threads to finish.

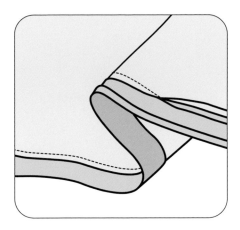

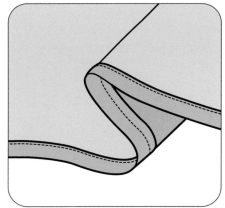

1 ▲ Bound hem
Prepare the hem and binding as in step 1 of the faced hem. If you are using purchased bias binding, the edges will already be folded under. Stitch the binding to the hem as described in step 2 of the faced hem.

2 Fold the strip halfway across its width and topstitch in place along the top edge, which means a narrow strip of binding will show on the right side.

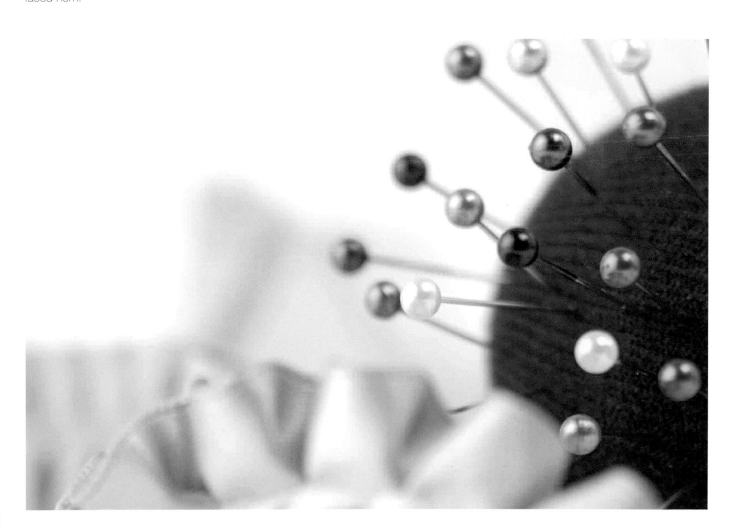

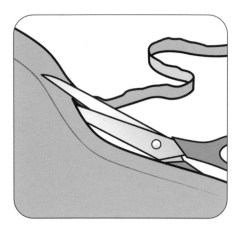

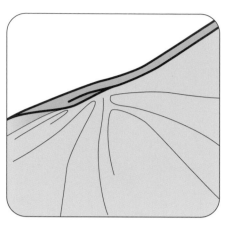

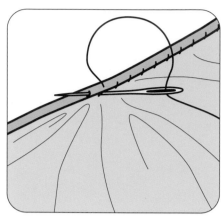

1 ▲ Hand-rolled hem
Mark the hemline with a pencil, then cut the raw edge of the fabric straight, trimming only a little at a time.

2 Roll the cut edge inward, until it encloses the raw edge completely. Work on only a small section at a time and keep the roll as small as possible.

3 Hold the edge very tightly over one finger and take two or three evenly spaced stitches onto the needle, picking up only one thread at a time. Repeat along the hem.

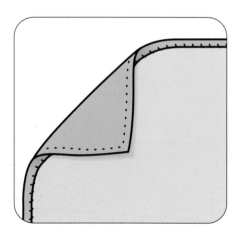

4 A hand-rolled hem should have evenly-spaced stitches and be neat on both sides. To make a sharp, neat corner, clip a small triangle at the corner, turn, and mitre carefully. Use a fine pin to hold the corner in position as you work.

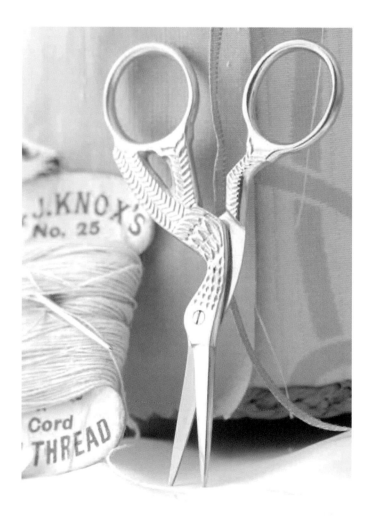

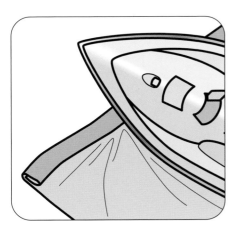

1 ▲ **Machine-rolled hem 1**
Turn under and press a single hem to an appropriate width for the fabric. Turn under again and press to make a double hem.

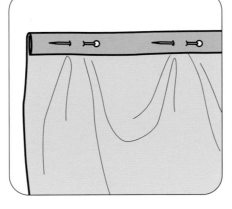

2 Pin the pressed hem in place, matching seams. Position the pins along the seam, with the points away from the direction you will be stitching. Tack at the corners.

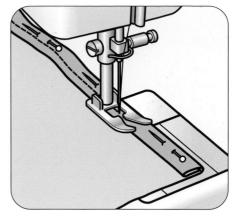

3 With the wrong side up, machine stitch the hem. Remove the pins as you work. When you have finished remove the tacking and press.

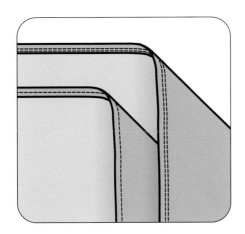

4 This hem is suitable for all weights of fabric, although it will be deeper on the heavier weights. For lighter weights, use method 2 overleaf, which will appear to be double-sided.

More tips for hemming

Some sewing machines can be fitted with a special foot that will roll the edge of the hem and stitch it at the same time. If you plan to make many projects with rolled hems, it will be worth investing in one.

Allow an extra deep hem on children's garments, so they can be turned down as the child grows.

If you are turning up a hem on a garment for an adult, cut off any excess fabric to avoid too much bulk at the hemline.

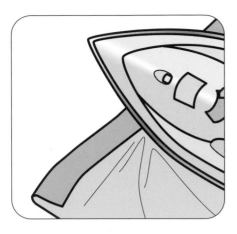

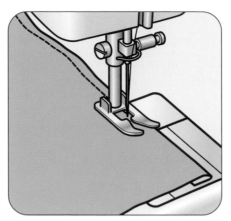

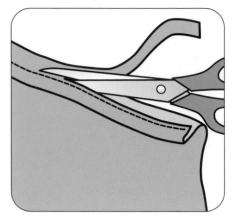

 1 ▲ Machine-rolled hem 2
Turn under and press a hem of around 18 mm (¾ in) to the wrong side, along the edge to be hemmed.

2 With the right side facing, machine stitch all along the edge approximately 6 mm (¼ in) from the fold.

3 Holding the stitching line open and using small, very sharp scissors, trim away the excess fabric as close to the stitching line as possible.

Achieving professional results

The hem is usually the last thing to be completed on a project, so you may be tempted to sew it quickly so the item is finished. However, as with all finishing techniques, the quality of your hem can make or break the whole look of your project so it is worth spending a bit more time to get it right.

Seams cut on the bias often drop, so allow the item to hang for a few days before measuring and turning up the hem. See page 127 for more information about working on the bias.

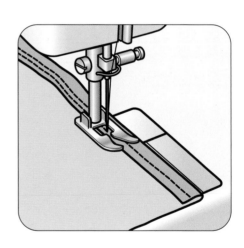

4 With the wrong side up, and working as close as possible to the first stitching line, stitch another line to prevent fraying.

Linings

Linings both neaten the inside of a garment, hiding all the construction seams, and improve its shape by holding the fabric in position. They also prolong the life of a garment by protecting the inside from wear and tear and keeping everything more stable. Since the lining is an extra layer that will add bulk, generally it is made in quite lightweight fabric.

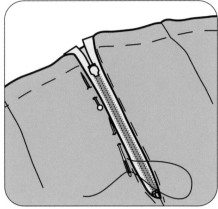

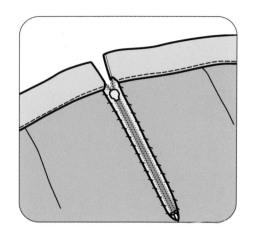

1 ▲ **Lining a skirt**
Make up the skirt, complete with zipper in place. Make up the lining pieces in the same way, leaving the seam open in the lining from the waist to the bottom of the zipper position.

2 Matching darts and seams and with wrong sides together, pin and tack the lining to the skirt along the waist. Fold under the seam allowance on either side of the zipper and pin and tack in place down the zipper sides.

3 Slipstitch the lining to the zipper tape, not too close to the teeth. Make sure the stitching does not show on the right side of the skirt. Add the waistband in the normal way, then finish the bottom hem as appropriate.

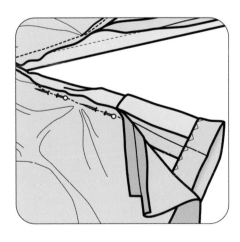

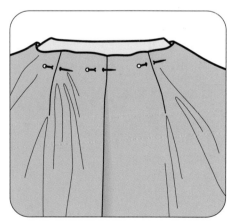

1 ▲ **Lining a jacket**
Finish the jacket, then make up the lining, adding an extra 2.5 cm (1 in) to the centre back width. Pin the lining into the jacket along one underarm and side seam wrong sides together, matching darts and seams, with seams pressed flat against each other. Pin then stitch seam to seam.

2 Pull the lining through to the wrong side of the garment and pin it in place along the neck edge and the facings. Do not pull tightly; allow a little slack as you work so the lining has some ease.

3 At the back, match the two shoulder darts. Make a small pleat in the lining fabric at the centre back to take up the extra fabric allowed on the width of the lining. Pin a corresponding pleat on the bottom edge.

Special hemline finishes

There are special ways to achieve a neat hemline finish in some circumstances.

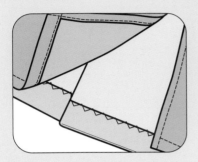

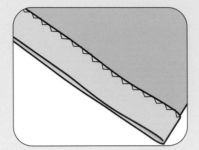

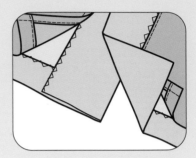

Kick pleat – if there is no centre seam in the garment, slit the lining to correspond with the pleat or split. Turn under a narrow double hem on both sides of the split, pin in position, and stitch. Hem the bottom.

Sewn-in lining – linings on skirts and trousers may be secured under the hem of the garment. Trim the lining a little shorter than the finished garment and stitch the hem of the garment to the lining.

Split skirt – a split is used if garment and lining have a centre back seam. Leave the bottom of the centre seam on the lining unstitched and clip the seam allowance on top. Turn under, pin, and stitch a double hem along both sides of the split. Hem the bottom.

4 Turn under any raw edges around the lining and slipstitch the lining to the jacket all round. You can now finish the other items, such as buttonholes on the jacket, although if you are making bound buttonholes they should be worked before the lining is added.

Lining tips

To secure a lining to a finished garment, turn under and pin the raw edge of the lining. Slipstitch all along the edge, taking care that the stitches do not show through on the right side of the garment.

Check that the garment fits correctly before lining or adding any finishing touches.

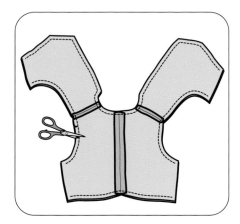

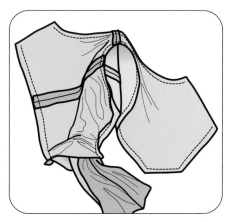

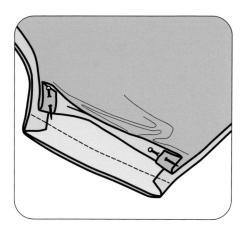

1 ▲ **Lining a waistcoat**
Join the centre back and shoulder seams on both the garment and lining pieces. With right sides together and matching seams, pin and tack the garment and the lining together. Stitch around all edges, except the four side seams under the armholes. Trim and clip curved seams and clip off any points.

2 Pull the lining through to the wrong side of the garment and pin it in place along the neck edge and the facings. Do not pull tightly; allow a little slack as you work so the lining has some ease.

3 Pin the side seams of the lining back out of the way. With right sides together, pin and stitch the side seams of the garment. Press gently.

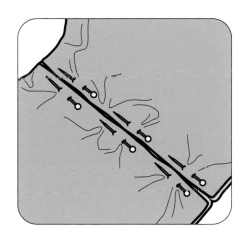

4 On the lining, fold under the seam allowance on each side seam and pin in place. Using slipstitch, catch the seam allowance on the garment as you stitch the lining seams together, but be careful the stitches do not show on the right side. Press and remove any tacking to finish.

More lining tips

White fabric can be quite translucent, so seams and other construction elements may show right through. Lining at least part of the garment will minimize the problem.

When choosing your lining fabric, select a colour to tone with the main fabric, or match one of the colours in the design.

If the garment is washable, make sure the lining is washable too—and that it will not shrink at a different rate and pull the garment out of shape.

Closures

Almost all garments require a fastener of some sort. Many people are daunted by the thought of inserting zippers, but once you become familiar with them they are fairly easy to handle. Buttonholes are often another area of concern, but practise will soon give you the confidence to work with them.

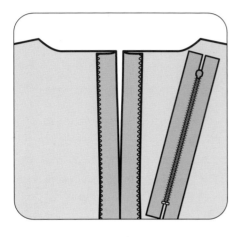

1 ▲ **Centre zipper**
Mark the zipper position on the seam, using the zipper as a guide. Stitch the seam to the bottom mark, leaving enough room at the top for a facing seam. Zigzag the raw edges.

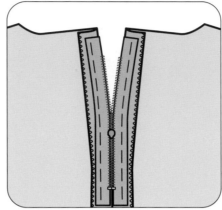

2 Place the closed zipper over the seam on the wrong side and pin in place. Tack along both sides of the zipper tape to hold it firmly in position while you work. Turn the garment to the right side.

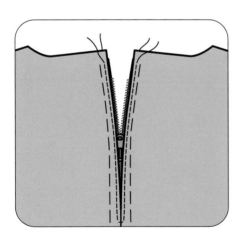

3 Using a zipper foot on the machine, start at the top and stitch down one side, across the bottom, and up to the top again to secure the zipper in place. Move the zipper slider if necessary to keep the seam straight, and keep the bottom corners nice and square.

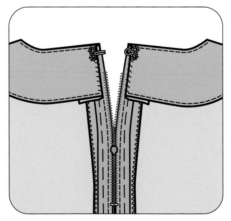

4 Add the facing or the waistband piece to the garment in the normal way and slipstitch the ends to the zipper tape. Make sure that no stitches or facings are likely to catch in the zipper teeth in use. Remove any tacking and add any other fasteners required.

Tips for closures

Always match the weight of the zipper to the weight of the fabric.

To insert an open-ended zipper, fold the lengthwise facings or seam allowances under and tack along the seamline. Insert the zipper as shown for centred zippers, stitching on the right side of the garment, then remove the tacking.

To shorten a zipper, sew the bar of a hook-and-bar fastening securely across the new end point, then cut the zipper below the bar.

To position a button, align the buttonhole band over the button band and insert a pin through the centre of the buttonhole. Mark the point on the button band.

Vertical hand-stitched buttonholes have a bar tack at each end, horizontal ones normally have buttonhole stitch worked in a semi-circle at the end nearest the opening.

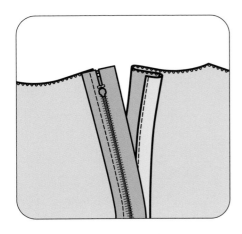

1 ▲ **Lapped zipper**

Stitch the seam to the bottom of the zipper and zigzag the raw edges of the seam allowance. Open the zipper and pin and tack it to one side of the seam allowance, which will become the underlap. Working from the wrong side, stitch this seam with the zipper foot on the machine. Strengthen the raw edge of the overlap seam with seam tape.

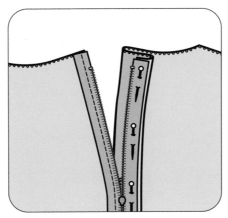

2 Fold the overlap edge to the wrong side of the garment. Pin and tack the zipper into position along both sides of the zipper tape, then close the zipper.

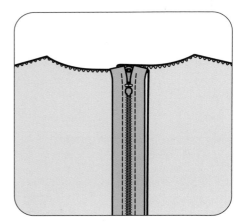

3 Again using the zipper foot on the machine, stitch the closed zipper in place on the overlap side and across the bottom. Remove the tacking. Check to make sure that the zipper slides easily when it is opened and closed, and that it is fully hidden in the seam.

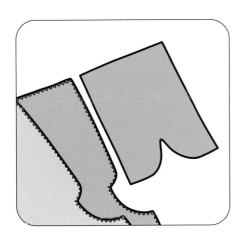

1 ▲ **Fly-front zipper**

Cut out and prepare the garment pieces. Finish all raw edges with zigzag stitch and tack all the zipper markings as shown on the pattern.

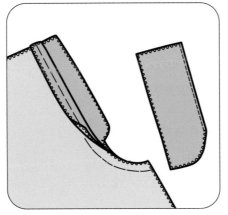

2 Fold the fly piece in half lengthwise, wrong sides together, and topstitch 3 mm (⅛ in) from the fold. Zigzag the other edges together. Stitch the curved garment seam, then fold the underlap to the wrong side and tack along the fold.

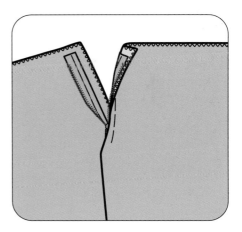

3 Open the zipper and align the teeth with the underlap fold. Pin, tack, and stitch the zipper on the underlap near the teeth, leaving room for the slider to move up and down. Close the zipper, fold the overlap along the tacked line, and tack through all layers of the overlap.

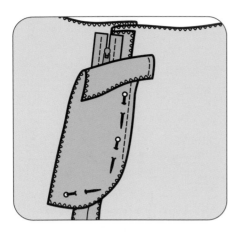

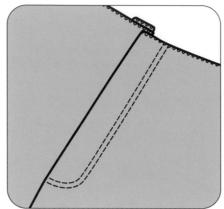

4 Pin the fly piece over the closed zipper, making sure that the curved edges match. Tack in position along the seamline.

5 Working on the right side, work a double row of topstitching to reinforce the finished fly, following the curved line of the tacking on the fly piece.

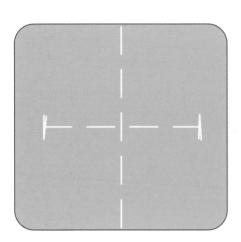

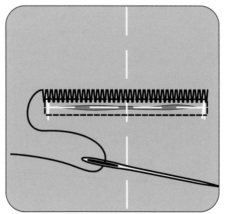

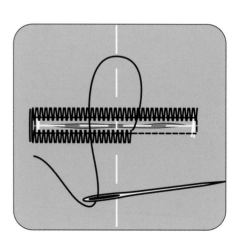

1 ▲ **Hand-sewn buttonhole**
Mark the buttonhole position on the wrong side of the buttonhole band and tack along the centre line to mark it. Tack along each side to stabilize the fabric while you work.

2 Slit the opening with sharp scissors or a seam ripper. Cut a piece of waxed thread more than twice the buttonhole length and lay it along the top edge. Work buttonhole stitch along the top edge, using a fine needle, and catching the waxed thread as you work.

3 Work a bar tack at the end, then repeat along the lower edge of the buttonhole. Make sure you catch the waxed thread in as you work, to strengthen the edge of the buttonhole. Keep your stitches as neat and even as possible for a professional finish.

Attaching buttons

Two-hole and four-hole buttons – secured by stitching through the holes into the fabric behind. With four-hole buttons, the two stitches required can be two parallel bars or worked as a small cross. Do not pull the thread too tight when stitching or there will be no room between the button and fabric for the extra layer of fabric on the buttonhole band.

Shank buttons – have no holes on the top surface, but instead have a small circle or handle underneath to stitch through, which also holds the button clear of the fabric surface.

Thread shank – required on thick fabric when stitching on buttons without a shank. Before beginning to stitch the button, place a matchstick or toothpick underneath to hold it clear of the fabric. When you have finished stitching, remove the matchstick and wind the thread around the loose threads beneath the button to create a thread shank before finishing off.

Military-style buttons – have a ring shank on the back with a metal pin. You will need to make a small eyelet hole in the fabric to thread the ring through, then the pin clips through the ring on the reverse to hold the button in place. To neaten the edges of the eyelet hole, work buttonhole stitch around it.

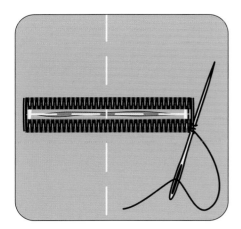

4 Make a few small straight stitches at the end to secure the end of the thread, then work another bar tack across this end. Trim the ends of the waxed thread and remove the tacking.

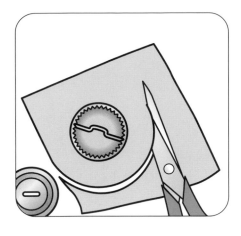

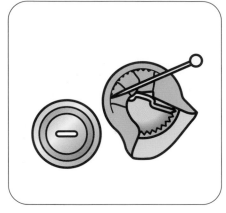

1 ▲ **Self-covering buttons**
If the button kit has instructions that differ, follow them instead. Using the button or the template provided in the kit, cut a circle of fabric around 12 mm (½ in) wider than the top of the button.

2 Place the button top in the centre of the wrong side of the fabric. Use a pin to push the excess fabric so that it catches on the teeth around the edge of the button top. Make sure all the fabric is securely held in place.

3 Line up the back of the button on the reverse of the button top and press it firmly into place until it snaps into position.

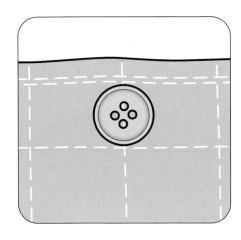

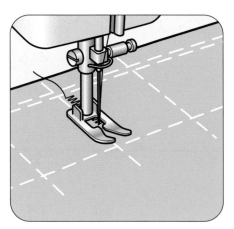

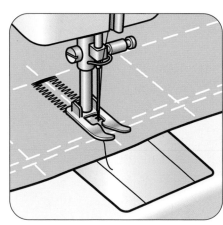

1 ▲ **Machine-sewn buttonhole**
Mark the centre position and length of the buttonhole by tacking guidelines on the button band, using the button as a guide.

2 Run a line of straight stitching on each side of the line of the buttonhole opening. Set the machine to medium-width zigzag and stitch a row of tight satin stitch along one edge.

3 Raise the foot and turn the garment 180°, then make a few long stitches across the full buttonhole width to reinforce the end.

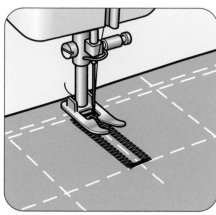

4 Repeat steps 2 and 3 to work the other side and end of the buttonhole. Set the stitch width at 0 to make a few stitches to secure the end of the thread.

5 Pull any loose ends through to the wrong side and trim close to the fabric. Using a seam ripper or a very sharp pair of scissors, slit the buttonhole open down the centre line.

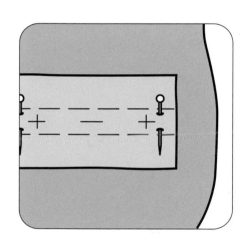

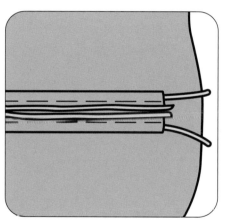

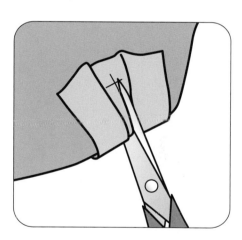

1 ▲ **Bound buttonhole**
Cut a patch 2.5 cm (1 in) wider and longer than the buttonhole and centre it over the marked buttonhole line. Tack 3 mm (⅛ in) from the buttonhole line on each side, working on the right side of the fabric.

2 Fold the patch to the centre along the tacked lines. Tack again to secure the folds in position. Machine stitch a rectangle the length of the buttonhole and 6 mm (¼ in) wide, working through all layers and centred on the buttonhole line.

3 Fold the buttonhole area of the fabric in half and carefully cut along the buttonhole line from end to end, being careful not to cut through any stitching.

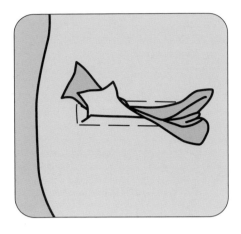
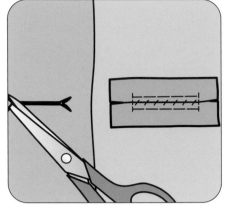
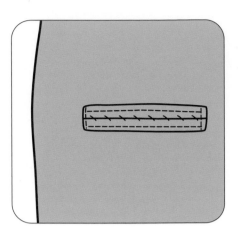

4 Pull the patch through to the wrong side of the fabric. Press it flat and slipstitch along the folds to hold the lips together. On the wrong side, pull the small triangle at each end to square the opening and stitch across to hold it in place.

5 With a small, sharp pair of scissors, slit a matching buttonhole in the facing, stopping 6 mm (¼ in) from the end and then angling the cut into the corners as shown.

6 Align the facing with the buttonhole, fold back the raw edges of the slit you have just made and pin and handstitch the facing to the buttonhole patch.

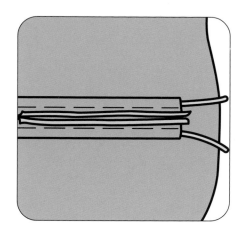

1 ▲ Corded buttonhole
Prepare the pieces as in step 1 of the bound buttonhole. In step 2, slide a length of cord under the fold at each edge and stitch in place. Then proceed as for the bound buttonhole.

Other fastening options

There is a wide range of other fasteners available so it is worth checking out what is on offer if you want something a bit different. If you want something eye-catching, look in antique stores or watch out for interesting fastenings that can be removed and reused from second hand clothes. If you want something unobtrusive, some common types are shown here.

Hook and loop tape – often also known by its brand name of Velcro®, this is a tape that comes in two halves, one with little loops and one with little hooks. It grips quite firmly for most applications but will not be suitable for heavy strain.

Metal popper snap – the knob on one side fits into a sprung hole on the other. Many types can grip very firmly, but in dressmaking they are usually used as a secondary fastening.

Plastic popper snap – as the metal version, but being transparent and less obtrusive. They are usually quite small so again will not cope with heavy strain.

Punch-in metal snap – these are used on commercial clothing, since no stitching is required to attach them. They are very effective when applied properly, but difficult to replace if they come off.

Heavy duty hook and bar – these will cope with considerable strain – in fact the fabric will tear or the stitching give way before they will break. Use double thread when stitching for extra security.

Lightweight hook and bar – a less heavy duty version, suitable to use at the top of zippers or as other secondary fastenings.

Hook and eye – the smallest version of the hook types, suitable for a wide range of uses.

Thread wrapped hook and eye – the thread hides the rather industrial look of the metal and these are used on lighter garments such as lingerie, or where the opening will be worn open so the fastenings will be on show.

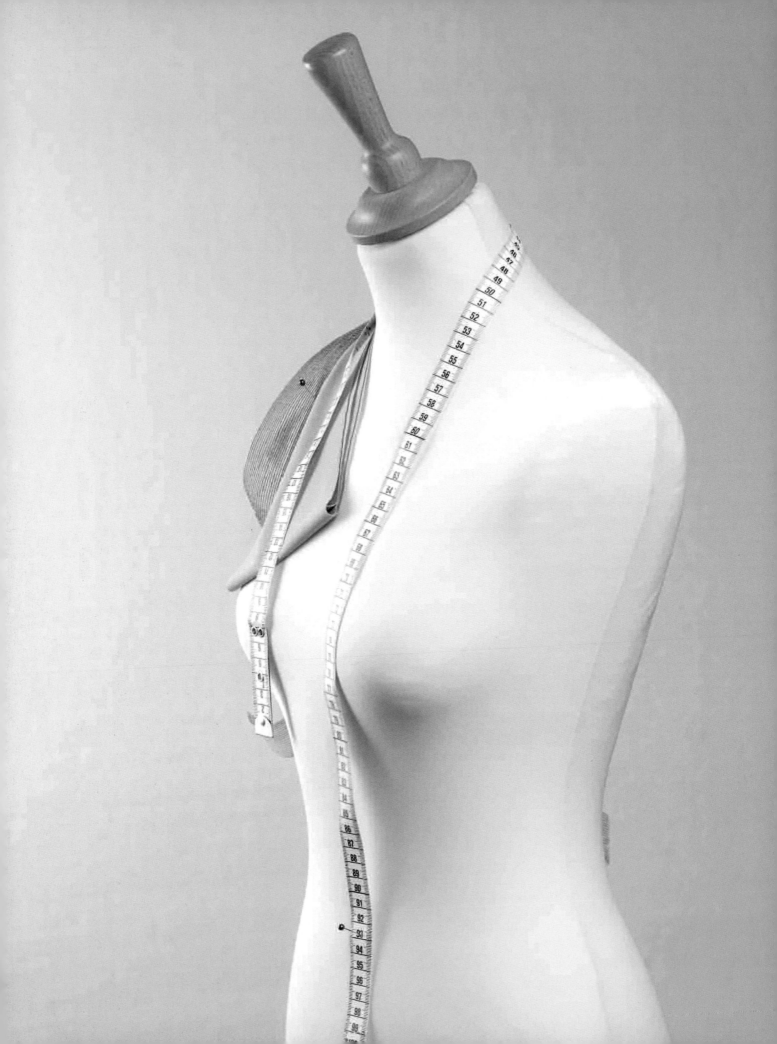

advanced tailoring

Tailoring is an advanced form of dressmaking that requires a strong grounding in sewing techniques and some experience before you tackle any projects. Many tailoring techniques are concerned with finishing and add a professional look to your garments, but you also need to learn how garments are shaped and moulded for a fully tailored effect.

jackets

When making a tailored jacket, choose a classic pattern that will not date quickly. Additionally, it is wise to avoid checks and stripes when starting out, since it is difficult to match the pattern across all the darts and seams. And if the pattern is not matched correctly, it could spoil the look of your carefully-made project!

Mounting and lining

Mounting and lining are extra layers of fabric used to support and add body to garments as well as to help them retain their shape. Mounting is included within the seams of a garment, supporting it so it stands away from the figure beneath. Lining is constructed separately and attached inside the garment at various points, both to hide construction seams and to help it keep its shape.

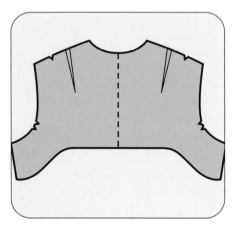

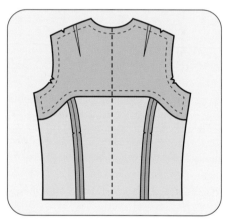

A few tips

Almost any fabric can be mounted, but generally only opaque fabrics are lined.

Mounting and lining should not be confused with interfacing, which is always used between the backing piece and the garment itself on facings, collars, lapels and cuffs.

If the garment you are lining is bulky, choose a lightweight lining fabric to avoid adding more weight.

1 ▲ **Back underlining**
Cut an underlining in a suitable fabric, such as batiste or preshrunk linen. Use the jacket's back pattern pieces, but if there are seams, pin the pattern pieces together on the seamline and cut the underlining in one piece about 25 cm (10 in) deep at the centre and shaped to fit round the armholes. Slash through the centre of the shoulder darts, lap one cut edge over the other with the seamline meeting in the centre, and stitch with a zigzag.

2 Make up the back section of the jacket if there are seams. Place the underlining over the wrong side of the back piece, matching centre lines and seam edges. Pin, then tack in place around the circumference, about 2.5 cm (1 in) from the outer edges.

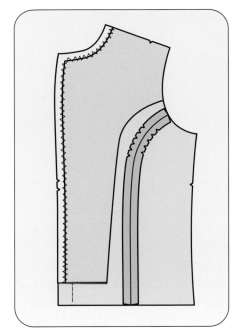

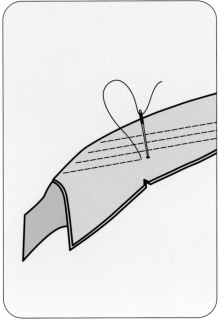

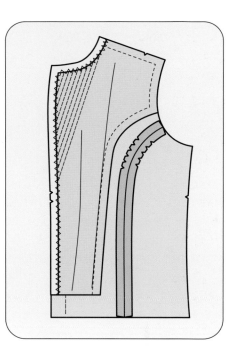

1 ▲ Front interfacing

Cut a strip of organza or similar lightweight fabric to fit around the front edge and the neckline, making it approximately 3.5 cm (1¼ in) wide and using the front interfacing piece as a guide to shape the edge. Pin the organza over the edge of the interfacing, extending it roughly 18 mm (¾ in). Stitch in place with zigzag stitching. Pin the interfacing over the wrong side of each jacket front, keeping the edge of the organza strip and the garment in line.

2 Establish the diagonal line of the roll of the lapel from the neckline to the top button, place a ruler between the two points, and mark the line on the interfacing with chalk. Pin the interfacing along this line, then stitch to the fabric with overlapping stitches using thread to match the fabric and only picking up one thread at a time. Roll the lapel over your fingers as you work, a technique that helps shape the roll of the lapel.

3 Begin each line of stitches at the top of the lapel and end at the seamline, working parallel lines from the roll line towards the point of the lapel. Tack the interfacing in place along the seamline. Finally, tack a couple more diagonal lines roughly over the main part of the interfacing—using very large stitches— to hold the interfacing in position.

Choosing fabrics

Mounting and lining fabrics do not need to be the same composition as the main fabric, but the colours should match.

Lay the fabric you will be using over different mounting or lining fabrics to assess the effect you will achieve before you buy and review the chart on page 120 for some useful suggestions.

advanced tailoring

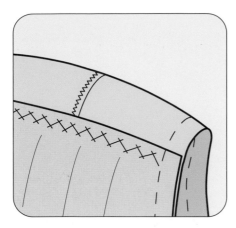

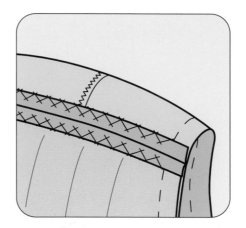

1 ▲ **Shoulder seams**
Join the front and back sections at the shoulder line, stitching through the main fabric only. Snip off the ends of the dart where they protrude into the seam allowance. Press the seams open. Remove the tacking along the shoulder and lap the front interfacing over the back underlining at the shoulder seam and pin in position. Turn right side out to make sure everything is lying smoothly. On the wrong side, herringbone stitch the lapped seam from the neckline to just short of the shoulder seam, stitching through the seam allowance of the main fabric only.

2 An alternative method is to make the shoulder seams as described in step 1 and trim the darts. Then trim off the seam allowances on both the front interfacing and the back underlining and slip the raw edges under the seam allowance of the shoulder seam on both sides. Pin in place, then herringbone stitch the seam allowance edges to the front interfacing on one side and the back underlining on the other.

Fabrics for mounting or lining

The fabric you use for mounting or interlining does not have to have the same fibre content as your main fabric, but it should match the colour. A few suggested fabrics:

Batiste	suitable for dry-clean cottons, lightweight wool, jersey, and loosely woven fabrics
Silk organza	suitable for most silk, light-weight wool, and lace
Taffeta	suitable for heavyweight silks, fine wool, chiffon, and lace
Rayon	suitable for silk, lightweight wool, jersey, loosely woven fabrics, and linen
Vilene	suitable for heavyweight fabrics and also used for interfacing
Voile	suitable for lace, lightweight silk, and chiffon

Tailored collar

Because the tailored collar is rolled into shape as it is made, it needs to be more solid than an ordinary interfaced collar. The lines of stitching on the undercollar hold everything firmly in place and help maintain the roll.

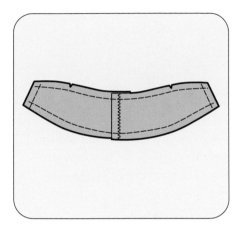

1   ▲   **Interfacing the undercollar**
Stitch the centre seam of the undercollar and press open. Lap the centre seam of the interfacing—matching any notches and seam lines—and zigzag stitch together. Mark a line around the interfacing 18 mm (¾ in) away from the edge. Trim the interfacing back to the marked line.

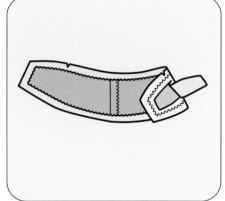

2   Pin the two halves of the undercollar pattern together and use it to cut a single collar piece in organza. Place the interfacing on top of the organza; it will be larger all around by 18 mm (¾ in). Stitch the interfacing and the organza together using a small zigzag stitch. Trim the organza away in the centre area of the interfacing.

Professional tips

Leaving a gap at each end of the seam when you stitch the undercollar to the jacket means no puckers will form when the facing is stitched on and turned to the inside.

If a back neckline facing is not provided as part of the pattern, you can cut one around 9 cm (3 ¼ in) deep, using the pattern for the back to shape the neckline and armhole.

3   Pin the interfacing to the wrong side of the undercollar. Establish the roll line and stitch parallel lines in a curve between it and the bottom collar edge, rolling the piece to shape it. Stitch the remaining area in parallel lines.

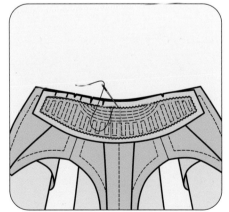

4   Pin the undercollar to the neck edge of the jacket, right sides together, working from the garment side. Ease the collar between markings as you work, then tack in place along the seam-line. Try the jacket on.

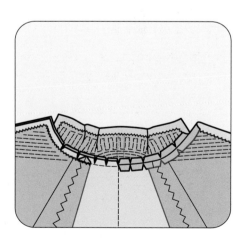

5   Stitch the undercollar to the jacket, starting 1.5 cm (⅝ in) from one edge and stopping the same from the other edge. Remove tacking, trim the seam allowance to 6 mm (¼ in), snip across corners and clip curved seams.

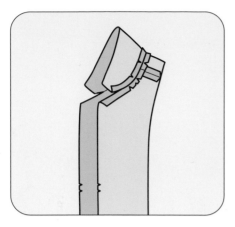

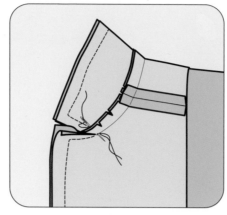

1 ▲ Facings and top collar
Join the front and back sections of the facing at the shoulder seams and press the seams open. Pin the top collar to the facing at the neck edge, right sides together, matching markings and easing the collar in between. Stitch in place, starting 1.5 cm (⅝ in) away from one edge and stopping the same distance away from the other edge. Pull the thread ends through to the wrong side, tie off, and trim. Clip into the seam allowance on curved sections so the seam will lie flat. Press open.

2 Place the facing and top collar over the jacket, right sides together, keeping seam edges open and matching markings and seams where possible. Pin around and down the sides of the facing. Tack, then turn the seam allowance on both top collar and undercollar away from the collar. Position the needle of the machine at the exact point on the collar seam where the stitching joining the collar and the facing ends. Stitch around the collar to the matching point on the opposite side, then stitch the facing seams, carefully placing the needle so the stitching begins at the end of the stitching joining the collar. Check the right side to make sure the seam matches perfectly, then repeat on the other side. Pull the thread ends through to the wrong side and make secure.

3 Remove tacking and press. Trim the undercollar seam allowance to 3 mm (⅛ in) and the top collar and organza strip to 6 mm (½ in). Clip into the seam allowances on any curved sections of seam and clip across points. From the top lapel to the top button, trim the main fabric seam allowance to 3 mm (⅛ in) and facing seam allowance to 6 mm (½ in). Reverse this layering below the top button.

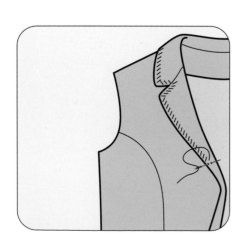

4 Turn the facing to the underside, easing out corners to a sharp point on collar and lapels. Tack in position with diagonal stitches to hold in place as you complete the jacket, making sure the facing is rolled to the back all along the edge. Do not remove this tacking until the jacket is complete. Roll the lapels and the collar into the shape needed when the jacket is worn and pin the facing and top collar in place along the roll line. The front facing is herringbone stitched to the interfacing after the sleeve has been set.

Two-piece sleeve with vent opening

Tailored garments are often made with a two-piece sleeve, which allows the sleeve to follow the natural bend of the arm at the elbow more easily. Sometimes a dart is also added to shape the sleeve further. Another advantage of the two-piece sleeve is that it is easy to add a vent at the cuff, which often has decorative buttons.

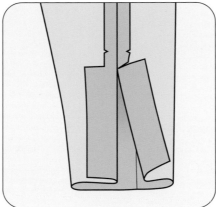

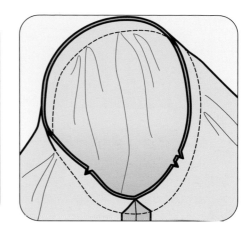

1 ▲ **Constructing the sleeve**
If there is a dart in the sleeve, stitch this first. Matching notches and raw edges, place the two sections of the sleeve right sides together and tack in place. Stitch the two pieces of the sleeve together along the front seam. Stitch along the back seam only to the point where the seamline turns at 90° to run across the top of the extended width of fabric at the cuff.

2 Slash diagonally into the seam allowance of the under section from the raw edge to the point where the stitching stops at the top of the vent opening. Press the seams open, running the seam crease continuously down the upper section of the vent piece only. Because of the cut you have made into the seam allowance, you can keep the under section flat to one side, although the seam above the cut is pressed open.

3 Turn the sleeve right side out and turn the garment inside out. Slip the sleeve inside the armhole and pin them together at the sleeve and garment underarm seams, shoulder markings, and notches. Tack into place, then stitch on the machine with the sleeve side up and being careful not to pull the fabric as you work.

Professional tips

Two-piece sleeves are often lined to hide the interfacing that is added to support the hem. If the sleeve is not lined, the raw edge of the hem should be turned over and hemmed normally.

A two-piece sleeve does not have an underarm seam; the seams are positioned at the back and towards the front.

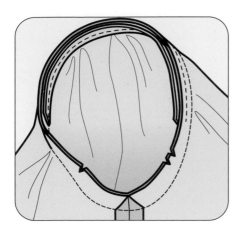

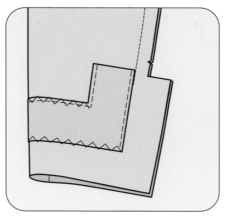

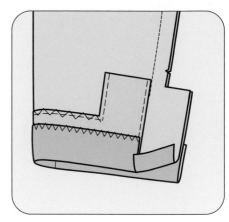

4 To reinforce the seam under the arm, stitch a second line of reinforcement stitching inside the first, within the seam allowance. Trim the seam allowance here close to the stitching, clip curves, then zigzag or overcast the edges. To maintain the roll of the sleeve head, cut a piece of thick fabric on the bias 3 cm (1¼ in) wide. Fold it lengthwise and then pin to the sleeve side of the seam allowance over the head of the sleeve between the notches. Keep the fold in line with the stitching line. Handstitch the strip in place to the seamline.

5 To give extra weight at the sleeve hem, cut a strip of interfacing the length of the lower hem of the sleeve and 2.5 cm (1 in) wider than the hem. Slide the interfacing into the hem, aligning the bottom edge and the crease of the hem. Herringbone stitch the interfacing to the jacket, being careful that the stitches do not show on the front surface.

6 Fold the bottom hem over the interfacing and tack near the fold. Herringbone stitch the hem to the interfacing, insuring that the stitches go through the hem and the interfacing only.

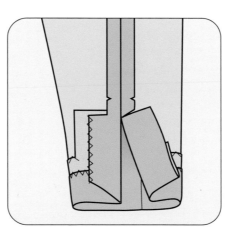

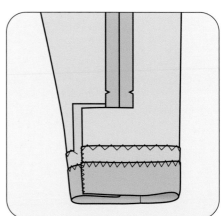

7 Make a neat mitre at the point where the upper section of the vent opening overlaps the hem, and press. Herringbone stitch in place the depth of the opening.

8 Wrap the upper section of the vent opening over the under section the depth of the seam allowance, making sure the lower edges are even. Pin in place. Still working on the wrong side, turn under the raw edge of the under section by 6 mm (¼ in) and hem in place to the underneath of the upper section.

Jacket hem

Before completing the hem of the jacket, try it on to be sure it is fitting correctly at key points and hanging properly. Ensure that the front points of the jacket are at the same level. The hem is interfaced to give extra body and weight.

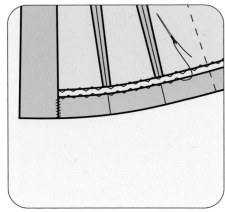

1 ▲ **Interfacing the jacket hem**
Turn the facing away from the jacket, fold and pin the hem. Tack in position, then trim the hem across the facing and seam to 12 mm (½ in). Cut a strip of interfacing the length of the lower hem and 2.5 cm (1 in) wider. Slide the interfacing into the hem, lining the bottom edge with the hem fold. Herringbone stitch the interfacing to the jacket, being careful the stitches do not show on the front.

2 Fold the bottom hem over the interfacing and tack near the fold. Herringbone stitch the hem to the interfacing as far as the facing seam, making sure that the stitches go through the hem and the interfacing only. Turn the front facing to the underside, easing it under slightly at the lower edge so it will not show on the front. Slipstitch in place, then work herringbone stitch over the cut edge the depth of the hem only.

evening wear

Making evening wear offers the opportunity to use luxurious and unusual fabrics that you may not get the chance to work with otherwise. Since they are only worn occasionally, evening wear items can also be much more dramatic than everyday wear and can include features that are less practical on everyday wear.

Making a boned bodice

A boned bodice has its own built-in support and does not require straps to hold it up. The strips of flexible material used are called boning, since they were once made of whalebone. They are inserted into casings running vertically down the bodice at intervals.

Professional tips

Make sure no boning lines run across the bustline, as this would flatten its shape.

The boning strips need to be at least 12 mm (½ in) shorter than the casing, or they will rub the ends of the casing into a hole.

Since casing around the bodice varies in length, measure, cut, and slide each boning strip before going on to the next. This will save time and confusion.

Cut the boning into a curve at the end as sharp points will tear the fabric.

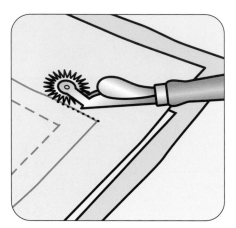

1 Cut and mark the sections of the bodice and stitch together following the pattern instructions. Mark the casing lines on the wrong side of the fabric with a tracing wheel and dressmaker's carbon.

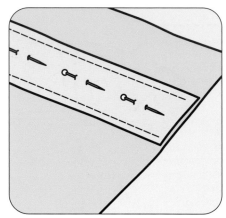

2 Place strips of casing tape along the marked lines and pin into place. Stitch along both sides of the tape using a medium to small stitch length to create an open-ended casing channel.

3 Measure the length of one of the casing channels. Subtract at least 12 mm (½ in) from this measurement and cut the boning length to match. Measure each casing individually, as they will vary slightly in length.

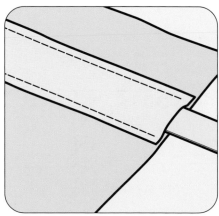

4 Slide the boning into the casing from the top edge. Finish the top and bottom edges of the bodice following the pattern instructions.

Bias skirts

Bias-cut skirts hang and flow around the body beautifully, making them ideal for evening wear. Despite a reputation for being challenging to sew, bias-cut garments are not too tricky as long as you follow a few basic rules. Bias seams curve very nicely around the body when sewn correctly, virtually eliminating wrinkles and improving the fit of a garment. Working on the bias requires a bit more time, a careful selection of fabric, and some alternate fitting and sewing techniques.

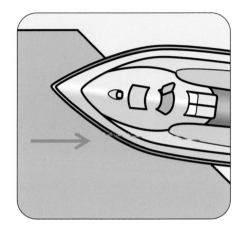

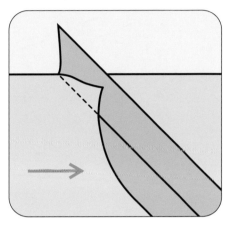

1 **Bias panel skirt**
Lay out the pattern pieces according to the pattern instructions, making very sure that all the straight of grain lines are lined up correctly as indicated. Press all of the fabric pieces, then check they still fit the shape of the pattern. Trim the edges if necessary.

2 Working with a 3.5 cm (1½ in) seam allowance, pin and tack together the first two panels down the centre line. Stitch the seam, then work the side seams. When stitching a bias-cut edge to a straight-grain edge, have the straight-grain edge uppermost, as it is more stable.

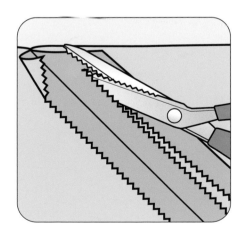

3 Carry on sewing the panels to each other until the skirt is finished. Trim the seams to 18 mm (¾ in) with pinking shears. Because bias seams do not fray, no other seam finishing is required. Add the waistband following the pattern instructions.

Professional tips

Bias garments need more fabric than those cut on the straight grain. Cut one layer at a time to avoiding distorting the grain.

Make sure any seams cut on the bias are as near to the absolute bias line as possible; seams slightly off the grain in either direction tend to disturb the drape of the garment and are difficult to tack and machine stitch neatly.

The fibres on bias-cut edges relax and open up, requiring a wider seam allowance. Use a 3.5 cm (1½ in) seam allowance on all main seams and a 1.5 cm (⅝ in) seam allowance at the neck.

Press each pattern piece before you begin to help remove a little of the stretch.

The key to smooth, vertical bias seams is to stretch them as you sew, using a stitch length of 2.5 to 3. The seam will look rippled after stitching but will press out nicely.

Bias-cut items change shape when worn, becoming longer and narrower.

Piping or binding works better than facings for necklines and armholes, since facings may fight with the fluidity of the bias-cut main piece.

Ruffled neckline

Add some extra interest to a simple scoop neck with a ruffle. There are many different options for the ruffle: it can be made in the same fabric as the dress, with lace, or even with be a double layer of two contrasting fabrics.

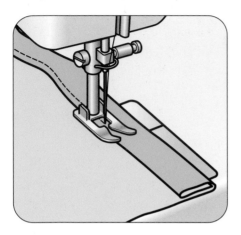

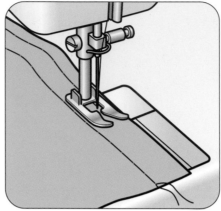

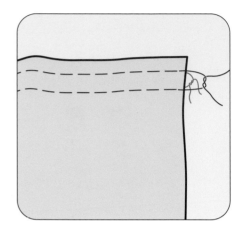

1 ▲ **Adding a ruffle with a neck facing**

Make up the main sections of the dress following the pattern instructions. Cut a strip of fabric the width of the frill or ruffle, adding 3 cm (1¼ in) for the seam allowances. Turn under a 6 mm (¼ in) double hem at the bottom of the ruffle. Press and topstitch in place.

2 Run a double line of gathering stitch (see page 38) along the top edge of the ruffle, one on the seam line and one within the seam allowance.

3 Take the two threads on the right side at each end of the stitching and knot together. Repeat for the two threads at each end on the wrong side.

Fabric for bias-cut projects

When choosing your fabric, remember that you need something smooth and reasonably stable that will hang well. Spend some time in the store observing how different types of fabric behave when pulled on the bias line. Heavily-textured fabrics will not work well, while stripes should be reserved for the very experienced.

Good fabrics for bias cutting include the following, which hang beautifully and are reasonably stable:

Fine cotton
Wool challis
Silk
Crêpe de chine
Georgette

Avoid the following fabrics:

Rayon – very elastic and unstable
Silky fabrics and polyester – slippery and hard to handle without great experience
Twills – lose weave definition on the bias
Duck, poplin, canvas, or similar – too heavy or stiff

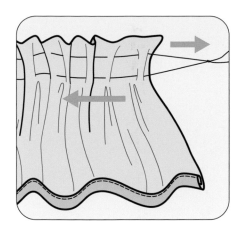

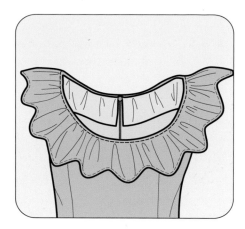

4 Holding the bobbin threads in one hand, ease the fabric into gathers with the other hand. When the frill is the length you need, adjust the gathers evenly and knot the threads at each end so they don't slip.

5 Pin the gathered edge to the neckline of the dress, with right sides up and matching raw edges. Add the facing, right side down. Stitch through all layers, being careful to keep the gathers even.

6 Turn neck facing to the inside and press. Hem in place along the back zipper and catch at the shoulders. Run a line of edge stitching along the periphery of the neck fold to prevent the ruffle turning through to the inside of the dress.

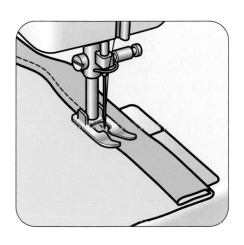

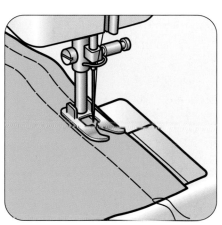

1 ▲ **Adding a ruffle without a facing**

Make up the main sections of the dress, following the pattern instructions. Cut a strip of fabric the width of the frill or ruffle, adding 3 cm (1¼ in) for the seam allowances. Turn under a 6 mm (¼ in) double hem along both long edges of the ruffle. Press and topstitch in place.

2 Run a double line of gathering stitch (see page 38) along the top edge of the ruffle, the first 12 mm (½ in) down from the top edge and the second 6 mm (¼ in) below the first line of stitching. Next follow steps 3 and 4 for adding a ruffle with a neck facing .

3 Finish the neckline of the dress with binding or turn and stitch a narrow hem. Pin the gathered edge of the ruffle to the neckline, with right sides up and matching finished edges. Stitch round the neckline with straight stitch between the two lines of gathering stitch so the gathers are even.

Decorative details

Adding different decorative details can completely change the look of a dress or outfit. With evening wear these details can add dramatic, large scale, or subtle effects.

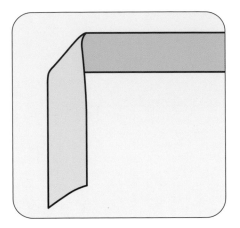

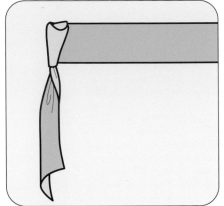

1 ▲ **Ribbon rose**
Fold the ribbon at right angles, leaving a 5 cm (2 in) tail.

2 Starting at the bottom left point of the fold, roll tightly about 3 to 4 complete turns to form a centre bud and a tight base for the rose.

Embellishment tips

Keep an eye out for interesting ribbons and motifs that can be used as decorative details.

Stitching on sequins or jewelled buttons is an inexpensive way of adding some sparkle.

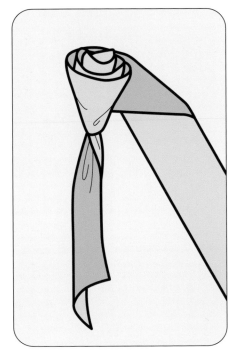

3 ◀ Holding the tail firmly in the left hand, fold the ribbon length to the outside at a sharp angle. Continue rolling until you almost reach the diagonal fold. As you near the end, fold the ribbon to the outside again at a right angle. Repeat this fold and roll process to form rose petals loosely around the bud and base. A gentle twist on the rolled tail will softly shape and tighten the rose.

4 ▶ When you have about 5 cm (2 in) of ribbon left, twist the ends straight down and along the first tail. Secure with a few stitches at the base.

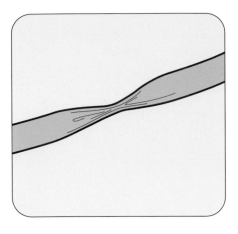

1 ▲ **Double bow**
Take a length of ribbon around 3 m (2¾ yd) long. Pinch the ribbon firmly between your thumb and index finger about 20 cm (8 in) from one end.

2 Make a 12.5 cm (5 in) loop—this will be half the size of the finished bow—and pinch together tightly. If the ribbon is finished only on one side, twist the length to the right side. Make a second loop and pinch it over the first.

3 Repeat this process, creating 4 loops on each side.

4 Make a centre knot by forming a small loop over your thumb. Pin and then stitch all of the loops together and trim any excess. Stitch two lengths of ribbon to the back of the bow for tails, if required.

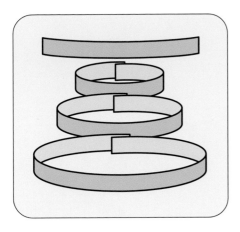

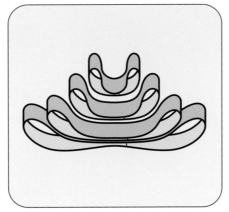

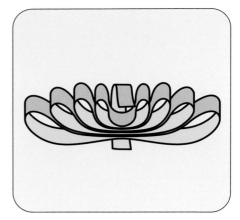

1 ▲ Dior bow
Cut 1.8 m (2 yd) ribbon into five lengths measuring 12.5 cm (5 in), 25 cm (10 in), 35 cm (14 in), 45 cm (18 in), and 55 cm (22 in).

2 Shape the four longer lengths into loops and overlap the ends at the centre. Stitch in place.

3 Flatten the four loops slightly and stitch together one above the other in descending order.

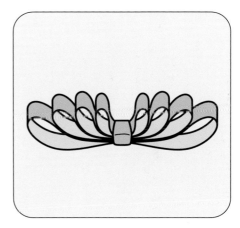

4 Wrap the smallest length of ribbon around the centre of the stacked loops and stitch to them the underside.

Choosing ribbons

There is a wide range of beautiful ready-made trims, ribbons and embellishments available that can be purchased from sewing stores. Look out for interesting antique trims as well—old clothes may well have embellishments in good condition that can be salvaged for future use.

Some inexpensive ribbon is not colourfast, so check a small length before stitching it to a garment that will be washed. If in any doubt, make sure the trim can be removed before laundering.

For extra sparkle on the Dior Bow, stitch a large crystal bead or a sequin in the centre instead of the final loop.

home furnishings

Making items for the home means you can create or match any colour scheme you like. Many home furnishing items are quite expensive, but even the larger projects—though their scale may seem a bit daunting—are often simple to make. This chapter takes you through preparation for your project and choosing a style and colours, and also explains how to make a wide range of household furnishings in easy steps.

preparation

However large or small your project, the first step is to assess exactly what you have and what you need. With most interior decorating projects there will be items reused in the new scheme, but many can be given a new lease of life with a throw, cushion, or slipcover. Even if you are just planning on changing the curtains, you need to take into account the other items in the room before choosing your design and the colour or pattern of the fabric.

Assessing furniture

When embarking on a change to your interior, start by assessing the furniture you already have. What condition is it in? Does it match? Can it be updated or recovered? You may find there are a few items that work well together, plus some odds and ends that do not really fit. Removing the latter and making the most of what is left is a good starting point, whatever you plan to do.

Choosing a style

If you are adding to an existing room or updating a few items within it, try to match the style of what is already there, or you may end up with a mishmash of conflicting items. You may choose to match the existing colour scheme, or if you are a bit bored with it, add accents in a different colour. Either way, you are working from a clear starting point and have some ground rules in place.

If you are redecorating an entire room from scratch you may have more choices, and the cost involved means that you need to take some care at the start to be sure that you get things right. Look carefully at what you have and how you use it—now is the time to get rid of items that do not work or that have seen better days. The style you choose is up to you: do you prefer a cosy, cluttered family style, or stark minimalism? Another thing to consider is how the room will be used. You may like the uncluttered look, but if you have small children it may be difficult to achieve. Lots of storage will be a must!

Planning

When planning a room, the first thing to consider is the furniture and other large items that need to be accommodated. They may be fine where they are, but could you create more space or make things look more open by moving things around a bit? Try drawing a scale plan of the room on graph paper and cutting out shapes of all the pieces of furniture. You can move the pieces around on the plan much more quickly than moving the items around the room. When you have a plan that seems to work, remember you are only working in two dimensions, so consider the height of all of the items before you make a final decision.

Professional tips

You don't need to knock down walls to create more space! Moving furniture around often makes the room appear bigger.

Warm colours make things appear closer, cool ones make them recede. Use this to create an airier or cosier space, depending on your needs.

Neutrals are safe, but can be boring. Add accent colours to liven things up, using items that are easy to alter when you need a change.

Look at colour samples in the room. The lighting at the store can make them look quite different.

Warm up north-facing rooms with reds, oranges, and yellows. Cool down south-facing rooms with blues, greens, and lilacs.

Creating a sample board

Once you have decided what needs to be in the room, you can move on to the colour scheme. The easiest way to visualize how the room will look is to create a sample board with all the materials on it. If you cannot choose between different colour schemes, you can easily do one board for each and see which one looks the best in the room itself. Start by covering a piece of cardboard with paper to match the wall colour; you may be able to get a large sample of the wallpaper or, if you are using paint, pots of colour and paint chips. Add scraps to represent the floor covering, upholstery, curtains and cushions, and any trims. Try to keep the samples in more or less the correct proportion to each other, or the effect may not be accurate.

Working with pattern

Using pattern is a great way to add extra interest to a room, but there are so many different types of patterns in different colourways that making a choice can be very difficult. The pattern can be printed or woven, and designs can be contemporary or traditional, geometric or floral, subtle or bold, large or small. Ultimately your choice is personal, but following a few general rules will help ensure success.

Keep it subtle

Subtle patterns are in toning colours and are usually small in scale. They tend to recede visually and are widely used as a background. They make small rooms seem bigger, but tend to disappear in large spaces. In larger rooms, combine them with broader designs.

Pattern repeat

If you want to use several different patterns together, make sure they match in either scale or colour.

Pick out one of the colours in the pattern and use that as the base colour for your scheme to tie things together.

▲ **Gingham check** – two-colour checks are usually subtle in general appearance, even when large in scale.

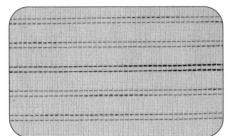

▲ **Narrow stripe** – when seen from a distance narrow stripes tend to merge into one colour, even if the colours contrast quite strongly.

▲ **Toile de Jouy** – the pattern here is very busy, but since it is only one subdued colour on a cream or white ground, the design tends to merge well with its surroundings.

▲ **Abstract pattern** – although this design is bold, as many abstracts tend to be, the muted colours mean it blends nicely.

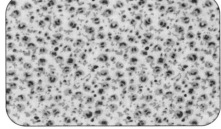

▲ **Small print** – in general, small-scale patterns are subtle, unless the colours used contrast very strongly with each other.

▲ **Repeated print** – repeating printed patterns can be in toning or contrasting colours and can look quite busy. The design can be large or small in scale.

Going for bold

Bold patterns are large in scale and usually feature strongly contrasting colours. They tend to overwhelm small rooms, but give large rooms a more intimate feel. You can soften bold designs by using plenty of neutrals with them. If you are mixing more than one bold pattern in the same room, make sure they work well with each other by choosing a limited range of matching colours or related designs. Too much pattern in a room will look very busy and the effect may be overpowering.

▲ **Woven motif** – the bold colours and large motifs in this pattern are dramatic, so use toning colours in other areas of the room.

▲ **Floral print** – large-scale floral prints need to be used in a way that allows the full effect of the print to be appreciated.

▲ **Ethnic print** – these often use bold designs and strong colours that can be combined in a range of ways.

▲ **Figurative print** – a pattern like this makes little sense unless you can see the whole design, so use it on flat cushions or covers.

▲ **Woven stripe** – the wide stripes here are in toning colours, but the stronger contrast of the narrow stripe makes the effect much more dramatic.

▲ **Plaid** – the colours are the critical factor with plaids; if they are toning the effect will be subtle as here, but if they contrast the design looks bold.

home furnishings

Working with texture

Apart from colour and design, the other factor to consider when choosing your fabric is texture. Depending on how it is made and finished, the surface can be smooth or highly textured, shiny or matte, flat or with a pile or nap. The surface also affects the colour; two pieces of fabric dyed an identical colour will look very different if one is shiny and the other napped.

Relaxing at home

Informal fabrics are ideal for family rooms used for relaxing, such as kitchens, breakfast rooms, bedrooms or a study room. Most informal fabrics work very well in contemporary settings. Types of informal fabric include heavy linens, hessian or burlap, corduroy and plain cotton.

Tips for textured fabrics

Shiny fabrics reflect light, making the room appear bigger. Matte fabrics absorb light, making the room cosier.

When joining fabrics with a pile, make sure the pile runs in the same direction on each piece or the colour will look quite different.

Do not cut off the selvedges when working with velvet, as it will fray badly. You will need to over-lock or zigzag any cut edges.

▲ **Hessian** – this cloth was originally used for sacks and is roughly woven from jute. It is inexpensive and hardwearing so is useful to cover large areas.

▲ **Indian hand-loomed cotton** – since it is woven by hand, this material has wonderfully natural and irregular look. It dyes very well.

▲ **Corduroy** – this is made with a ribbed nap and has a pleasantly tactile surface. It is hardwearing so is great for areas of heavy use.

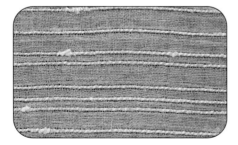

▲ **Linen hopsack** – this type of linen is quite stiff, and best used for upholstery projects

▲ **Canvas** – a strong, tightly woven cotton fabric, canvas is tough and rather stiff, but has a smooth surface. It is often used in a natural cream colour.

▲ **Linen union** – similar to canvas in both weave and strength, linen union is a mix of cotton and linen and has a rough surface texture.

Out on show

Formal fabrics tend to be used in rooms for entertaining, such as dining rooms or sitting rooms, but they work well in any period interior. Most formal fabrics are luxurious as well as expensive, but often just a little goes a long way. You can combine them with a large quantity of less glamourous fabric without losing their effect.

▲ **Damask** – traditionally made from silk, damask has a slightly embossed texture that is created by the weaving.

▲ **Velvet** – this fabric has a fine pile across the surface that runs in one direction, changing colour depending on which way it is hung or stroked.

▲ **Crewelwork** – a kind of embroidered fabric that is often stitched by hand and frequently features elaborate and traditional floral patterns.

▲ **Indian dupion silk** – a pure silk with a deep shine and a richly textured surface, created by using the threads from two silk worms that have nested together.

▲ **Moleskin** – a soft fabric with a short pile made of hardwearing cotton. It is stronger than many formal fabrics.

▲ **Chenille** – traditionally made from either wool or silk, chenille has a double-sided pile and is soft to handle. It also drapes very well.

Professional tip

To make the most of formal fabrics, use them on something that will be a focal point within the room. An expensive fabric used for a scatter cushion will add drama to the plainest sofa.

Fabrics for home furnishings

Fabrics used for home furnishings can look very similar to those used for dressmaking, but they tend to be much more hardwearing. Curtain fabrics need to drape well and can also be used for bedcovers or cushions. However, most curtain fabrics are unlikely to withstand the wear if used for a slipcover or upholstery. Upholstery fabrics tend to be thicker and stiffer and look great on a chair, but they may not hang as well as a curtain. Some fabrics are dual use—check the label to see the manufacturer's recommendations—or may be available in a choice of weights.

Linings and base fabrics

These are the practical fabrics used to back curtains and line projects, and are often neutral in colour.

▲ **Thermal lining** – used as both lining and interlining in one layer, when making both separately would add too much bulk. The silvery side faces the wrong side of the curtain fabric, so when made up thermal lining looks like normal lining.

▲ **Calico** – an inexpensive fabric made from unbleached cotton, calico—known as muslin in North America—is used for lining and backing or for simple curtains and covers. It is available in several widths and weights.

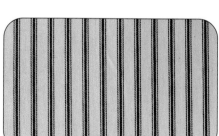

▲ **Sateen** – a tightly woven cotton with a slight sheen, sateen is often used to line curtains and to back bedcovers and cushions because it holds its shape well. It is available in a limited range of colours and can be used to make simple soft furnishing projects.

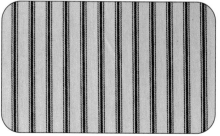

▲ **Ticking** – originally used to cover mattresses, its tight weave is designed to keep the stuffing in. It is now often used as an upholstery fabric, as its simple stripes in white or cream combined with blue, black, or grey have become very fashionable.

Laundering tips

Use washable fabrics for curtains in active rooms like the kitchen.

Slipcovers are easy to remove and wash, and save having the furnishings professionally cleaned.

Some fabrics have a finish that will be removed by laundering; these need to be dry-cleaned.

Neutral and simple patterns

These fabrics can be used as the basis of any interior design scheme. You can then add bolder colours or designs as accent pieces on items that are easy to recover when you feel like a new look. Neutral fabrics often have surface texture or muted patterns to add interest so if you are using a selection in one room, make sure they go together.

▲ **Herringbone weave** – this sample of herringbone weave is made of strong cotton and is highly textured and stiff. This weave is quite heavy, so fabrics tend to be more suitable for upholstery.

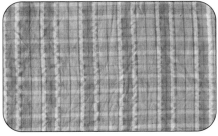

▲ **Cotton check** – patterns that are woven into the fabric, like this simple two-colour check, are often reversible, making them ideal for unlined curtains. However, this example is also a strong weave that is good for upholstery.

▲ **Voile** – this translucent, light fabric can be made from cotton, silk, or man-made fibre. It can be printed or woven, and is used for secondary curtains or for the main curtains in more informal areas.

▲ **Hessian** – a rough, open-weave fabric made from natural jute, hessian— known as burlap in North America—is usually plain but it may be dyed or have a pattern woven into it. It is used as curtaining or to cover large areas.

◀ **Linen** – woven from the fibres of the flax plant, linen can be smooth or rough, finely woven or quite coarse. The heavier weights are very hardwearing and good for upholstery, while the lighter weights drape beautifully when used for curtains.

Using neutrals

All-neutral schemes can look boring—make sure to add some accent colours to spice things up, or to incorporate strong textures.

Neutrals come in different tones—don't assume two beiges will go together without checking in the correct lighting conditions.

If using pale colours in a family room choose washable fabrics and removable covers, so they will be easy to pop in the machine to keep everything looking fresh.

home furnishings

Printed and woven patterns

These fabrics will usually make more of a statement, so they need to be selected and used with some care. Different geometric patterns often work well together, and geometrics can be successfully combined with florals, but too many different florals can look messy. Woven patterns may be double-sided, but printed patterns usually have a right and wrong side.

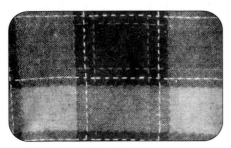

▲ **Wool check** – this fabric is woven in a diagonal weave called twill, but also has a woven grid of stripes in two thicknesses. Twill is quite hardwearing, though not as strong as a plain weave.

▲ **Tapestry** – originally hand woven, but machine-woven versions can look rich and elaborate, like this example here. Traditionally hung on walls, tapestry looks great when used on seating, too.

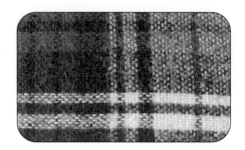

▲ **Woven blanket** – blankets are made from combed fibres, which makes for a soft, insulating texture. The fabric can be used to make throws or bedcovers, or to cover casual cushions, but is not practical for curtains.

▲ **Plaid** – a woven design, plaids—also known as tartans—originally denoted different clans in Scotland. They drape well and are ideal for all kinds of soft furnishing projects.

▲ **Paisley** – the name of this fabric comes from the town of Paisley in Scotland, where it was originally made. Its swirling tear-drop motifs were popular on woollen shawls and printed cotton, and were based on the designs found in traditional Indian shawls.

▲ **Chintz** – a traditional furnishing fabric, chintz usually has an elaborate printed floral design on a plain cream or white ground. It is made of cotton and is used for both curtains and upholstery.

▲ **Cotton print** – cotton fabrics take dye so well that they lend themselves to the creation of crisp and delicate designs, such as the one above. They are also suitable for more experimental printing techniques.

▲ **Silk damask** – damask was traditionally woven from pure silk, but is now available in a wide range of fibres. The silk version is truly luxurious, however, with a wonderful sheen and an interesting texture. It also hangs extremely well.

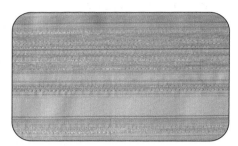

▲ **Striped velvet** – velvet does not have to be plain; it can be woven in patterns as well. This example has woven stripes of muted colours, offering both subtle pattern and interesting texture.

▲ **Printed linen** – linen is available in a wide range of plain colours, but weaves with a smoother surface can also be printed. This patterned linen has a bold design with limited colours that would work with many different schemes.

▲ **Taffeta** – pure silk taffeta can be woven with different colours in the warp and weft, changing the iridescent colour depending on how the fabric is viewed. It is fine and delicate with a crisp handle, so is best for curtains and cushions.

▲ **Velvet** – like other fabrics, velvet can be printed with a design, but the richness of its surface means that simple patterns tend to look best.

Using patterned fabrics

When selecting pattern, bear in mind how it will be used. If you plan on making curtains, gather a length up to see if the design still looks good.

If you want to make something small, like a cushion, from a large-scale pattern see if you can make a feature of just a section of the design.

Trims and embellishments for home furnishings

Trims, tassels, and buttons are a great way to add interest and detail to home furnishing projects, or to customize bought items easily. There is a wide range available: solid or multicolour, textured or smooth, wide or narrow, elaborate or simple. Choosing the right one for your project is largely a matter of personal taste.

Traditional trims

Period furniture is often trimmed with braid to hide the pins holding in the fabric, while traditional curtains usually have cords, fringe, and tassels.

Most of these are sewn on by hand, but some can be added by machine.

1. Rope – twisted in one or more colours and sewn along edges by hand.

2. Rope with an inset – this has a flat extension that is set into seams in the same way as piping.

3. Decorative braid – available in a wide range of colours and designs and is suitable for many uses.

4. Gimp braid – usually in toning colours, it is chosen to match the upholstery and is traditionally used to hide fixing nails.

5. Fan braid – comes in many colours and is sewn by hand or machine to decorate the edges of many types of soft furnishing projects.

6. Looped fringe – fringe can be looped or single strands depending on how it is manufactured. It is sewn to the edges by hand or machine.

▲ **Fringe** – fringes come in a variety of lengths and weights, and may be one colour, as here, or multicoloured.

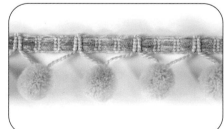

▲ **Bobble fringe** – a fun fringe for a casual project, these bobbles give a retro 1950s feel.

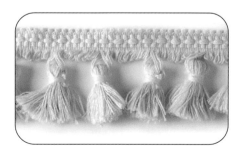

▲ **Braid with tassels** – tassels are more three-dimensional than fringing, and are easy to add to any project with this tassel braid.

▲ **Tufts** – easy to make from any kind of yarn, tufts can be used to hold layers of fabric together in a decorative way.

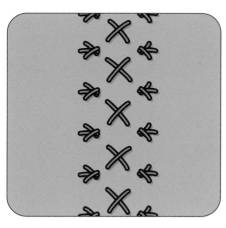

▲ **Embroidery** – even quite simple stitches can add beautiful texture to a project if they are well made.

▲ **Appliqué** – simple shapes can be cut from a contrasting fabric and applied to a background to create a design.

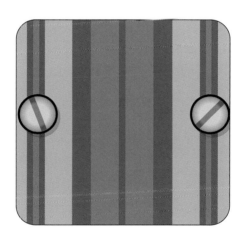

▲ **Buttons** – although they are generally used to fasten fabrics, buttons can also be used decoratively.

Surface decoration

Applying other fabrics, motifs, or stitching to the surface of a soft furnishing project adds both interest and texture. They can be used to spice up bland fabrics and to create projects with individual style.

When choosing your trim, you should generally try to match one or more of the colours in the design. Contrasting trims can look very effective, but only if they form a reasonable proportion of the project area.

If the fabric you are using is washable, make sure the trim can be laundered too.

Measuring

Whatever you plan to make, accurate measuring right at the start is vital for a professional finish. The following pages explain how to measure a wide range of household items to be sure you are working with all the information you need. A rough sketch of the item to put the measurements on will be useful, otherwise you may forget which measurement is which.

Measuring windows

When you are calculating the amount of fabric you need, be sure to allow for pattern repeats, hems and headings, and fullness. When working out the width, sheers and lightweight fabrics will need up to three times the width of the window, while heavily patterned fabrics may need only twice the width.

Height – vertical measurements

a. ceiling or top of pole to floor

b. ceiling or top of pole to window frame

c. ceiling or top of pole to sill

d. top of glass area to sill

e. horizontal sash to sill

Width – horizontal measurements

f. ends of pole, track or rod

g. outside edge of the window frame to the opposite edge

h. inside edge of the window frame to the opposite edge

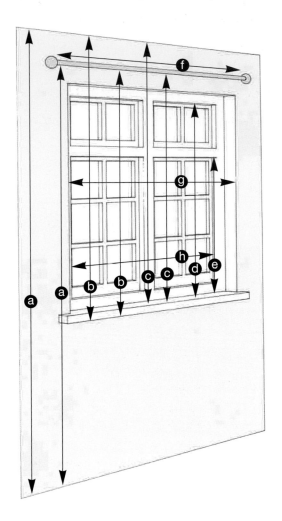

Tips for measuring

Try to fit the curtain fixtures before you start measuring. It is easier to measure from the top of a fixed pole or track than guessing placement.

The type of heading you require may also affect the fabric needed (see pages 167–173).

Don't forget that curtain tracks need extra length on either side of the window to keep the curtain clear of the window when open.

Use a metal tape to take measurements. Fabric tapes can stretch in time and give inaccurate results.

Glossary of measuring terms

Finished width – the full width of the area that a completed curtain or blind is intended to cover.

Cut width – the width of the fabric after the selvedge has been removed.

Fabric width – the purchased width of the fabric.

Finished drop or drop – the full length of a completed curtain or blind from the very top to the very bottom. Also sometimes called the drop.

Cut drop – the finished length plus hem, heading, and pattern repeat allowances. The measurement to cut before assembling the curtain or blind.

Widths – multiples of the cut width of the fabric. With the exception of a very small window, you will probably need to join more than one width of fabric to make up the finished width.

Selvedge – the tightly woven edge of the fabric. It reacts differently to stitching and washing, so should be cut off before measuring the cut width of curtains and blinds.

Recessed window – a window set into a hole in the wall. Curtains or blinds can be hung inside the recess or across it.

Flush window – a window set level with the face of the wall. Curtains or blinds are hung across it.

Support – the mechanism from which a curtain or blind is hung, including tracks, poles, rods, rails, and laths. The support can be mounted on the wall over the window frame, on the frame, or inside the recess.

Measuring for tiebacks

To work out the best position for a tieback, hold the curtain back with a spare piece of fabric at different levels to see which one looks right. It should sit about two-thirds of the height down from the top. Then pull the curtain back with the spare length of fabric until it makes a nice rounded curve, not too tight or too loose. You can then measure the fabric piece to see how much you need for the tieback. See also pages 187–188 for more details on tiebacks and holdbacks.

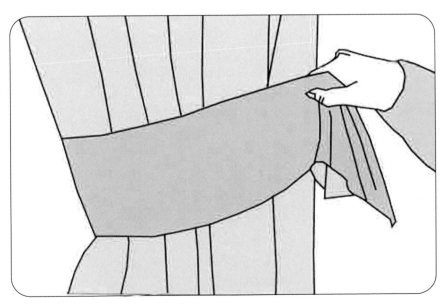

Measuring for valances or pelmets

Valances or pelmets are the decorative band across the top of a curtain. They serve four purposes: to block light, retain warmth, conceal the curtain support, and add an extra touch of style. Flounced valances can be adjusted as they are hung, if necessary, but flat valances need to be measured accurately because they are difficult to change when they are finished. Measure the depth of the board, allowing enough fabric to turn over the edges but making sure the excess fabric will not impede the movement of the curtain. Then measure the length, including the returns at each end.

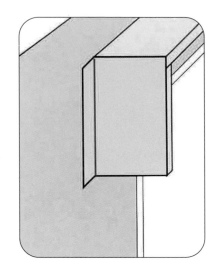

Estimating fabric

There are basic guidelines that you can follow to help you work out how much fabric you need in a given situation:

Cut drop

1. Measure the finished drop.
2. Add 30–40 cm (12–16 in) for hems plus twice the depth of the heading.
3. Check the pattern repeat if you are using patterned fabric, and divide the finished drop by the repeat.
4. Round up to the nearest round number, then multiply the repeat by that number. This is your cut drop.

Final amount of fabric to buy

1. Measure the finished width of the curtain.
2. Allow 2–2 ½ times the finished width for medium-weight to heavyweight fabrics and 2 ½–3 times the width for sheers or lightweights.
3. Divide the result by the width of the fabric.
4. Round up to the nearest number to get the number of widths. Multiply the cut drop by the number of widths to get the final amount of fabric needed.

An example:
1. Finished drop = 230 cm (92 in)
2. Add 30 cm (12 in) = 260 cm (104 in)
3. Pattern repeat 35 cm (14 in)
   260 divided by 35 = 7.42
4. Nearest round number is 8
   35 cm (14 in) x 8,
Therefore the cut drop = 280 cm (112 in)

1. Width of window = 150 cm (60 in)
2. Multiply by 2 ½ times = 375 cm (150 in)
3. Fabric width 120 cm (48 in)
   375 divided by 120 = 3.125
4. Nearest round number = 4
   multiply the cut drop by the number of widths
   280 cm (112 in) x 4
Therefore the final amount of fabric = 1120 cm (448 in)

Measuring for different types of curtains and blinds

Before you even begin to measure, you need to decide exactly where your curtain or blind will go. If the supports are not already in position, you must decide if they are to go above and across the window, or on the window frame, or from side to side of the window recess. Is the curtain or blind to be sill length, below sill length or floor length?

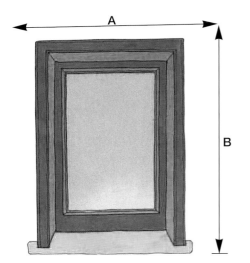

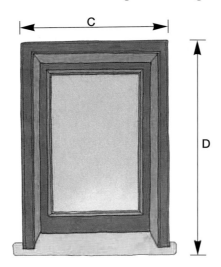

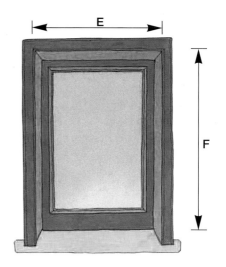

Measuring for a curtain or blind that hangs from a support on the wall.

The track or pole should be positioned 10–30 cm (4–12 in) above the frame and extend 20–25 cm (8–10 in) on each side.

A. Width of the window plus side extensions

B. Top of the support to the bottom of the drop, if this is the sill

Measuring for a curtain or blind that hangs from a support on the window frame

The track or pole should be the width of the window.

C. Width from one outer edge of the frame to the other

D. Top of the support to the bottom of the drop, if this is the sill

Measuring for a curtain or blind that hangs between the sides of the window recess

The track or pole should be the width of the recess.

E. Width from one side of the recess to the other

F. Top of the support to the bottom of the drop, at the sill

French doors

French doors, also known as French windows, are full-glazed external doors that can open outward or inward. If they open outward, treat them like normal casement windows. If they open inward, supports must be long enough so the curtains can be pulled back out of the way of the doors.

Another option is to mount a fixed curtain or a blind over the glazed portion on the door itself.

Bay windows

There are two ways of handling a bay window. Option one is to have a separate curtain and support for each window, but this can leave gaps at the corners. Option two is to have one pair of long curtains that open from the middle, which can look more attractive but requires an angled track. Some types of track can be bent on site to fit, otherwise a curved track can be ordered from a supplier.

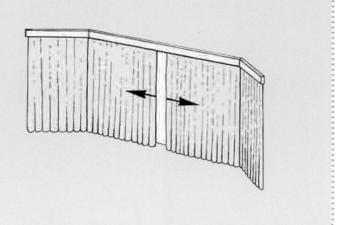

Measuring for blinds

Like curtains, blinds can be mounted above and across the window, on the window frame, or from side to side of the window recess. Generally follow the instructions for measuring curtains, but with the following changes:

If the blind is to go across the window you will not need to allow as much extra on the sides; add only a maximum of 10 cm (4 in) on each side.

If the blind is to go in the window recess take at least two width dimensions at different levels and use the smaller one—or the blinds may be too big!

Types of blinds

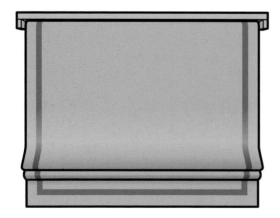

Roman blind – this sits flat against the window and draws up into straight and regular pleats when closed.

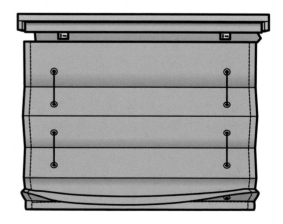

Eyelet blind – a variation of the Roman blind in which the draw cords show on the face

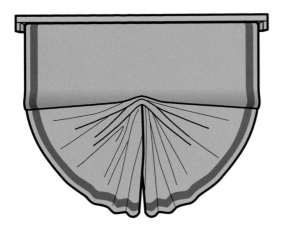

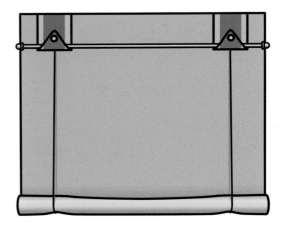

Fan blind – another variation of the Roman blind in which the fabric is drawn up at the centre to form a rounded fan shape at the bottom.

Roll-up blind – with this design the fabric collects on a roller, which may be at the bottom, as shown here, or at the top.

Measuring furniture

Trying to estimate how much fabric you will need to cover a piece of furniture can seem complex, but if you look at it as a series of flat rectangles it becomes much simpler. Just measure each rectangle and then add seam or hem allowance as appropriate.

Tips for estimating fabrics

Fabric widths vary, so you will not be able to come up with an accurate quantity until you know which fabric you want. When you collect swatches for consideration, jot down the width and the pattern repeat so you have them at hand when you have made your selection.

Make a scale diagram to calculate how much fabric you will need, especially if the pattern repeat is large. Draw up a rectangle the width of your fabric and cut out scale pieces the size you need so you can move them around to find the ideal cutting layout.

Better to buy too much fabric than too little. You can always use the extra to make matching accessories.

Ovals and circles should be measured as rectangles and squares. Use the diameter as side measurements.

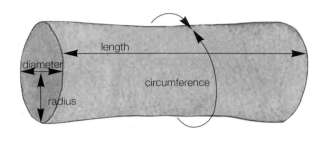

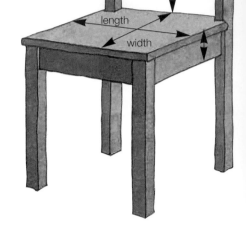

▲ Measuring for seat cushion covers or throws

Bolster cushion – if it has separate ends, first measure the circumference and length, then the diameter. If it does not have separate ends, find the centre one end and measure from that point to the same point at the other, then the circumference.

▶ Fitted squab cushion and back cushion

Measure the width and depth of the chair seat. Make a template to use as a pattern if the seat is not square. If you are making a box cushion, measure the depth of the seat to estimate how deep the cushion should be. For the back cushion, also measure the height and width of the back, but remember to allow for ties to attach the cushion.

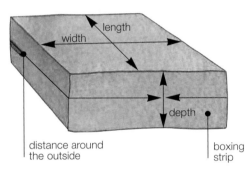

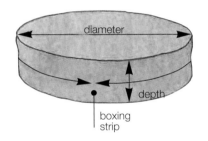

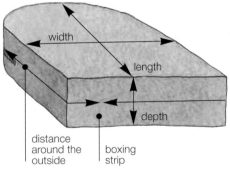

◀ Box cushions – for these you will need three pieces of

fabric: top, bottom, and side strip. Measure the length and width, or the diameter, to work out the top and bottom, and the depth and distance around the outside or the circumference, to work out the side strip. Make a template for complex shapes.

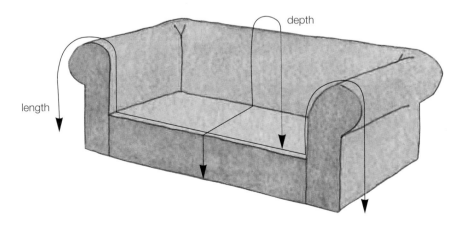

◀ Sofa throw – if the arms are to show,

measure the width of the seating area and the distance from the floor to the back of the seat, then up and over the back to the floor on the other side. Add a little extra so the throw can be tucked into the back. to secure it. If you want the throw to cover the arms, for the width measure straight up from the floor, over the arm to the seat, across the width, then up and over the arm to the floor on the other side.

Measuring for slipcovers

Simple wooden chair – measure each section of the chair as indicated by the arrows, remembering to add seam allowances. Make a toile in a cheap fabric and tack together roughly to check the fit. Make any adjustments necessary for a perfect fit then take the toile apart and use it as a pattern to cut the chair cover.

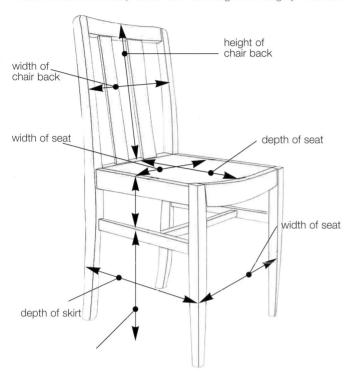

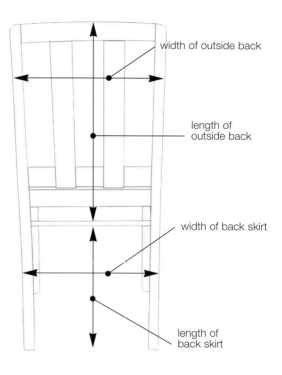

Simple padded chair – measure as for the wooden chair and again make a toile. For curved surfaces you may find it easier to use a fabric tape, but check it against the metal one to make sure it is accurate.

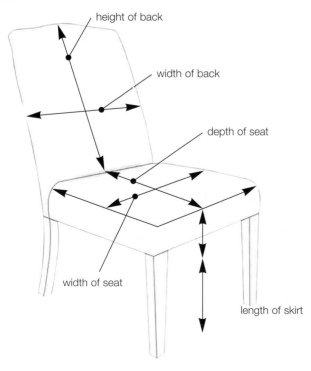

Simple sofa – measure as for the padded chair and again make a toile. For a more complex sofa you will have to spend some time fitting the toile to the shape. (See pages 232–237.)

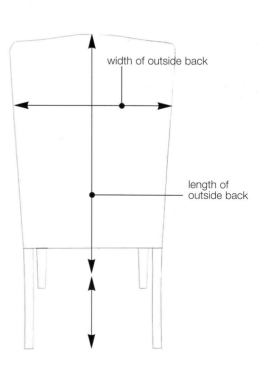

home furnishings

Measuring tables

Rectangular or square table – measure the length and width first, then add the drop for the skirt plus an allowance for the hem to all four sides. Any sort of angular geometric table is measured in the same way. If you are making a short-skirted tablecloth, allow at least 10 cm (4 in) for the skirt drop, as any less will probably look too skimpy.

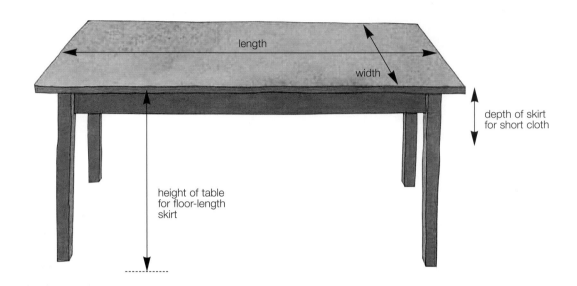

length

width

depth of skirt
for short cloth

height of table
for floor-length
skirt

Circular table – measure the diameter then add the drop plus a hem allowance to both sides. Fold the fabric you are using into a square (see page 160 for full instructions). Find the centre of the square and use a pencil on a string to draw a circle the correct diameter for the full tablecloth. Check the circumference before you cut.

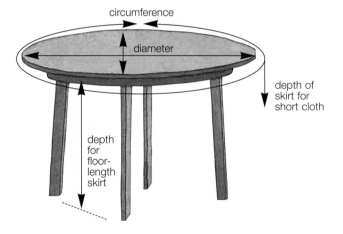

circumference

diameter

depth of
skirt for
short cloth

depth
for
floor-
length
skirt

Table setting

Tablecloths can be quite thin but if you do not want to use placemats as well, protect polished surfaces with a thick layer of felt or a heat pad concealed under the tablecloth.

Measuring beds

Headboard cover – measure the width of the headboard and from the top of the mattress to the top of the headboard. Double these measurements to get both sides. Measure the thickness of the headboard and add this amount to each side of the width measurement and to the top of the depth measurement, plus seam allowances and hems.

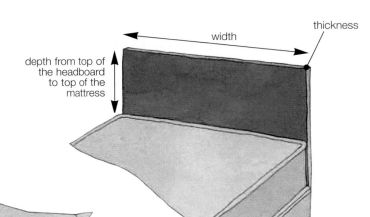

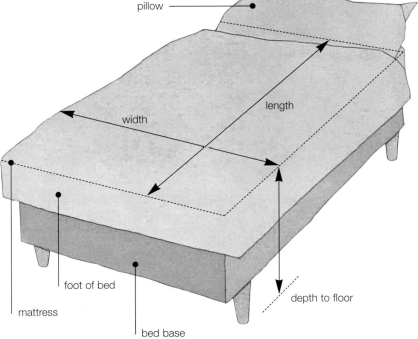

Bedcover – measure on a made bed, with all blankets and pillows in place. Measure the length of the bed and add 60 cm (24 in) (to go around the pillows) and the depth from the top of the mattress to the floor. Measure the width of the bed, and add the depth from the top of the mattress to the floor on each side. Add a hem allowance all around.

Bed valance or skirt – cut the skirt separately from the flat piece. Measure the width and the length of the bed base for the flat piece, adding a seam allowance all around. For the length of the valance, start measuring 15 cm (6 in) in at the head as indicated, then down the bed length, across the width, up the other side and 15 cm (6 in) in at the head again. For the depth, measure from the top of the base to the floor, plus a seam and hem allowance. For a ruffled or pleated valance, multiply the length by two.

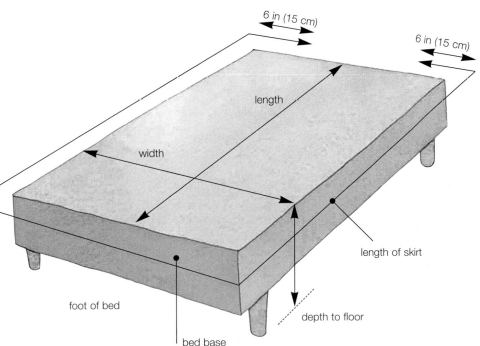

Preparing and cutting

Accurate cutting is a must if you want your projects to look professional. Start by making sure that the fabric is absolutely straight and square to the grain before you begin, and be careful not to stretch it out of shape as you work. Mark the cutting lines and use very sharp scissors. Cut in smooth strokes, not in little jerky movements.

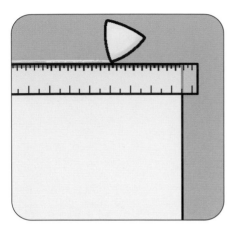

1 ▲ **Cutting on the grain**
To find the straight of grain, align the edge of a piece of paper with the selvedge. Place a ruler along the opposite edge and draw a line along it in chalk. This line will be on the straight of grain.

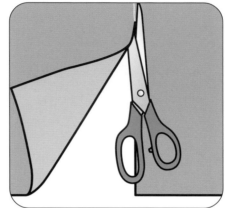

2 When cutting, turn the fabric around so that you are facing the direction in which you want to cut. Use sharp dressmaker's shears and try to keep the fabric as flat as possible as you cut.

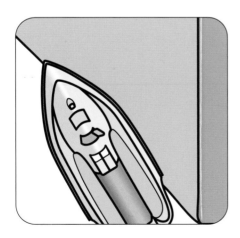

1 ▲ **Cutting on the bias**
Make sure both the selvedge and the bottom edge of the piece of fabric are straight and square to each other. Mark the straight of grain line as described in step 1 of cutting on the grain, then align the bottom edge with the line and press.

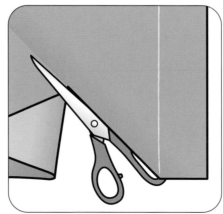

2 Turn the fabric so you are facing the direction you wish to cut and open the fold. Cut carefully along the pressed crease, making sure that you do not stretch or distort the fabric as you work.

Fabric cutting tips

Fabrics that shrink should be washed and ironed before you begin. Follow the manufacturer's care guidelines for laundering.

If the edge of the fabric is not straight, level it before you begin as described on page 160.

Always cut the fabric on the straight of grain, unless the pattern says otherwise.

Cutting on the cross grain or bias will give more flexibility, but the fabric will need to be handled with care as it will distort easily.

Preparing the fabric

Before you begin to cut, unroll the fabric and check along its entire length for any flaws in either the weave or the pattern. If there is a problem, the shop where you bought it should allow a return or exchange—but usually only if you have not started to cut. If the flaw is not serious you may be able to cut round it, but

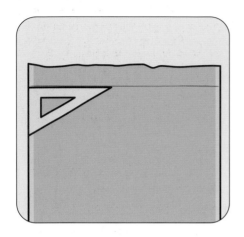

Straightening the fabric edge

Use a set square as illustrated to find the straight edge of the fabric at right angles to the selvedge. Check the weave; in some cases the fabric may have twisted during weaving. If so, pull out a thread across the width to establish the straight of grain, then pull the fabric gently in the opposite direction of the twist to straighten it.

Planning around the pattern repeat

The lengths of fabric needed for each drop of a curtain must be carefully planned to start and finish at the same point on the repeat, or you will not be able to match the repeats across seams. Measure and mark the cutting line for each drop along the length with chalk before starting to cut. Check that the repeats are the same in each length, then cut each drop.

Cutting curves and circles This method is a quick and easy way of marking and cutting a symmetrical circle from a piece of fabric. You will need a pin, a piece of string a little longer than the radius of your circle, and an erasable marker. Remember to check the marker on a scrap piece of fabric first, to make sure the marks can be removed.

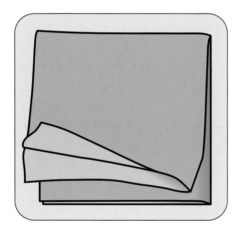

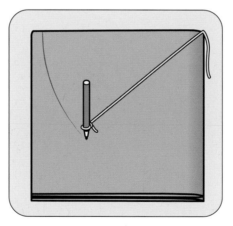

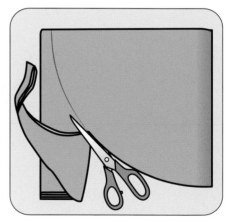

1 After preparing the fabric as described on page 159 and above, fold it in half lengthwise, then in half again widthwise so you have four layers of fabric. Tie one end of the piece of string to the marker.

2 Measure and mark your radius along both folded edges of the fabric and on a diagonal line from the folded corner. Place the marker on one of the marks, and pin the other end of the string securely at the folded corner.

3 Holding the string taut, draw a quarter circle from one folded edge to the other, running through the mark on the diagonal in the middle. Pin the layers of fabric just inside the line, then cut through all four layers.

Cutting difficult fabrics
Sheers

To cut loosely-woven fabrics on the straight of grain, pull out a thread across the width and use the line created as your cutting line.

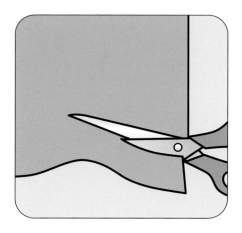

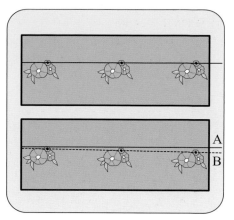

For perfect results

Velvet frays very badly, so make sure you oversew or zig zag stitch along all raw edges.

Slippery fabrics are easier to cut accurately if you sandwich them between two layers of tissue. Use a flat surface and pin the layers together if you are cutting more than one at a time.

Velvets

When cutting velvet, do not use the tips of the shears or you will create a series of jagged edges and damage the pile. Make short and deep cuts using the main part of the blade, so the scissors will follow the line of the thread and the line will stay straight.

Patterns

In a woven fabric, just make sure that the widthwise threads are at a right angle to the selvedge. A good way to do this is to line up the selvedge with the side edge of a table, with the end of the fabric overhanging the table end. Crease the overhang along the table end to make a line at right angles to the selvedge; then you can check the widthwise threads against the crease line.

With a printed pattern things may be more complex, as the pattern may not run exactly along the straight of grain. With a small repeat this may not matter, but with large repeats it can be obvious. In this case you must cut to the pattern repeat and not to the true grain line, or your project will look wrong when it is finished.

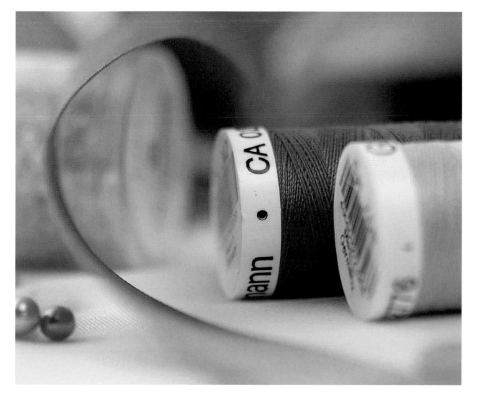

curtains

In addition to providing privacy and insulation, curtains provide the finishing touch to a window. Without curtains the room seems positively bare! Apart from all of the fabric possibilities, there are also many different designs to consider. What you choose will not only depend on your personal taste, but the style of your room and the type of windows you have as well.

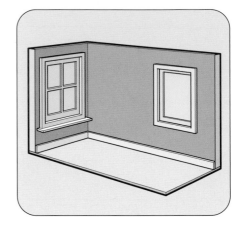

Pairs of identical windows on the same wall – these can be treated as one unit or as two separate windows, depending on how close together they are. The treatment for both should be identical, or they may have an unbalanced appearance.

Two different windows on the same wall – to tie these windows together visually, work from the height of the taller window and dress both to the same levels. If they are close enough together they can be treated as one unit.

Two or more different windows in the same room – where the windows are far apart and quite dissimilar they can have different treatments, but use the same fabric and trimmings to tie them together.

French doors – these will probably need to open for access, so any treatment must bear this in mind. Simple curtains are easy to draw back, while a blind could be added to the door for privacy.

Window considerations

The shape of the window has a bearing on the style of curtain that will look best. Round and square windows may need special treatments.

Make sure that the window treatment you choose does not greatly restrict the amount of light that the window adds to the room, unless blocking light is your aim.

Some windows, such as those in ceilings and in home offices where light levels need to be controlled, work better with blinds than curtains.

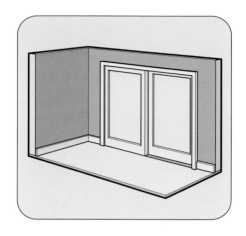

Windows or sliding doors taking up all or most of the wall – there may not be much room for curtains and the expanse will make them bulky. Opt for simple sheers or dress curtains that do not draw at the sides, plus blinds for privacy.

Bay windows – these are usually covered with one or more sets of curtains on a curved track. You may also run the curtains across the face of the bay if you don't mind losing the floor space when they are closed.

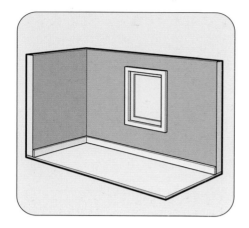

Single window in a wall – this offers the most options for dressing, since you can use virtually anything you like as long as it fits the style of the room. Dramatic statements work well in larger rooms, but keep it simple for smaller ones.

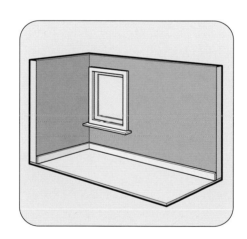

Window close to an adjacent wall – it is difficult to keep this symmetrical because one side of the window has no room to pull back the curtain. Try using a blind or any asymmetrical window dressing.

Window close to a ceiling – here you may have to mount the support either on the window frame or on the ceiling. Adding a pelmet can visually shorten the top of the window if it is very tall.

Window in a deep recess – if the recess is very deep you may be better off choosing a design that is mounted on the frame or between the sides of the recess. Keep things simple and consider a blind instead of a curtain.

home furnishings

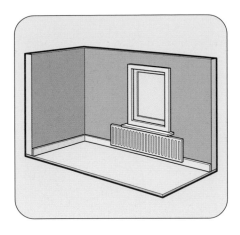

Window with a radiator beneath – floor-length curtains will block some of the heat from the radiator. One option is decorative full-length dress curtains with a blind that comes to the sill for warmth and privacy.

Window on the stairs, where the floor is uneven – here the issue is being able to reach the curtain or blind to close it. Make sure the closing mechanism of a blind can be reached easily from the upper level and consider pull cords for a curtain.

Curtain supports

Just as with window dressings, there is an impossibly wide range of supports available. Do you want concealed or visible, period or contemporary, wood or metal, pull cords or none? To some extent the style of your room and your fabric may influence your choice. There are so many types available that we can show only a few examples here.

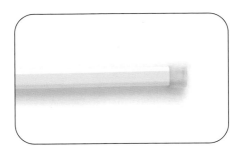

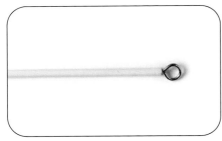

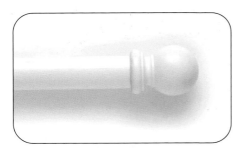

Tension rod – this is held in place by tension within a window recess, so there is no need for fixings. It will only hold sheers or very lightweight curtains.

Spring wire – this is usually attached to the window frame with small hooks and is mainly used for sheers, which are threaded onto the wire.

Pole – supports like this wooden pole are designed to be seen and come in both wood and metal and in a variety of finishes and styles.

Café curtain rod – usually placed halfway down across the window, this is used to hold half curtains, which you do not usually draw.

• *Metal track* – this type of track is not designed to be seen and is purely functional. The side view is discreet and can also be obscured with a pelmet or heading.

Plastic track – like a metal track this is functional rather than decorative. A plastic track is stable when in place, but bends easily round corners to fit awkward spaces.

Track tips

With a corded curtain track, decide which end is easiest to access and position the pull cords at that end.

Heavy curtains need a hefty track to support their weight, and the track itself must be firmly fixed to the wall to withstand constant pulling.

Double tracks are useful if you want dress curtains and sheers on the same window.

Curtain supplies

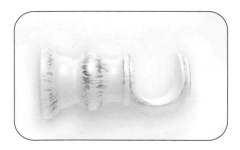

Wooden curtain rod support
This support is screwed to the wall and the wooden curtain pole drops into it. It is easy to fit, but the pole is not secured and may slide out.

Metal curtain rod finial
Finials for curtain rods provide a decorative touch at each end. There is a wide range of designs available, some with matching holdbacks.

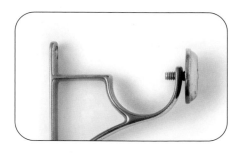

Metal curtain rod support
This metal pole support has a screw-in fitting on the front, which can be tightened against the pole to hold it firmly in place.

Small metal cord hook
This type of small metal hook is fixed to the wall at the side of a blind—or sometimes a curtain—to hold the excess pull cord in place.

Wooden curtain rod finial
Finials not only add decoration but also prevent the curtain sliding off the end of the rod.

Plastic curtain hooks
Plastic curtain hooks like these slide into the heading tape on curtains, then hook over the loops hanging from plastic track. A similar item is available for metal tracks.

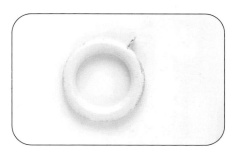

Wooden curtain ring
These rings are threaded onto wooden curtain poles. The curtain is fitted with hooks—plastic or metal—which hook over the small metal ring.

Curtain headings

The heading of a curtain or blind is the edge that runs across the top and is attached to the support. Curtain headings are usually much wider than the window, so they need to be gathered together or pleated to control the excess fabric. Many seemingly complex headings can be created easily by using special tapes that either have several cords to pull at required intervals, or pockets in which to insert special hooks to make the pleats.

Casing – this is the simplest type of heading; it is just a tube at the top of the curtain or blind. It works best for lightweight curtains that do not need to be drawn.

Goblet pleats – a formal heading, goblet pleats look best in plain, heavy fabrics. The curtains need to be full length to balance the visual weight of the heading.

Gathered heading – one of the plainest headings, it is suitable for many types of curtain and some blinds. It is made using a narrow heading tape.

Box pleats – a very geometric look, box pleats work in formal rooms whether they are period or contemporary. The fabric needs to be light to medium in weight.

Pencil pleats – this heading is made using a wide tape that has several cords across it to pull the heading into a series of vertical folds.

Handsewn hooks – here the hooks are stitched individually at intervals across the heading. The final curtain will look very simple and hang more or less flat.

French pleats – a very traditional heading style, French pleats can be made by hand or by using a special tape with spaced hooks.

Heading tapes and hooks

Heading tapes and hooks should be selected with care; ask the sales consultant for advice if you are not sure which you need. Make sure you buy the tape long enough to avoid joins. Also, match the type of hook to the tape you choose.

Curtain heading tips

Heading tapes have woven guidelines to help you keep your stitching straight.

When measuring heading tape, allow the finished width of the curtain plus at least 5 cm (2 in) at each end to turn under.

After pulling the cords to get the heading to the required width, knot near the curtain to hold in place and then wind the excess around your fingers and tuck it behind the heading tape at the end. NEVER cut the cords—you will need to let the heading out again whenever the curtain is laundered.

If your curtain is narrow you can stitch over the cords at the leading edge and only pull up one set of cords to gather. If the curtain is wide, it will be quicker to gather from both ends.

Eyelets – these eyelets are punched at intervals across the heading and then threaded with a cord. The look works best in an informal room.

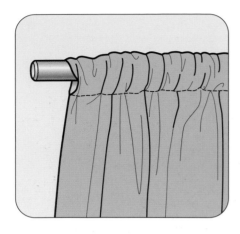

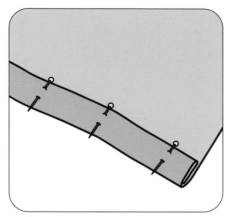

▲ Making a casing

This is the simplest type of heading. The pole or rod just slides through the tube of fabric. If the curtains are quite lightweight they can be gathered along the pole. Blinds may also have a simple casing heading.

1 Measure the width of the rod, then turn a double hem twice this width across the top of the curtain. Pin and press in place.

2 Stitch along the bottom fold on the machine, removing the pins as you work. At each end, work backstitch to secure the threads.

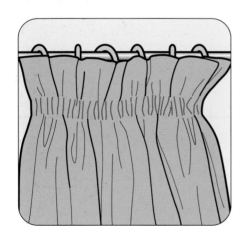

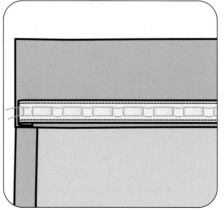

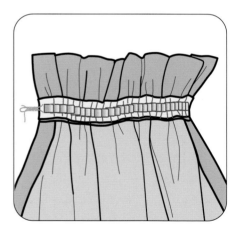

▲ Making a gathered heading

The gathered heading is almost as simple as the casing, but allows curtain hooks to be used so the curtains will be easier to draw. Gathering tape is available in several different widths and usually in both white and cream.

1 Fold the top of the curtain over to the depth of the heading. It should be at least 2.5 cm (1 in); here it is 5 cm (2 in). Position the gathering tape over the raw edge.

2 Stitch along the guidelines on either side of the tape. Knot the cords at one end and pull up the curtain to the required width. Knot the cords at the other end to secure.

Pencil-pleat heading

▲ Pencil pleats are thin, straight pleats that run evenly across the full width of the heading, creating a generous fullness in the curtain beneath. For closely spaced pleats, as shown here, you will need the curtain to be at least three times the width of your window.

More curtain heading tips

Try to choose the type of curtain and heading you want before selecting your track. If you already have tracks in place, consider your options before going to the expense of changing them.

Full headings need a massive amount of fabric if they are to look good. Remember this means the drawn back curtain will also be wider than with a simple heading, so allow extra at each end of the pole or track so the open curtain clears the window opening.

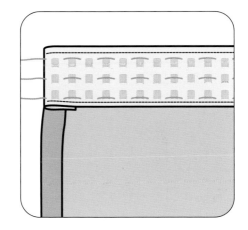

1 At the top of the curtain, fold over a single hem slightly narrower than the width of the heading tape. Align one edge of the tape with the top edge of the curtain, covering the raw edge, and pin in place across the curtain. Tuck each end of the tape under, but pull the cords free. Stitch the tape to the curtain along the top and bottom edges.

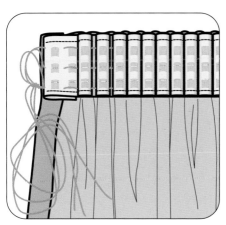

2 Knot the loose cords at one end and pull on the other end to gather up the fabric into even pleats. Spread the pleats along the full width of the curtain until the curtain is the width required. Knot the cords at the other end, wind the excess cord around your fingers. and tuck in behind the tape.

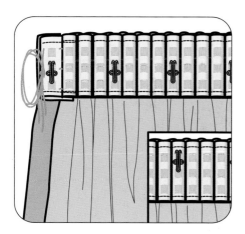

3 Slot the hooks into the tape. There is usually a choice of two or three levels for the hook depending on whether you are using a track that the heading should cover or a pole that you want to show. Place one hook at each end of the curtain and space the others around 7.5 cm (3 in) apart.

home furnishings

Box-pleat heading

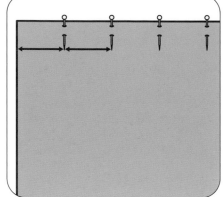

Box pleats do not need heading tape. They must be set up by hand, but they are simple to do. They will give a flat, tailored style to your curtains that looks great in a modern room with classic plain fabrics that are not too bulky.

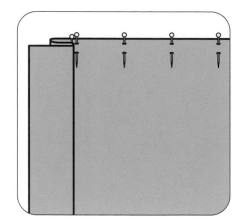

1 Measure across the finished width of the curtain and divide it into equal amounts across the top, marked with pins. You need three pins for each pair of pleats, so the total number of pins (not spaces) across the heading should be divisible by three.

2 Fold the fabric along the line of the first pin and then bring the fold over to meet the second pin.

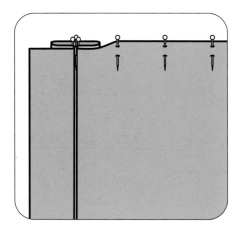

3 Fold the fabric along the line of the third pin and then bring the fold over to meet the second pin.

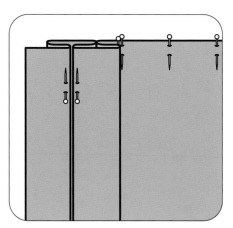

4 Fold at the fourth pin and the sixth pin, and bring the folds to meet at the fifth pin. Continue in this way across the full width of the heading.

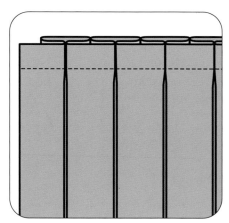

5 Stitch across the top of the curtain about 2.5 cm (1 in) from the top, keeping the pleats square. Remove the pins and press the pleats. Fold over the top of the curtain and finish on the reverse by making a hem or binding.

French pleats

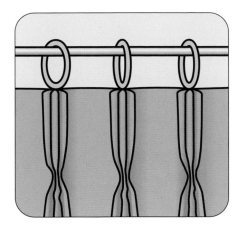

French pleats are also known as pinch pleats. They consist of a group of pleats pinched together at the base and fanning out at the top, with a flat area between. Tape is available to create French pleats, but making them by hand creates a more professional finish.

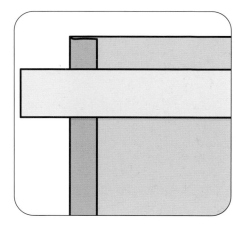

1 Fold over the top edge of the curtain to the wrong side to make a deep hem and press. Cut a length of fusible buckram 15 cm (6 in) longer than the curtain width.

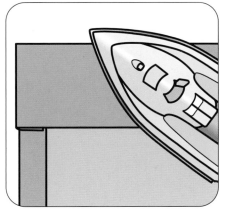

2 Open up the fold and place the buckram along the pressed line. Make sure the bottom edge of the buckram is along the fold.

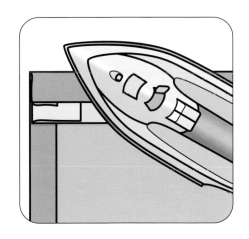

3 Fold in the extra buckram at each end, then fold over the extra fabric above the buckram. Press to hold in place.

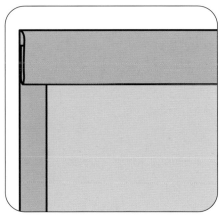

4 Fold over the buckram tape, so the line you first pressed is now back at the top of the curtain. Press across the width of the curtain again.

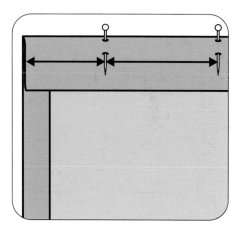

5 Measure the finished curtain width. This measurement must be divided evenly into space, pleat, space across the curtain with the pleat width a bit bigger than the space. For instance, if the space is 13 cm (5 in) the pleat should be around 18 cm (7 in). Place a pin at each measure.

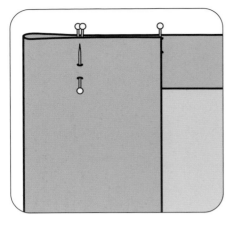 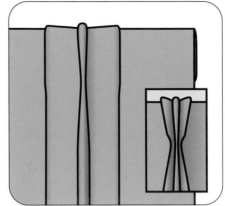 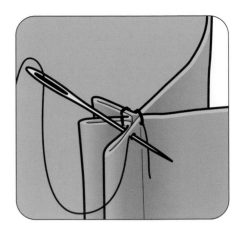

6 On the wrong side, fold at the first pin and bring it to meet the second. Pin along the width of the buckram to secure. Fold the third pin to the fourth and repeat across the curtain. On the right side, stitch down the line of each pleat the depth of the buckram.

7 Still working from the right side, flatten each pleat slightly over the centre seam. Pinch the centre up into a pleat, then pinch a pleat on each side. Adjust until you have three even pleats.

8 Work stab stitch through the base of each triple pleat to hold it firmly in position, pulling the thread tight and fastening off after each one. Close the top of each fold separately with slip stitch.

Goblet pleats

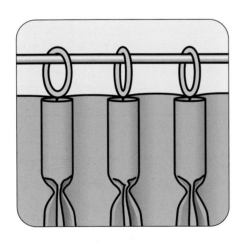 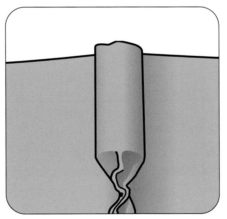 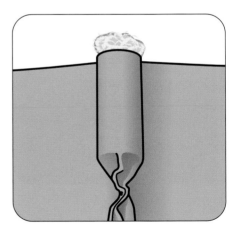

Goblet pleats make an elegant formal heading, but they are quite heavy visually so this style needs to be used with care. The goblets are padded to create their solid, rounded shape.

1 Follow steps 1-6 for French pleats. Working on the right side, pinch together the base of the French pleat you have just made and work a few stab stitches to secure in place.

2 Pad out the rounded shape of each goblet with a roll of wadding or other soft material, pushing it right down to the bottom of the pleat.

Handsewn hooks

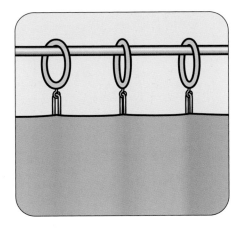

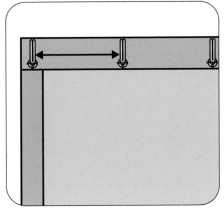

1 Measure the finished width of the curtain and divide into equal spaces. The exact space will depend on the width of the curtain, but should not be more than 15 cm (6 in).

2 Mark each measure with a pin. Stitch a hook at each mark, either with the end protruding over the top of the curtain or fully concealed behind it.

Handsewn hooks give a flat heading that can add a touch of understated elegance to a curtain. This type of heading works well on café curtains, but can also be used on full-length curtains. The hooks can be on show or be concealed behind the curtain.

Lined and interlined curtains

A traditional curtain has both lining and interlining, which are attached so they all move as one entity. This means that the completed curtain will hang beautifully. For a truly professional finish follow the steps carefully. Three layers does make quite a substantial curtain, so if you need something lighter omit the interlining layer.

Lining tips

See page 148 for how to measure the window, and page 150 for how to estimate quantity.

Lining should be 10 cm (4 in) narrower than the curtain measurement.

Interlining should be 10 cm (4 in) shorter than the curtain, but the same width as the curtain measurement.

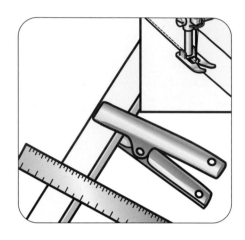

1 Join widths to make up the lining. Fold up a hem of 3 cm (1¼ in) and press against the edge of the table with a metal ruler to set the fold. Fold up the same width again, and press. Stitch the hem. Lay the interlining flat with the main fabric on top, aligned so the top is 8 cm (3 in) above the top edge of the interlining.

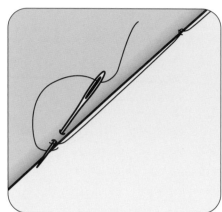

2 Fold the main fabric back on itself in a straight line down the centre of the curtain. Work interlocking stitches 10 cm (4 in) apart to attach the two layers. Repeat across the curtain at intervals of around 40 cm (16 in). Carefully turn over the entire curtain, so the interlining is now on top.

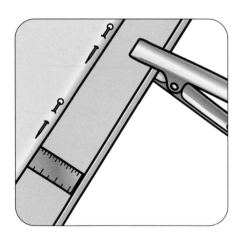

3 Fold the interlining back by 5 cm (2 in) along the length of the leading edge of the curtain. Measure at regular intervals to make sure the line stays straight. Pin the interlining in position.

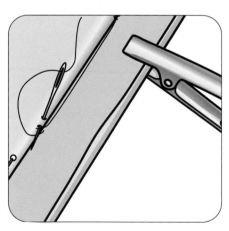

4 Work interlocking stitch along the fold you have just made, working the stitches around 5 cm (2 in) apart. This will secure the leading edge, since the edges are handled more than other parts of the curtain.

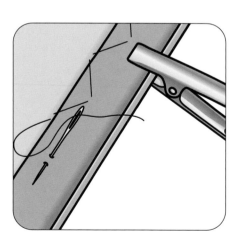

5 Fold the edge of the main curtain fabric over the interlining and anchor it in place with stitching, making sure that it does not show on the right side of the curtain. Repeat steps 3–5 on the other side of the curtain.

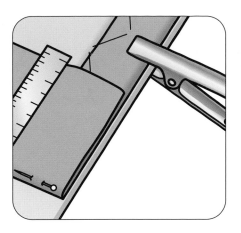

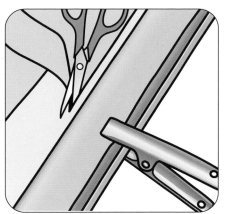

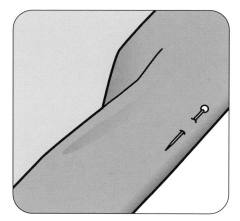

6 Fold the main fabric up by 12 cm (4⅜ in) over the interlining along the bottom edge of the curtain and pin in position close to the line of the fold.

7 Turn the hem you just made back on itself and fix in position. Here we have used a fabric clamp. Trim off 3 cm (1¼ in) of excess interlining, straightening up the edge as you go if necessary.

8 Release the edge of the hem and fold it under along the raw edge by 3 cm (1¼ in), fixing in place by moving up the pins along the fold line. The edge of the hem should cover the raw edge of the interlining. Leave the last 30 cm (12 in) unpinned at both ends of the hem.

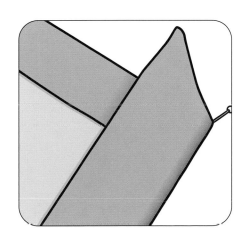

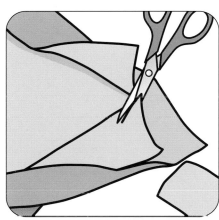

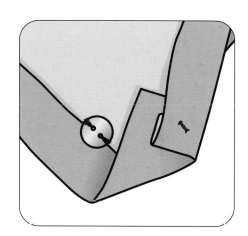

9 Lay each corner of the hem on a flat surface and check that the corner is a perfect right angle, gently smoothing out any wrinkles with your fingers. Mark the corner with a pin.

10 Open the corner so you can cut away the excess interlining to reduce bulk. Then, using the pin as a guide so that you do not cut too far, snip off the main fabric diagonally across the corner.

11 Using double thread, stitch a curtain weight into each corner. Fold the main fabric hems back over the interlining, making a neat mitre at the corner, and stitch the hem in place.

home furnishings

12 Place the lining on top of the curtain, right side up, aligning the raw edge with the leading edge of the curtain at the side but leaving 3 cm (1¼ in) of the main hem showing at the bottom. Clamp or pin in place.

13 Fold the raw side edge of the lining over by 3 cm (1¼ in), aligning the bottom corner with the corner fold of the main fabric. Slipstitch the lining to the main fabric along the leading edge, stopping around 20 cm (8 in) from the top of the curtain.

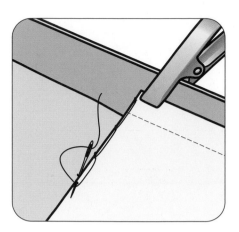

14 Fold the lining back around 40 cm (16 in) from the edge and work interlock stitching down the fold. Repeat across the curtain as in step 2. On the far side, trim off the excess lining fabric, and repeat steps 12 and 13 on this side.

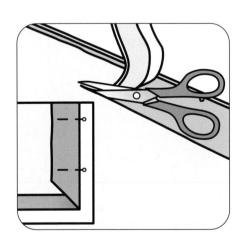

15 Measure the finished drop of the curtain up from the finished hem and mark across the heading of the curtain on the wrong side. Trim off the excess lining and interlining to this line, but DO NOT trim off the main fabric. Fold over the main fabric along the cut edge you just made, turning the corner under at a 45° angle. Pin along the fold.

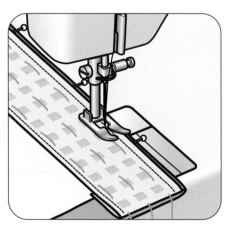

16 Stitch the chosen heading tape in place across the top of the curtain, following the instructions on page 168.

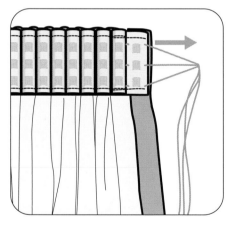

17 Pull the cords to gather the heading up evenly across the width. Knot the cords securely and hide the excess behind the heading tape.

Tube lining

This type of lining is stitched to the curtain at each side by machine, right sides together, to make a tube, which is then turned right sides out for the hem and heading to be added.

This is much faster than hand stitching the side seams, but means that the curtain cannot be interlined. However, if you want a lighter-weight curtain, this technique may be ideal.

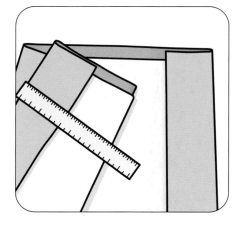

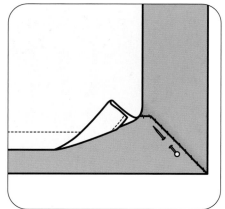

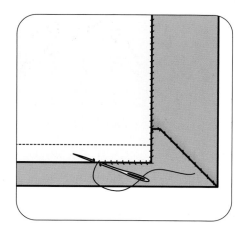

1 Cut the lining the same length as the curtain, but 20 cm (8 in) narrower. With right sides together, stitch the curtain to the lining on each side, stopping 15 cm (6 in) from the bottom. Turn right sides out and measure each side so the lining is centred on the curtain, then press.

2 Measure the required length, turn up the bottom hem on the main fabric, and pin into place. Turn up a double hem on the lining so it is 4 cm (1½ in) shorter than the curtain, then machine stitch in place. Mitre the corners at the hem of the main fabric and hem in place by hand.

3 Slipstitch the last few inches of each side of the lining to the main fabric, folding and catching the bottom corners neatly. Add the chosen heading as described on pages 167–173.

More lining tips

If you want coloured linings for your curtains, you can use cotton sateen or a similar type of fabric instead of actual lining material. However, make sure the lining can be laundered in the same way as the main fabric.

Lined curtains will last longer than unlined ones, as the lining helps the fabric to stay in shape. However, sometimes simple, unlined curtains are lighter and less fussy.

If you want to line purchased ready-made curtains, the easiest method is to use a loose lining as shown on page 178.

Sometimes the lining will show on the right side—if you want to make lined swags (see page 186), for instance, or when the main curtain is a dress curtain that is permanently held back in folds. In this case it is worth using a better-quality fabric for the lining that coordinates with your main fabric.

Loose linings

Here the lining is made as a totally separate piece to the curtain itself and just hooked onto the back of it, which is very useful if the lining needs to be laundered separately for any reason. It is also a good technique to use if you want to add lining to a curtain that is already made up. Again, with this technique, it is not possible to have interlining.

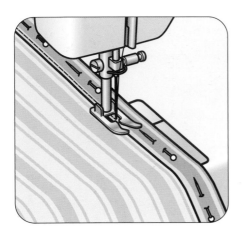

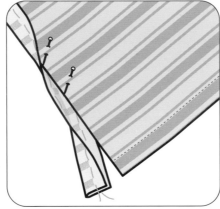

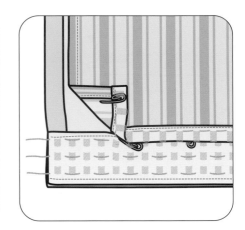

1 Cut and make the curtain and the lining the same length, but make the lining narrower by the width of the side hem. Turn under a double hem along both sides of the lining and machine stitch in place.

2 Pin and tack a length of gathered heading tape to enclose the raw edge of the top of the lining. Stitch the tape in position. Finish the curtain completely, including adding the heading.

3 Insert hooks into the tape of the lining and then fix the lining to the back of the main curtain, using the bottom row of slots. The lining can now be hemmed to a suitable length so it does not show below the curtain.

Café curtains

Traditional café curtains have a scalloped or crenellated heading, through which the rods are threaded. The shapes used can be anything you desire, just draw up the relevant template and follow the steps illustrated on this page. Some possible variations are shown on page 180, but use your imagination to come up with your own ideas.

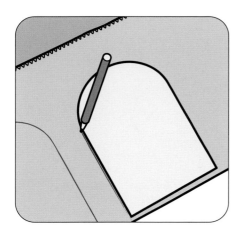

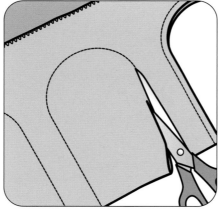

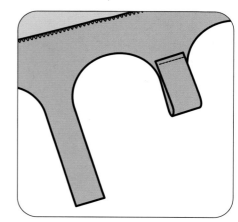

1 Make a template to work out the shape of the scallops evenly across the width of the curtain. Cut the curtain drops and join widths as required, then zigzag the raw edges at the top and bottom. Fold over the top edge to the right side to a level 6 cm (2 ½ in) deeper than the depth of the scallop, and mark the scallops across the curtain width.

2 Pin around the edge of the middle section of each scallop, then stitch each scallop around the marked line. Using sharp scissors or dressmaking shears, cut out the scallops and trim the fabric to within 9 mm (⅜ in) of the stitching line. Clip curves and trim all corners, being very careful not to cut through any of the stitching.

3 Turn the top layer right side out— the edge you folded over has now become a facing along the top edge. Press gently, then fold each tab to the back and stitch to the main curtain to make a channel across the top of each leg of the scallop. Turn under a narrow double hem along the sides and topstitch in place.

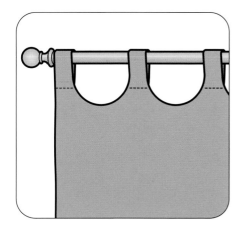

4 Thread the curtain onto the rod and measure the level for the bottom hem. Turn under a single hem along the bottom edge of the curtain and either topstitch or hem in place.

Tips for café curtains

On small windows, café curtains can just be threaded onto a tension rod.

Café curtains were designed to give some privacy to diners in the window from people walking past in the street, but at the same time let a maximum amount of natural light into the room.

Café curtain heading variations

Tied heading – here the curtain has been edged with a contrasting fabric, and ties in the same fabric have been added to attach the curtain to the rod.

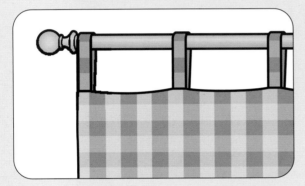

Tabbed heading – these narrow tabs can be made separately and inserted into the seam between the curtain and a facing. This allows you to use a matching or contrasting colour.

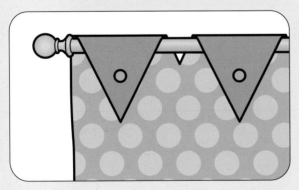

Triangles – these jaunty triangles have been made in the same way as the scallops, but are faced in a contrasting fabric and then folded to the front and secured with buttons.

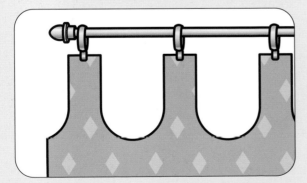

Scalloped with rings – instead of folding over the tabs at the top, here the curtain is clipped to café curtain rings.

Sheer curtains

Simple sheers obscure an unattractive view but let in lots of natural light. Since they are translucent, a basic construction method works best so that not too many seams show through.

If you want a gathered heading you can buy translucent heading tape to use on this type of curtain, which will be much less obtrusive than the solid kind.

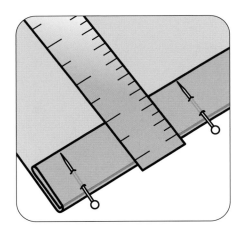

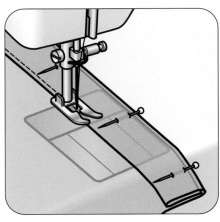

1 Measure and cut the fabric for the sheers. Fold up the bottom edge by 2.5 cm (1 in) and pin. Crease the fold with a metal ruler, then turn up by the same amount and crease again.

2 Stitch very close to the top folded edge. Fold the heading in the same way as the hem, but folding half the heading measurement each time. Zigzag along the raw side edges.

3 Carefully insert the rod down the casing you have made at the top, trying not to snag anywhere as threads will pull easily. Hang the curtain, then even out the gathers along its width.

Tips for sheers

When measuring up for sheers with a casing heading, the drop will be the finished drop plus 5 cm (2 in) for the hem, plus twice the diameter of the rod, plus 6 mm (¼ in) for the seam allowance on the heading. The width will be at least 2 ½ times the length of the pole—but do not make the curtain too much wider than this.

Sheers also work very well with a tabbed heading (see page 180), which is just threaded onto the pole. With a tabbed heading you can also achieve interesting effects by alternately threading the tabs of two different coloured sheers onto the pole, to get an attractive layered effect.

Curtain valances

Valances or pelmets cover the top of the window and hide both the support and the heading of the curtain, as well as blocking any light coming in over the top of the curtain. Make sure they are long enough to allow enough spare space at each end to also conceal the operating mechanism of the curtain.

Tips for valances

There are special valance supports that clip to ordinary curtain tracks to hold the valance, or you can buy a double track.

You can easily make your own flat or boxed pelmet from plywood or fibreboard.

A flat valance can be fixed across the top of a window recess, while a box valance has returns that will hide the ends of the curtain support.

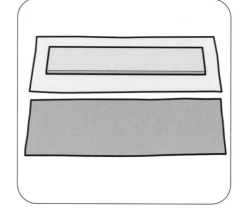

1 ▲ **Flat valance or pelmet**
Measure and cut the board, wadding, and fabric. You need to allow enough wadding and fabric to cover the board and wrap around to the back on all four sides.

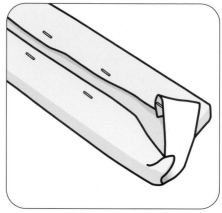

2 Attach the wadding to the board using staples, glue, or tacks. Fix the two long edges first, then reduce bulk at the corners and fold over the two short edges.

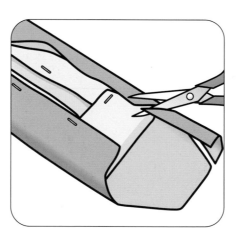

3 Wrap the fabric around the board and secure it as for the wadding, turning under the corners neatly on all sides.

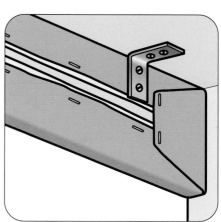

4 The finished valance can now be fixed across the top of a window recess, or attached to the wall on brackets if the ends of the curtain support will not be visible.

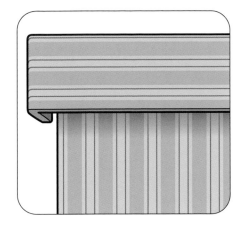

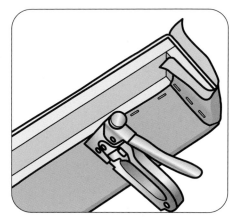

▲ **Box valance**

As the name indicates, this type of valance is a three-sided box fitted over the top of the curtain and track.

1 Make up a box with top and three sides. Cover with wadding as for the flat valance, but do not cover the edges that will rest against the wall.

2 Cut a piece of fabric large enough to cover the box completely and staple, glue, or tack it into position on the inside, pulling the fabric taut on the outside.

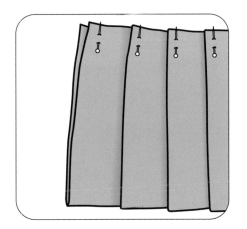

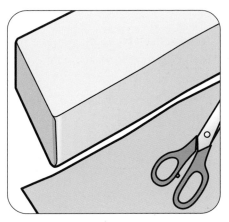

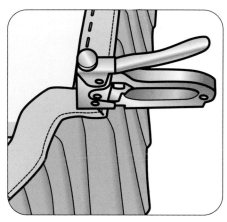

1 ▲ **Box-pleated valance**
Cut a strip of fabric long enough to pleat across the front of the box, and twice the height of the box plus an extra 10 cm (4 in). Fold over a hem at the short ends, and fold the whole strip in half lengthways, wrong sides together. Mark, press, and pin the pleats as described on page 170, and stitch across the top raw edges.

2 Cut another length of the main fabric wide enough to use as a binding for the top edge. With right sides together, pin and stitch the binding to the top of the valance. Turn the strip to the wrong side, turn the raw edge under, and stitch both the short and the long edges.

3 Fold the binding strip over the top edge of the box and staple it into position. Turn the corners carefully, folding the binding into a neat pleat at each corner before stapling it into position.

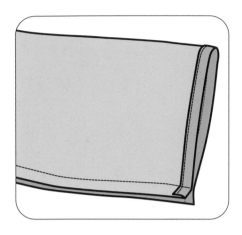

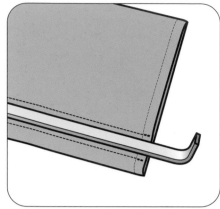

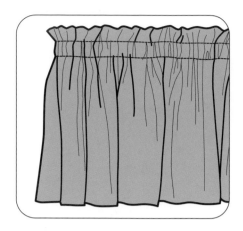

1 ▲ Gathered valance
Measure a piece of fabric the same width as the curtain plus seam allowances and twice the depth of the desired valance plus seam allowances. Turn over to the wrong side and hem both the short ends. Fold in half lengthways with right sides together and stitch the long edge to make a tube.

2 Turn the tube right side out and press with the seam flat across the centre of the back. Measure two parallel lines twice the depth of the curtain track and mark along one long edge to make a casing, making sure that it does not line up with the seam on the back. Stitch the lines to create the casing.

3 Slide the track carefully into the casing, being sure not to snag the fabric on any edges. Spread the gathers evenly along the length of the track. Working with the fabric double means that the right side of the fabric will show on both sides of the valance.

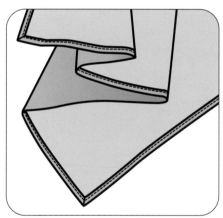

1 ▲ Simple swag
Use a fabric that drapes well and hang one width over the window to estimate the length required. Take down.

2 Level the edges and trim any selvedges. Turn under a hem around all four sides, backstitching at the corners to secure.

Tiebacks and holdbacks

Tiebacks are lengths of fabric attached to a hook (or something similar) on the wall and designed to hold the curtain back out of the way when it is drawn. They also add an extra decorative touch. Holdbacks serve a similar purpose, but are made of a solid material such as wood or metal and are fixed to the wall, so the curtain can be hooked behind them.

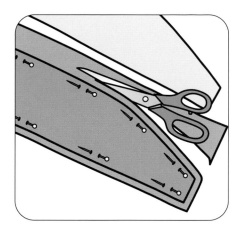

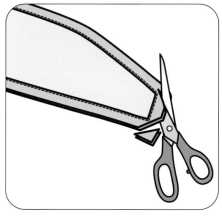

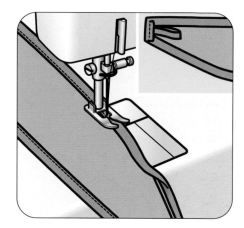

1 ▲ **Basic tieback**
To determine the length of the tieback, loop a fabric tape measure around the curtain and pull it back to the approximate position. For the shape, make a paper template. Cut each tieback two times in fabric with seam allowances added, and once in iron-on interfacing.

2 Place one piece of fabric wrong side up and iron the interfacing on top. Place the other piece of fabric against the first, right sides together, and stitch all around the edge, using the interfacing as a guide to the stitching line and leaving a gap to turn the right side out. Notch the curves and clip across the corners.

3 Turn the tieback right side out and slipstitch the gap closed. Press gently. On the reverse of the tieback, stitch bias binding all around. Fold over the edges, then topstitch in place along the front side. On the front, stitch a fabric loop at each end to hook over the wall fastening.

Tips for tiebacks

Tiebacks come in many materials and designs. They can be made from the same fabric as the curtain, or in a coordinating colour, and may have cords and end tassels and be trimmed with a range of embellishments.

There are also many possible tieback shapes. Ideally it should match the style of the curtain, but there are many variations on this.

Most tiebacks are shaped in a simple crescent, but this basic shape can be altered by making it more angular, or by softening the edges with scallops or fringing.

Embellishments add another variation: the fabric can be pleated, the two halves laced together, or the tieback can be a cord threaded with chunky beads.

Using cords makes a narrower tieback for smaller curtains, but cords can also be twisted, plaited, knotted, or just wound into a thick rope.

Plaiting lengths of the fabric used for the curtains also makes a great tieback. See page 188 for instructions.

home furnishings

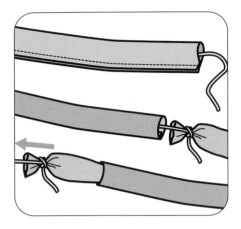

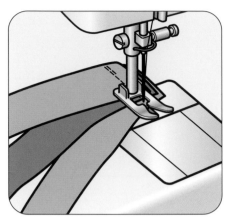

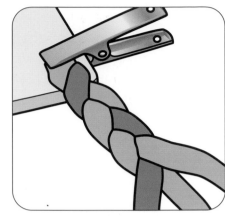

1 ▲ Making padded plaits

Cut three long strips of fabric, two from the curtain fabric and one from a contrasting or toning fabric. Fold each strip in half lengthwise around a long piece of string and stitch the long side into a tube and across the end to secure. Pull the string to turn the tube right side out. Cut off the sewn end, but DO NOT remove the string. Tie one end of the string around a strip of padding and use it to pull the padding into the tube.

2 When the tube is full of padding, cut off the string and trim the padding a little shorter than the tube. Repeat for the other three tubes. Stack the three tubes on top of one another with the contrasting one in the middle, then stitch across to attach them at one end.

3 Clamp the stitched end to a table or chair back and plait the tubes together firmly. When you reach the other end, stack the ends together as in step 2 and stitch across to hold them all together. Fold under the raw ends and hand sew a metal ring to each end to attach the tiebacks to the wall.

Holdbacks

Holdbacks are made from wood, metal, or plastic and are secured to the wall or window frame next to the curtain.

Wooden holdbacks

These usually work best in a classic room. They are almost invariably round, with a short stalk at the back to hold them away from the wall and to provide a space for the curtain to sit within. They often have a turned decoration on the front face, which is usually made to match the finial of the curtain rod.

Metal holdbacks

These are traditionally made of polished brass or wrought iron, but may also be chrome or stainless steel. They are usually in the form of a large hook, which is fitted facing away from the curtain on each side, so the curtain can be slid into the open end of the hook and held back. However, they can also be round, like the wooden ones described left. Metal holdbacks are also often made in designs to coordinate with the pole

blinds

A window blind can be the simplest window covering, but it can also be quite complex, with ruched fabrics and trims. If the blind is to be used with curtains, or in a room that also has curtains, match the style of the curtain for the blind.

Estimating fabric for different types of blind

Blinds require some slightly different methods of measuring, depending upon the type of blind you plan to make. The fabric you will be using also may need taking into account. Decide on which type of blind you want, then check the table below. For further information on estimating quantity for different styles of blind, see the tip box on page 190.

BLIND TYPE	CUT WIDTH	CUT DROP	NOTES
BLINDS WITH A ROLLER TOP	Finished width measurement + 10 cm (4 in) for the inside hems	Finished drop measurement + 5 cm (2 in) for base hem + 25 cm (10 in) for attaching top of blind to wall	Allow additional lining fabric for rod casings. Each casing measures 12 cm (4 ½ in) deep by the width of the blind.
BLINDS WITH A PLEATED TOP	Finished width measurement + 10 cm (4 in) for side hems + 10 cm (4 in) for returns + around 20 cm (8 in) for each pleat	Finished drop measurement + 5 cm (2 in) for base hem + 25 cm (10 in) for attaching top of blind to wall	Allow additional lining fabric for some fullness at the bottom, and perhaps another 20 cm (8 in) on the drop.

Fabric considerations

Almost any fabric can be used for a blind, but some lightweight types may need to be stiffened.

Blinds can be economical with fabric—but some styles need almost as much fabric as a curtain!

Panel blind

Panel blinds are simple and unstructured, without rods. The rings are sewn in rows beginning 10 cm (4 in) from each side edge. The bottom ring should be 5 cm (2 in) from the base, the highest 20 cm (8 in) from the top, with around 15 cm (6 in) for each space between the rings.

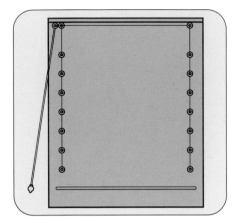

▲ **Panel blind with rod**

This simple blind has one rod positioned about 15 cm (6 in) above the bottom to give it weight. Sew two rows of rings as for the panel blind, with the bottom one 15 cm (6 in) above the rod.

▲ **Inverted pleat blind**

This blind is looser and fuller, with no rod. It has a row of rings up each side, 10 cm (4 in) from the edge, with the bottom one 5 cm (2 in) from the base, the highest one 45 cm (18 in) from the top, and intervals of around 30 cm (12 in) between.

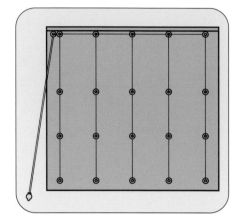

▲ **Austrian blind with inverted pleats**

The position and spacing of the rings on this heavily ruched blind is the same as the simpler inverted pleat blind shown left, with the rows running up each inverted pleat as required.

Cording a blind

Roman and Austrian blinds work through a system of cords threaded up the back of the blind. The same principle applies to all types, but the position of the rows of cording varies according to the style of blind. Cords are secured in small rings anchored at the base of the blind and threaded through rows of rings to its top, where there is anther set of stationary rings. The cords are then threaded across the top of the blind to one side and attached to a weight.

Tips for measuring up for blinds

When measuring a recess for blinds, take several measurements at different levels and work to the smallest.

For a roller blind, measure the width and the drop of the window. There may be no need for seam allowances if the fabric is stiffened so it will not fray.

For a Roman blind, measure the width of the window and for the length use the window height plus the depth of the top allowance, bottom casing, hems, and seam allowance.

For an Austrian blind, measure the width of the window, multiply by 2 or 2 ½ and add seam allowances. For the length measure the length of the window, multiply by 2 or 2 ½ and add hems. Allow more if you are using lightweight fabric.

Cording a Roman blind with dowels

In this version of the Roman blind, dowel rods are inserted into casings across the reverse of the blind so it pulls up into neat folds. The casings are stitched into the lining and should be positioned 10 cm (4 in) above the base of the blind with the highest one at least 35 cm (14 in) below the top and intervals of 23–30 cm (9–12 in) in between.

1 Stitch a small curtain ring to each casing all the way up the centre, then stitch a second row 5 cm (2 in) away from each side. Wide blinds may need an additional row or even more.

2 Screw an eye into the top lathe of the blind in line with each row of rings. Screw an extra eye 2.5 cm (1 in) from the edge on the side to which the cords will be threaded.

3 Cut a cord for each column of rings that is twice the length of the blind plus the width. Tie a cord to each bottom ring and thread it through each ring in the column above. Take it through the extra eye at the side of the lathe after threading it through any eyes it passes on the way.

4 With the blind fully extended, take the cords through a brass drop weight. Trim them evenly and knot them securely. You may need to add a single cord below the weight.

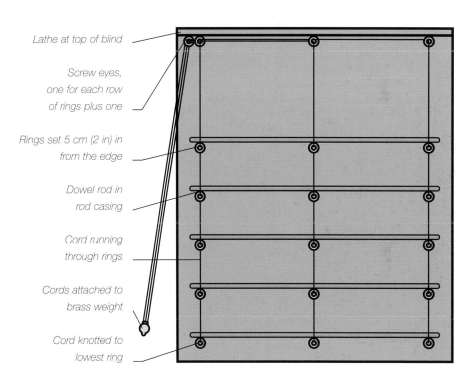

Lathe at top of blind

Screw eyes, one for each row of rings plus one

Rings set 5 cm (2 in) in from the edge

Dowel rod in rod casing

Cord running through rings

Cords attached to brass weight

Cord knotted to lowest ring

Why choose Roman blinds?

Roman blinds are very economical with fabric, but look attractively full when pulled up into pleats at the head of the window.

Roller blind

Roller blinds are simple panels of fabric that roll onto a tube or cylinder at the top or the bottom of the blind. A top roller may be spring-loaded. Roller blinds are often made of stiffened fabric, but there are kits available that mean you can use your own fabric to match the rest of the scheme.

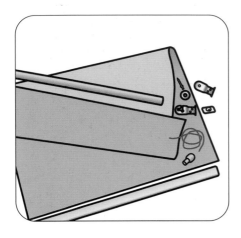

1 Measure, mark, and cut a length of fabric following the manufacturer's instructions in the kit. Make sure the kit has all its parts, including a spring roller, a slat for the bottom, cord, and small pieces of hardware.

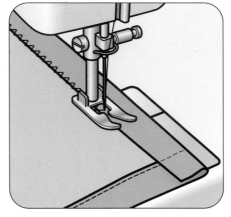

2 Turn under, pin, and stitch a narrow hem on both sides of the length of fabric. Zigzag a single hem along the raw edge at the top.

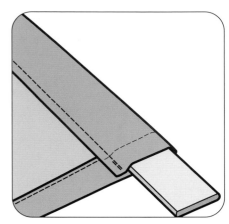

3 Turn up, pin, and stitch the bottom edge to make a casing wide enough for the bottom slat. Insert the slat and slipstitch the end of the casing closed to hold it in place.

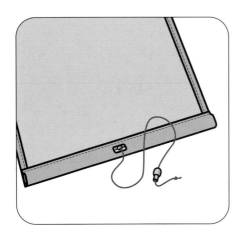

4 Attach the pull cord mechanism to the centre of the back of the slat. Thread the finial onto the cord and knot the end. Spray the blind with a coat of protective stiffener, if desired.

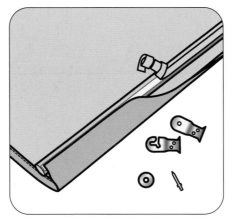

5 Attach the top edge of the fabric to the spring roller. The type illustrated has a self-adhesive strip onto which fabric can be pressed. Some kits may have fixings that use staples or small tacks instead.

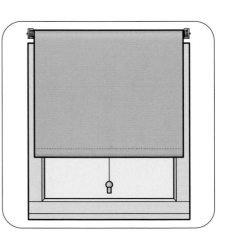

6 Mount the brackets on the window frame, wall, or ceiling following the manufacturer's instructions. Roll the blind up and insert the end prongs into the brackets; pulling the blind up sets the mechanism.

Decorative finishes

Although roller blinds are quite simple in concept, they do not have to be plain or boring. The bottom edges can be finished with almost any type of different trim, or shaped. A few ideas are shown below, but in effect the possibilities are almost endless. Fabric also makes a big difference—you can make a roller blind in almost anything, including lace.

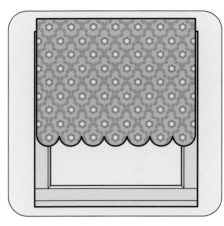

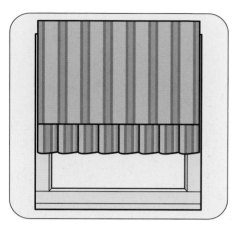

▲ Scalloped edge

The scalloped edge of this blind was made and faced like the café curtains on page 179, then topstitched. The casing for the bottom slat is a separate strip.

▲ Pointed edge

Here the pattern of the fabric has been used to create an effective and dramatic edging. The edges could be faced, turned back in a narrow hem, or bound.

▲ Pleated edge

The bottom trim of this blind is a separate strip of fabric that has been box-pleated and applied to the bottom of the casing to make a stylish edge.

Roman blind

A Roman blind looks very similar to a roller blind when it is open, but closes in a different way. Strips of tape on the back pull the blind into neat horizontal pleats at the top of the window when the cords at the side are pulled. Roman blinds are ideal for windows that need a decorative dressing, but are not suitable for curtains.

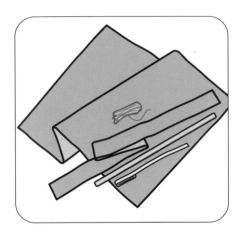

1 Measure out the fabric and cut one piece for the blind, plus a heading strip the width of the blind and around 7.5 cm (3 in) deep. You will also need several metres of Roman blind tape (or plain fabric tape and small curtain rings), thin cord, a wooden slat for the bottom, and a mounting board.

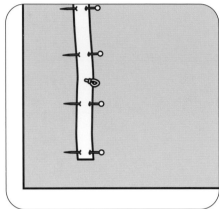

2 Mark guidelines on the wrong side of the blind for three vertical tapes—one each side and one in the centre; use more if the window is very wide. Pin the tape over the lines and stitch in place along both long edges. Be careful not to catch the loops in the stitching.

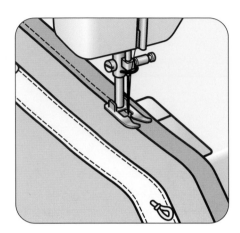

3 If you are using ordinary tape, work step three with the tape instead and stitch a small curtain ring at around 10 cm (4 in) intervals up all three lengths of tape. Turn under, pin, and stitch a narrow double hem along each side edge of the length of fabric.

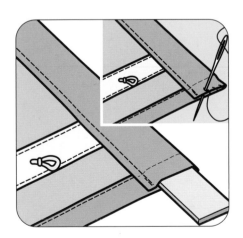

4 Turn up the bottom edge, turn under the raw edge by around 6 mm (¼ in), and stitch on the top fold to make a casing across the bottom for a slat. Slide in the slat and slipstitch the ends of the casing closed.

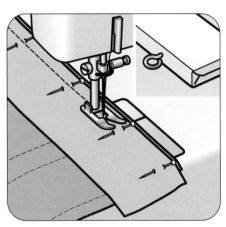

5 Finish the top edge by stitching on the heading strip, right sides together, and turning over to bind the edge. On one narrow edge of the mounting board, screw an eye to align with each vertical length of tape.

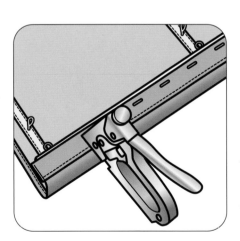

6 Using a staple gun or tacks, secure the top bound edge of the blind to the side of the mounting board that will rest against the wall. Wrap the blind over to hang down the front of the board.

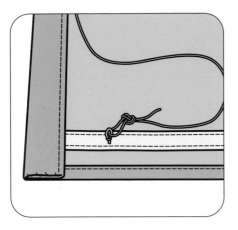

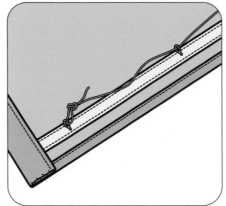

7 Slip the end of a length of cord through the bottom loop or curtain ring on one of the vertical tapes. Secure the cord with a strong knot at the end; it will need to be very firm as it will take the full weight every time the blind is pulled up.

8 Thread the cord up through each loop in the tape, making sure that you leave enough cord at the top to stretch across the width of the blind. Repeat for each vertical tape across the blind.

9 Thread the top of each cord through the screw eyes in one direction along the mounting board. Knot them together at the edge. Trim, then attach a separate length of cord to the knotted end to make a pull.

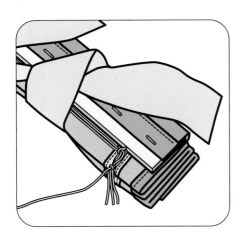

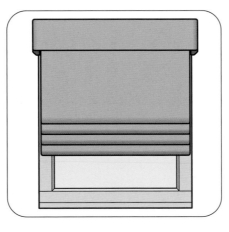

10 Fold the blind into even accordion pleats, aligning the tape loops, and tie loosely with cotton tape at each end. Leave it wrapped on a flat surface for a day or two to set the folds.

11 Screw through the mounting board directly into the window frame or wall, or mount the board on brackets. Mount a cleat hook on the pull cord side. Note that the matching valance on this window covers the top to reduce light and draughts.

Pull cords

A wide range of decorative finials for pull cords can be purchased, or you can make your own using large beads or found objects.

A cleat hook mounted to the wall is ideal for securing a Roman blind at a set level. These hooks are usually made of metal and come in a variety of sizes and colours.

Making a mounting board

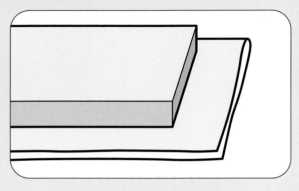

1. Cut a piece of 2.5 x 5 cm (1 x 2 in) board to the desired length. Measure the width all around the board and cut a length of lining fabric to that size, plus seam allowances.

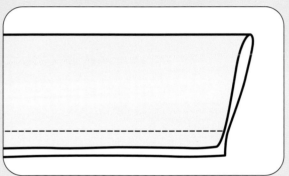

2. The length of fabric required is the length of the cut board, plus a 5 cm (2 in) seam allowance at each end. Fold the fabric in half lengthwise and sew the long edges. Turn right side out.

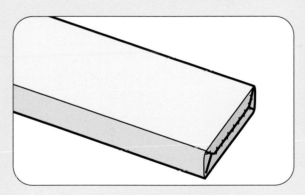

3. Slide the board into the fabric tube and turn the ends neatly. Mitre the corners and slipstitch in place to secure.

cushions and pillows

Cushions and pillows can be used to add accents of colour to a room and to soften the edges of hard furniture. Since they are quick and easy to make they can be changed more easily than other items. Adding embellishments gives them some originality and a more luxurious look.

Zippers in furnishings

The most common closure used in home furnishings is the zipper. It is used to close cushions and seat covers, and is usually inserted before the item is assembled as it is easier to work on flat fabric. If you haven't inserted a zipper before, follow these easy steps for perfect results every time.

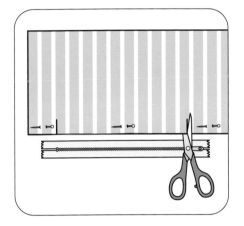
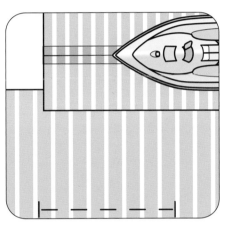
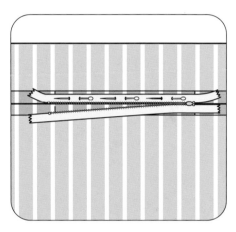

1 **Inserting a zipper**
Line the zipper up in position against the raw edge and clip the seam allowances of both layers to mark the two ends. With right sides together, and aligning the cuts, pin the pieces together and stitch from each cut to the edge, backstitching at the cut end to secure.

2 Machine tack the opening between the two cuts closed. Slitting through one of the stitches every inch or so will make the tacking easier to remove later. Press the seam open.

3 Lay the fabric flat with the seam allowance on the bottom piece folded upward. Open the zipper and pin it face down with the teeth very close to the seamline and edges with the cuts.

Tips for choosing and fitting zippers

Zippers should be inserted at the bottom of the cushion or the back of the seat cushion.

Match the weight of the zipper to the weight of the fabric you are using.

Continuous zippers can be purchased by the metre (yard) and cut to the length you require. Stitch over the end to make a stopper.

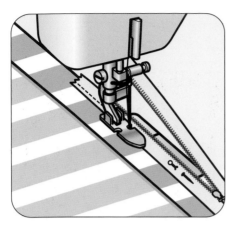

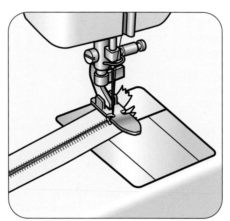

4 Using the zipper foot on the machine and keeping the needle on the left, stitch close to the teeth, backstitching at each end. Turn and repeat steps 3 and 4 to stitch the other side.

5 Remove the tacking, turn the fabric to the right side, and press gently, being careful not to iron over the zipper itself. Continue making up the rest of the item in the normal way.

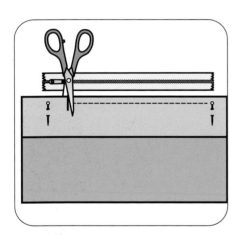

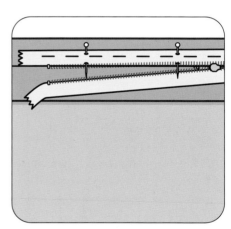

1 ▲ **Putting in a continuous zipper**
Place the pieces of fabric right sides together on a flat surface. Cut the zipper to match the length of the opening. Machine tack the opening closed as described in step 2 of inserting a zipper on page 199.

2 Make a stop at the end of the zipper by stitching several times over the end of the teeth, or by stitching the bar of a hook and bar fastening securely over the teeth.

3 Open the zipper and pin it face down centred over the seam. Stitch in place as detailed in steps 3 and 4 of inserting a zipper on pages 199–200. Close the zipper and repeat the stitching on the other side. Remove the machine basting so the zipper can be opened and closed. Topstitch at the ends of the opening to secure.

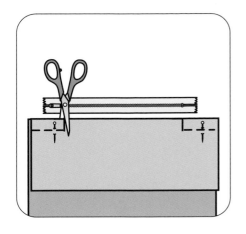

1 ▲ Making a lapped zipper
Clip into the seam allowance of both pieces of fabric to mark the length of the zipper opening. Place the pieces right sides together and stitch from each cut to the side edge. Follow step 2 on page 199 of inserting a zipper to machine tack the opening.

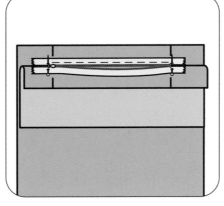

2 Lay the fabric flat with the seam allowance on the bottom piece folded outward. Open the zipper and pin it face down with the teeth close to the seamline and top and bottom aligned with the cuts. Using the zipper foot with the needle on the right, machine tack 6 mm (¼ in) from the teeth.

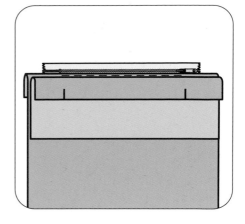

3 Turn the zipper face up and fold under the stitched side of the zipper. Stitch very close to the edge of the fold through all the thicknesses.

4 Turn the work round and lay the other seam allowance flat. Close the zipper and machine tack the unstitched side in place. On the right side, with the needle to the left of the zipper foot, topstitch over the bottom of the zipper, along the side 12 mm (½ in) from the seam and at the top. Remove tacking.

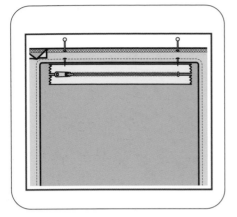

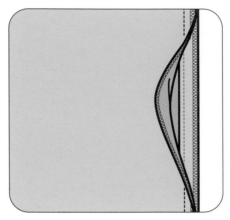

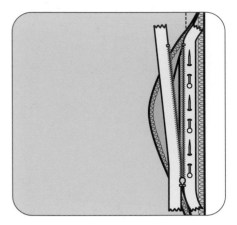

1 ▲ Inserting a zipper into a piped seam

Zigzag along the raw edges of the fabric and place pins to mark the position of the zipper. Stitch the front and back pieces together, right sides together, from the corner to the pins.

2 Stitch as close to the piping cord as possible. Fold back the piece of fabric that does not have piping.

3 Open the zipper and place face down on the piping, with the teeth of the right side on the cord. Pin in place and at the top.

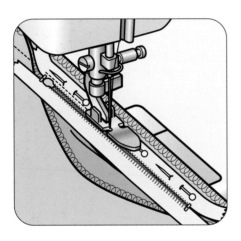

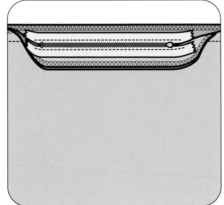

4 Close the zipper and stitch the pinned side in place as close to the teeth as possible. Lift the needle as required to make sure everything is lined up correctly.

5 Turn the work round and line up the zipper with the inner edge of the zigzag stitching. Stitch the second side, working as close to the teeth as possible but making sure the slider will still move freely. Remove tacking.

Circular cushion with overlap closure

Using an overlap closure is a neat and simple way to close the cushion without having to add a zipper or buttons, and without stitching closed so the pad cannot later be removed for laundering. Contrast piping around the edge will add some extra colour to a plain cover. The overlap closure can also be used for any other shape of cushion.

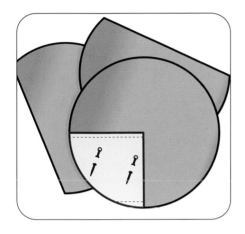

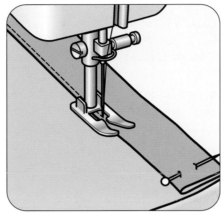

1 Make a circular paper pattern to the size of cushion you want, plus seam allowances. Cut three fabric circles, then trim a strip about ⅓ of the width off the edge of two of them to create the overlapping back piece.

2 Fold back a single hem on the straight edge of one of the back pieces, press, and zigzag stitch to hold in place. Turn under and stitch a double hem on the straight edge of the other piece.

3 Add the contrast piping around the edge of the circular front piece, following the instructions on page 212. Make sure the piping is positioned just inside the seam allowance all around, then join the ends.

Tips for making cushions

Cushions can be made in almost any shape or size; there is a wide range of standard cushion pads or pillow forms available or you can even make your own by making up a shaped cover in lining fabric and stuffing with fibrefill or feathers.

For a quick new look, add embellishments—such as braid, buttons, tassels or appliqué—to a plain purchased cushion cover.

Cushions do not need to be made of very hard-wearing fabric as they can easily be recovered. This means you can use delicate silks, lace, and embroidered fabrics to add a touch of opulence to your room.

Feather-stuffed cushions are luxurious and will plump up beautifully, but if you suffer from allergies a synthetic filling may be a better option.

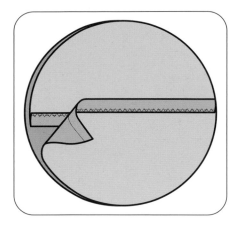

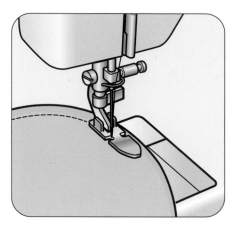

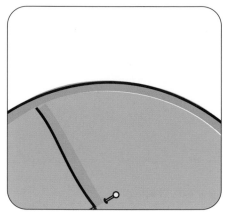

4 With the front piece right side up, lay the hemmed piece right side down on top, then the zigzagged piece on top of that, also right side down. Pin and tack the edge through all of the layers.

5 Using the zipper foot on the machine, stitch around the edge of the cushion, working as close to the piping as possible. Zigzag the raw edges of the seam allowance.

6 Turn the cover right side out through the overlap hole and insert the cushion form through the same hole. The form can easily be removed if the cushion needs to be laundered.

Square cushion with zipper

This cushion has a zipped opening, but the overlap type would work just as well on this shape; the two methods are interchangeable. The gently rounded corners are better for a square cushion with piping or added trim such as a ruffle.

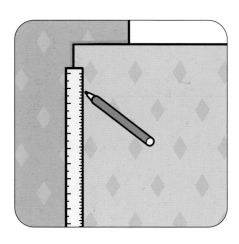

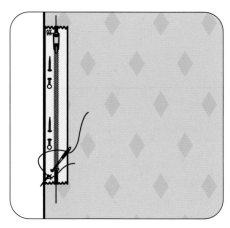

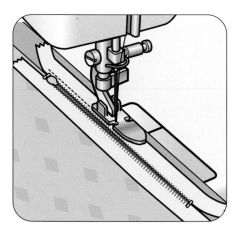

1 Measure and cut two pieces of fabric to the size of the cushion plus seam allowances. Mark a line 12 mm (½ in) in from the edge on the wrong side of one of the pieces.

2 Use a zipper 5 cm (2 in) shorter than the cushion size. Centre the zipper over the line just marked, then pin, tack, and stitch in place. Backstitch at both ends of the seam to make sure it is secure.

3 If you are adding piping around the cushion, apply it to the edge of the second piece of fabric. Tack and stitch the second piece to the zipper, with the trim resting right against the teeth.

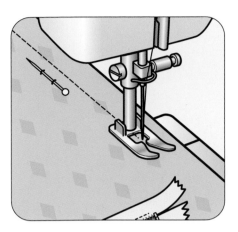

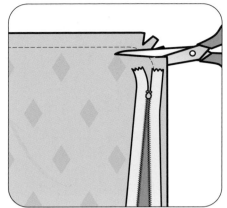

4 Open the zipper, then pin and stitch the two pieces with right sides together around the remaining sides, beginning and ending just short of the zipper. Use backstitch to secure the ends of the seam and zigzag the seam allowance.

5 Trim back the seam allowance all round, being careful not to cut through the stitching. Trim and notch the curved corners. Turn the cushion right side out through the zip and insert the cushion form.

Heart-shaped cushion cover

For very unusual shapes you can make your own pad or form as well as the cover. Make a template, which you can also use for the cover. This heart-shaped cover has lush curves and is fastened with tie ribbons, which are decorative enough to be on the front or the back of the finished cushion.

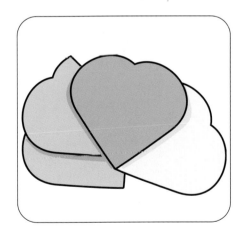

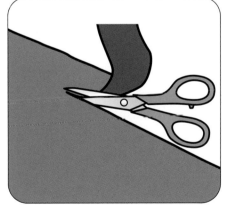

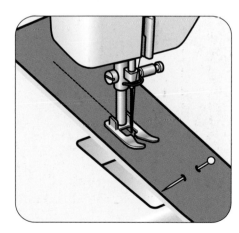

1 Using the enlarged template pattern, cut a piece of fabric for the front of the cushion. Fold one side of the template back by around ⅓ then use it to cut two overlapping back pieces.

2 Mark the centre fold line on the back pieces and the seamline on the front piece. Measure two long strips in a contrasting fabric to make the ties; they should be around 6 x 35 cm (2 ½ x 14 in). Mark the seamline along all edges.

3 Fold a tie in half along its length with right sides together and pin. Stitch across one short edge and the long raw edge. Turn the tie right side out and press. Repeat to make the other tie.

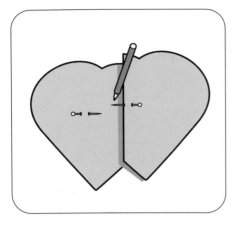

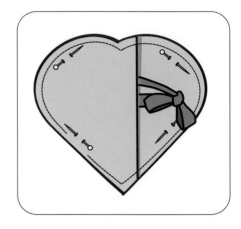

4 Mark where the ties are to go on the back pieces of the cover, using a couple of tacking stitches. One should be on the overlap piece on the centre fold line, the other should be on the underlap where the two sides will meet.

5 Fold the edge of the underlap piece to the back along the centre fold line. Zigzag along the raw edge. Turn and stitch a narrow double hem on the edge of the overlap piece. Pin the ties in place and stitch, neatening their raw ends at the same time.

6 Place the front piece right side up, then place the overlap on top, right side down, covered by the underlap, also right side down. Take care to align all edges. Pin and then stitch around the edge of the heart, leaving a small gap for turning.

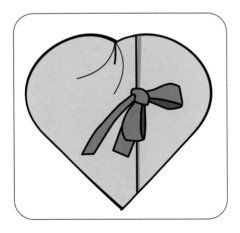

7 Turn the cover right side out through the gap left in the side. Press, then insert the heart-shaped cushion form. The ties are formed into a pretty bow on the back, which could also be used as the front.

Template tips

Use heavy paper to make the template. For symmetrical shapes like this heart, fold the paper over so the two halves will be identical.

For the cover, use the same template but add an extra 6 mm (¼ in) seam allowance.

Decorative techniques for cushions

Trims, buttons, and other embellishments can be used to add detail to your cushions and to tie them in further with your main colour scheme. Embellishments can also be used to personalize plain store-bought cushions, which will make them look much more original and expensive.

1 ▲ **Corded edge**
Wrap one end of the cord with masking tape. Stitch the cord to the edge of the cushion by hand, making a stitch through the cord and then through the fabric. At the end, wrap tape around the other end of the cord, allowing the two ends to overlap.

2 Unpick around 2.5 cm (1 in) of the seam next to the overlapped cord. Remove the tape from the cord and slip the ends into the gap in the seam, overlapping them slightly. Slipstitch the seam closed, securing the cord at the same time.

Scalloped effect

You don't have to attach the cord all along its length—for an interesting scalloped effect, try attaching it at intervals, allowing small loops of cord between each fastening point. Don't make the loops too big, or they will continually be catching on things.

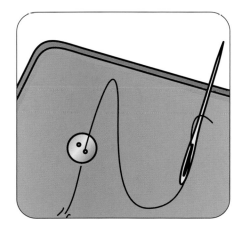

1 ▲ **Buttoning**
Use an upholstery needle and a long length of doubled thread. Fasten the end and push the needle through to the other side of the cushion. Make a couple of stitches, going through the back of a button each time. Fasten off securely.

2 You can use a decorative button, as here, or a covered button. The cushion can have a button on one or both sides. The cushion here has an attractive plumpness as the stuffing is not too full.

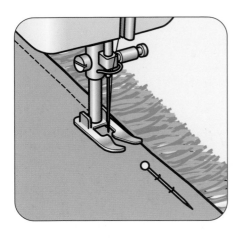

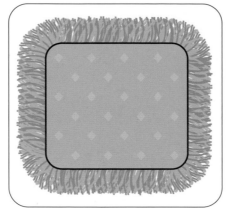

1 ▲ Fringing
Pin the fringe around the front edge of the finished cushion cover, then tack if necessary. If the fringe has a narrow braid, one line of stitching will be enough; if the braid is wider, stitch along both edges.

2 Fold over the final end before stitching in place. If you use a fringe with heavy braid it will disguise the lines of stitching very well, but you can also make the stitching a part of the design.

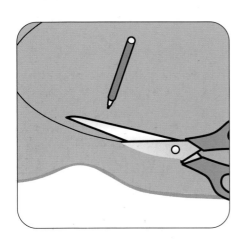

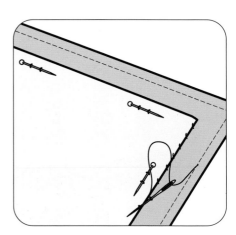

1 ▲ Tapestry insert
Turn the finished cover wrong side out and mark the size of the tapestry piece in the centre of one side. Cut out the square the width of a seam allowance inside the marked line.

2 Press the seam allowance to the wrong side all around the window, clipping as necessary. Press the tapestry and trim back the raw edges to 2.5 cm (1 in) or less. Pin the tapestry into the window all round.

3 Check that the tapestry is centred within the window then stitch in position. Backstitch around each of the corners to strengthen them. Turn the cover right side out through the zipper opening.

Tie-on chair cushion

This pretty ruffled cushion goes very well with the traditional style of chair shown here, and makes it much more comfortable to sit on. The ruffle also softens the hard edges of the chair visually, but you can add piping instead if you prefer, for a more tailored look. This type of chair could also be fitted with a shaped box cushion.

1 Measure the chair seat as indicated: a–b from back to front; c–d across the middle; e–f between the arms. Make a template of the shape in paper, adjusting it until it fits the chair exactly. Add seam allowances.

2 Use the template to cut two pieces of fabric for the cushion and cut four strips for the ties. Measure the sides and front of the cushion, multiply by 2–2½, add a seam allowance, and cut another strip for the ruffle about 5 cm (2 in) wide plus seam allowance. Fold ties in half lengthwise right sides together, pin.

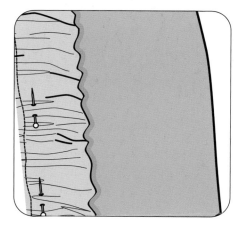

3 Make up the ties, turn right side out; hem and gather the ruffle. Turn over and stitch a double hem on both cushion pieces between where the ties will be attached at the back. Pin the two seat pieces right sides together, with the ruffle and ties in place but neatly tucked inside and not caught up anywhere.

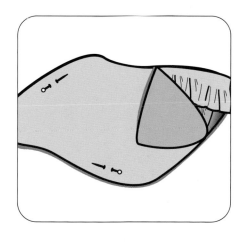

4 Tack around to hold everything firmly in place, starting and stopping at the ends of the double hem made in step 3. Pin small squares of hook and loop tape (Velcro®) along the double hem on each piece, aligned to match, and stitch them all down.

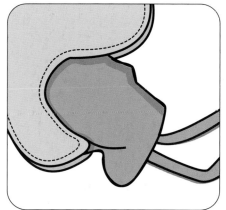

5 Sew the seam around the cushion, again starting and stopping at the ends of the double hem made in step 3. Turn the cushion right side out through the back opening and insert the cushion form.

6 Tie the cushion to the back supports of the chair.

Box cushions

A box cushion has a separate strip of fabric running around between the top and bottom pieces, which covers the depth of the cushion form and is known as a box strip. This type of cushion is usually used as seat cushions, but it could be a floor cushion as well.

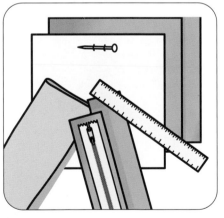

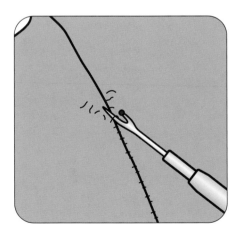

▲ **Square box cushion**
The instructions here are for a square cushion, but exactly the same technique is used to make an oblong, round or shaped one.

1 **Square box cushion**
Cut two seat pieces and one strip the full depth and the length of three sides of the form, plus seams. Cut two strips the length of the box form but only half the depth, plus seams. Make two strips of piping the length around the outside edge.

2 Place the narrow strips right sides together and mark where the zipper is to go. Stitch to the end of the zipper at each side, then tack the seam between. Pin, tack, and stitch the closed zipper, taking care that it is centred over the tacked section of seam. Remove tacking.

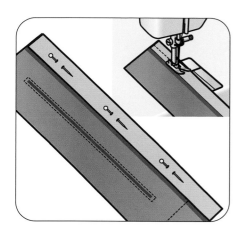

3 Stitch one short end of the long strip to one short end of the zippered strip, right sides together. Press the seam open, then tack and stitch the piping all around one long edge, with the raw edges aligned and the piping facing in.

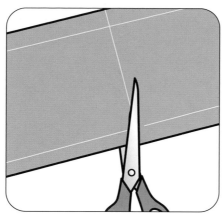

4 Stitch piping to the other long edge in the same way. Mark where the corners of the form will fall and clip into the seam allowance at all four. Stitch the other two short ends together, press the seams open, and clip corners.

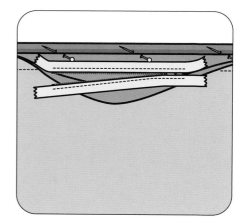

5 Pin and stitch a seat piece to the piped strip with right sides together. Open the zipper and pin the other seat piece to the other side of the strip, making sure the piping is straight. Stitch both seams.

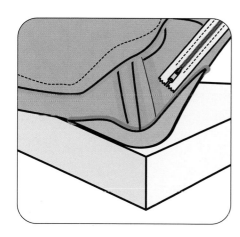

6 Trim the seam allowances and clip all corners to remove bulk, being verycareful not to cut through any stitching. Turn the cover right side out through the zipper opening, and insert the cushion form.

Box cushion tips

Box cushion forms are available in a range of sizes, but if you can't find one to fit your seat have a piece of thick seating foam cut to shape.

Use a zipper that is 5 cm (2 in) shorter or less than the back edge of the cushion—any shorter and it will be difficult to get the rather solid box form through the gap.

For a quick and easy box cushion, cut two squares of fabric the size of the form, plus half the depth, plus seam allowances all round. Insert the zipper and stitch, right sides together. Fold so the seam runs up the centre to the point of a corner, then stitch across the corner diagonally. The seam should be the depth of the form. Repeat on the other four corners and trim them off. Turn right side out and insert the form.

Bolsters

A bolster is a long, cylindrical cushion, used at the head of a bed or a chaise longue, or on a sofa. Bolster cushion forms can be purchased in several diameters and lengths, or you can make your own. To make your own bolster cushion form, follow the instructions below, using plain fabric and omitting piping. Use quite a firm stuffing for a bolster.

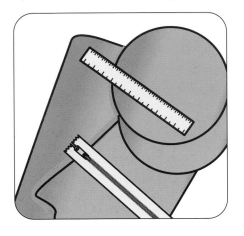

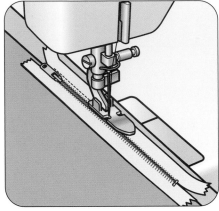

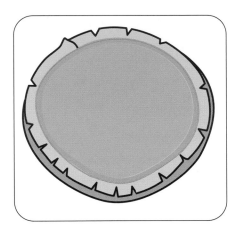

1 ▲ **Piped bolster with zipper**
Measure the bolster and cut one piece of fabric the length and circumference, plus seam allowance all round. Cut two circles the same diameter as the ends, plus seam allowance, and make a length of piping twice the circumference plus seam allowance.

2 With right sides together, fold the main piece of fabric lengthwise and pin. Centre the zipper on the seam and mark its ends. Stitch the seam from the edge to the end of the zipper on each side. Tack the rest of the seam and insert the zipper as described on page 199.

3 Apply piping around the edges of the end pieces with the piping facing inward and the ends overlapping slightly into the seam. Clip the curved seam all round so the end will fit onto the main piece smoothly.

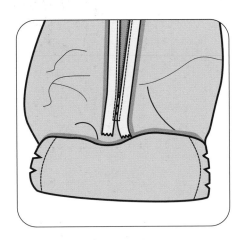

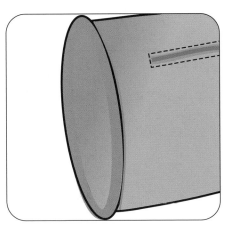

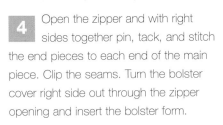

4 Open the zipper and with right sides together pin, tack, and stitch the end pieces to each end of the main piece. Clip the seams. Turn the bolster cover right side out through the zipper opening and insert the bolster form.

bed linens

Although bed linen is now quite inexpensive and there is a wide range of designs available, you still may want to make something a bit special or to coordinate your linens with the rest of the room. You may also have a bed that is not a standard size or has some unusual feature that makes finding bedding difficult.

Sheets

The main problem with making sheets is finding fabric wide enough to sew them without a seam. If you just want to add a trim, you can purchase a plain sheet as the basis.

Achieving a coordinated look

To make a flat sheet, just purchase a length of fabric the correct size and turn up a double hem all round.

For a fully-coordinated look, trim the pillowcases and make a valance to match your sheets (see pages 215–217 and 219–221).

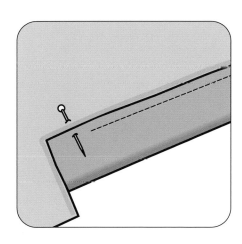

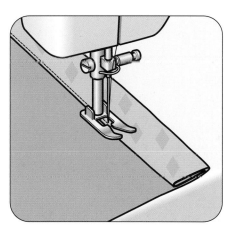

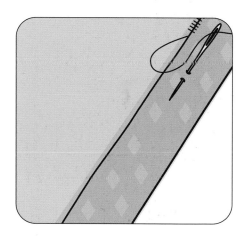

1 ▲ **Decorative border sheet**
Measure the depth of the desired border at the top of the sheet. Clip both side edges to mark the lower edge of the border. Turn under and pin a double hem below the clip all around the sides and bottom of the sheet. Stitch the hem.

2 Cut a strip of border fabric the width of the sheet fabric before hemming and the depth of the desired border plus seam allowances. With right sides together, pin the border to the top edge of the sheet and stitch the sides and top edge.

3 Turn the border over to the wrong side of the sheet and press. Turn under the raw edge at the bottom and topstitch to secure, or run satin stitch along the edge to cover and secure it. When the bed is made, the border is folded back to the right side.

home furnishings

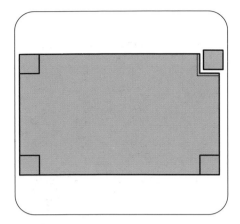
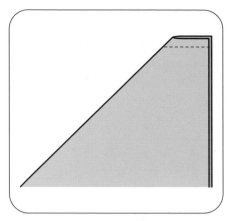
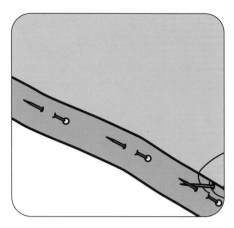

1 ▲ **Fitted sheet**
The fabric piece needs to be the size of the mattress, plus its depth, plus 10cm (4 in) for seam allowances and underlap. Measure the depth of the mattress and mark right-angled squares of this depth plus seam allowance in each corner of the fabric. Cut out the squares.

2 With right sides together, position the cut edges of a corner together and then pin and sew. Do this on all four corners. Press seams open and finish the edges. Cut a length of 12 mm (½ in) wide elastic twice the length plus twice the width of the mattress, less 25 cm (10 in).

3 Turn up a casing around the raw edges of the sheet wide enough for the elastic. Pin and stitch, leaving a small gap 15 cm (6 in) from either side of each corner. Thread the elastic through the casing, then overlap the ends and stitch them together.

Try the fitted sheet on the bed. The corners should fit neatly over the mattress and the sheet should be taut across the bed. You can make a fitted sheet from a purchased flat sheet if you cut off the top and bottom hems first.

Trims and embellishments

Almost any type of purchased trim can be used to decorate sheets, and most of the decorative techniques in this book can also be used.

Piped corner – particularly useful for tailored pillowcases.

Piped seam border – a simple trim that can be turned back to make a deep border.

Plain contrast border with lace overlay – the contrast band highlights the delicate pattern of the lace.

Lace with a contrast insert – many lace bands have loops that can be used to thread ribbon.

Broderie anglais or eyelet lace – this trim has a slight gather so also adds a delicate ruffle.

Pillowcases

Pillowcases not only protect the pillow but are also often decorative as the pillow is displayed on top of the bed as an extra feature. Although pillowcases are not expensive to buy, they can easily be made to match the other bed linens on show instead of the sheets hidden beneath, which will coordinate with the main scheme better.

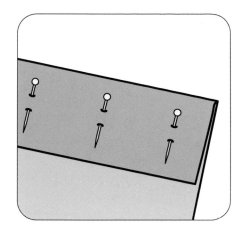

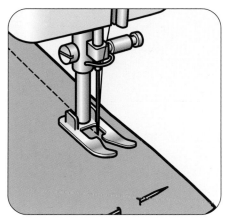

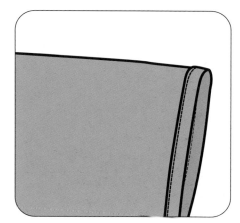

1 ▲ Top-opening pillowcase
Measure the pillow and cut a piece of fabric measuring twice the length plus hems, and the width plus side seam allowances. Turn and pin a deep hem at each short end of the fabric. This pillow will be stitched with a French seam.

2 With WRONG sides together, fold the fabric in half widthwise and pin and stitch a seam along both long edges. Turn it inside out so the right sides are together and stitch both long seams again, being careful to enclose the raw edges completely.

3 Turn the finished pillowcase right side out again and slide the pillow through the open end. This simple pillowcase is ideal as a basic canvas on which you can stitch any kind of embellishment.

Tips for making pillowcases

Decorated pillowcases are a thoughtful gift for a new bride or homeowner.

Extra pillowcases are always useful. You may need more pillows on the bed for a guest, or want a little lift while reading in bed.

Bought pillowcases can be trimmed in the same way that sheets can—see page 213 for steps. You can also add trims as described for cushions on pages 207–208, but make sure the centre of the pillow, where the head will rest, is clear and smooth or it will be uncomfortable.

If you want to make a pillowcase as shown above but with a plain seam instead of a French seam, do not fold the flap in step 1. Instead, fold it over the opening, like the flap of an envelope, before the long side seams are stitched. When the pillow-case is turned inside out, the flap on the inside will cover the raw edges of the seams at the opening.

Pillows do not have to be oblong or square, they can be any shape you like, as long as they are still comfortable. Don't be afraid to experiment.

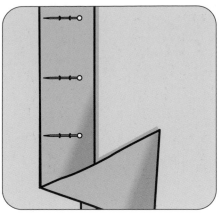

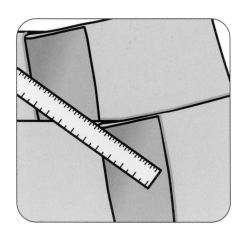

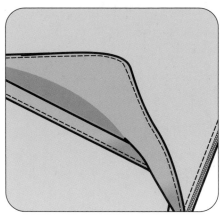

1 ▲ Back-opening pillowcase
Cut one piece of fabric the size of the pillow plus seam allowances all round for the front of the pillowcase. Cut two pieces each two-thirds of the length of the pillow and the same width, plus seam allowances all round, for the two overlapping pieces at the back.

2 Make a narrow double hem along one long edge of one back piece and a 4 cm (1½ in) hem along one long edge of the other piece. Lay the deep hemmed piece right side down and the narrow hemmed piece right side down on top, overlapping the hemmed edges so the size of the two pieces together is the same as the front piece. Pin them together along the overlap.

3 Lay the front piece right side up and align the joined back over it, right sides down and matching all raw edges. Pin and stitch around all four edges, then zigzag stitch to finish off all raw edges. Remove the pins and turn the pillowcase right side out. Insert the pillow through the slit in the back.

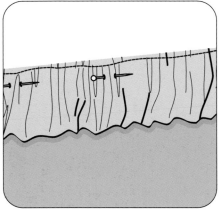

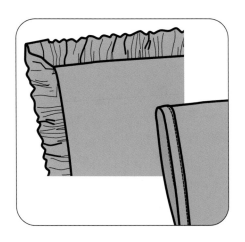

1 ▲ Ruffled pillowcase
Cut three pieces of fabric for the pillowcase as described in step 1 above. Cut a ruffle strip to the desired width plus seam allowances and twice the length of all four sides of the pillow added together. Stitch the short ends of the ruffle together to make a ring and stitch a narrow double hem on one long edge. Run a double line of gathering stitches along the other edge.

2 Pin the ruffle around the edge of the larger front pillowcase piece, matching raw edges and with the ruffle turned to the inside. Machine tack the ruffle all around. Make up the back section of the pillowcase as described in step 2 of the back-opening pillowcase above.

3 Lay the front piece right side up and align the joined back over it, right side down and matching all raw edges. Pin and stitch around all four edges, then zigzag stitch to finish off all raw edges. Remove the pins and turn the pillowcase right side out. Insert the pillow through the slit in the back.

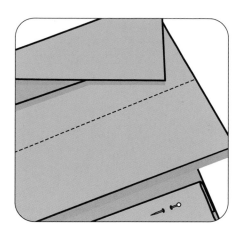
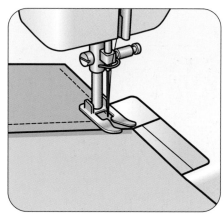
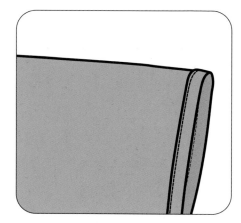

1 ▲ **Housewife pillowcase**
Measure the pillow and cut a piece of fabric measuring twice the length, plus hems, plus an extra 7.5 cm (3 in) for the flap, and the width of the pillow plus seam allowances. Turn and pin a deep hem at one short end of the fabric and a narrow hem at the other. Fold back the narrow hem edge by 7.5 cm (3 in), WRONG sides together, to make the flap.

2 Fold the fabric in half widthways, right sides together and with the deep hem edge tucked under the flap made in step 1 so the hemmed edge sits up against the flap fold. Pin and stitch a seam along both long edges.

3 Turn the finished pillowcase right side out again. The flap will be on the inside; simply slide the pillow inside through the open end and tuck the flap over it. This pillowcase is a wonderful choice if the pillows will be on full view, as the flap conceals the end of the pillow.

Duvet cover

A duvet cover is basically a very large pillowcase, so therefore its construction is very simple. The only complex thing is that you are working with very large pieces of fabric so you will need a lot of space. If you use different but coordinating fabrics for the front and back the duvet can be reversible, and folding back the leading edge will add extra interest to your colour scheme.

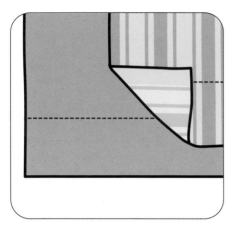

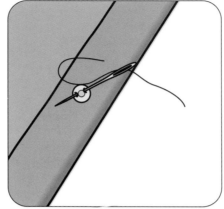

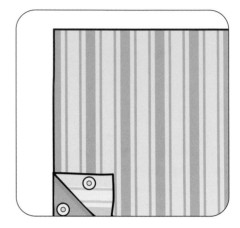

1 ▲ **Duvet cover**
Measure the duvet and cut two pieces of fabric the length and width, plus seam and hem allowances. Turn under a deep hem along one short edge of each piece and stitch in place.

2 Stitch one half of a series of snap fasteners along the inside of one of the hemmed edges, spacing them out equally along the edge.

3 Stitch the other half of the series of snap fasteners along the inside of the other hemmed edge, making sure to align them with the first set.

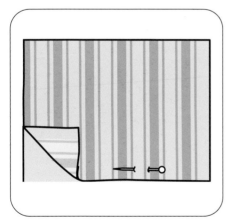

4 Join the fasteners. With WRONG sides together, pin the remaining three sides of the cover together.

5 For extra strength, stitch a French seam around the three sides, following the instructions on page 215.

Duvet cover tips

Fastenings on a duvet should be easy to open so the duvet can be laundered, but firm enough so they do not fall open in use.

If you don't want to make the whole duvet cover from scratch, buy a plain one in the right basic colour and add a trim of coordinating fabric.

If you have purchased a duvet cover and want curtains to match, buy a large extra cover and take it apart for curtain fabric.

Fitted bedspreads and valances

A fitted bedspread or valance has a flat top piece over the bed, with skirt pieces at the side that reach the ground. The bedspread fits over the top of the entire bed and is removed for sleeping, while the valance sits under the mattress to cover the box spring or legs of the bed, and so it is left in place most of the time.

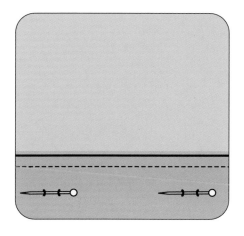

1 ▲ **Flounced bedspread or valance**

Measure the bed and cut a piece of fabric for the deck to the size plus seam allowances and 5 cm (2 in) for the hem. Turn a deep double hem at the top and stitch in place.

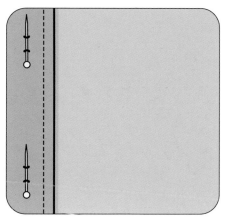

2 Cut the skirt 2½ times the length of the two sides of the bed added to the width, joining fabric as necessary to make up the length. The depth is the deck to the floor, plus seam and hem allowance. Press seams open, hem the short ends and one long edge.

A few tips

A bedspread will need to be laundered more than a valance, so check the care instructions on the fabric. If you have a purchased duvet set but there is no valance in the range, buy extra sheets or another duvet and take it apart to get the material to make a matching valance.

A flounced bedspread or valance will soften the shape of the bed, but a tailored one gives a crisper look.

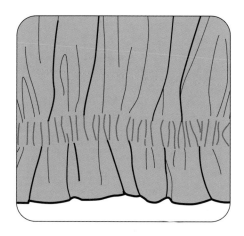

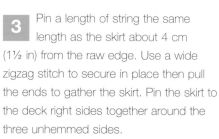

3 Pin a length of string the same length as the skirt about 4 cm (1½ in) from the raw edge. Use a wide zigzag stitch to secure in place then pull the ends to gather the skirt. Pin the skirt to the deck right sides together around the three unhemmed sides.

4 Stitch the pieces together, adjusting gathers evenly. Trim the top of the skirt to 12 mm (½ in) and the raw edge of the deck to 4 cm (1½ in). Fold over and pin the raw edge of the deck to enclose the top of the skirt and machine stitch in place all round.

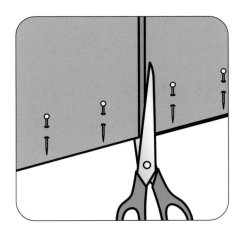

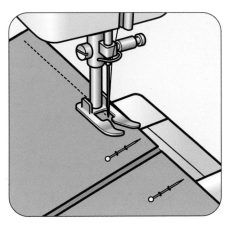

1 ▲ Tailored bedspread or valance

Cut a piece of fabric for the deck, turn a deep double hem at the top, and stitch in place. Cut the skirt the length of the two sides of the bed added to the width, plus 40 cm (16 in) for the corner pleats. Hem short ends and one long edge. Mark two corner pleats, each 5 cm (2 in) wide and press the folds. Pin in position and snip 12 mm (½ in) down the centre of each pleat. Tack each pleat closed.

2 Pin the skirt to the deck right sides together along the short unfinished side. Stitch the short side only, working from the centre of one end corner pleat to the centre of the other end corner pleat.

A few more tips

Box valances are designed to act as fitted sheet and valance in one, as the deck fits over the mattress instead of underneath it. The skirt is therefore longer, from the top of the mattress to the floor.

Even beds with headboards and footboards can be fitted with a valance. Either make head and foot the same, with a gap across both ends for the boards, or leave a slit for the footboard leg.

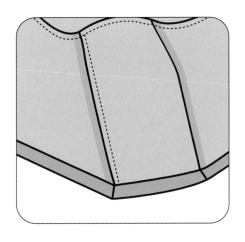

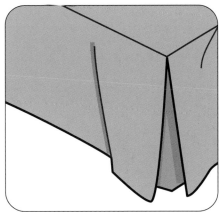

3 Pin and stitch the long sides, making sure that the pleat is folded back so the top of it will be caught in the stitching as you work. Backstitch at the corner pleats to secure and finish the edges.

4 The finished spread has neat pleats at each corner and gives a stylish look to the bed. For the bedspread you can also add piping to the seam joining the deck and the skirt, though it is not worth doing this if you are making a valance as it will be hidden.

home furnishings

table linens

This is one area of home furnishings where it really is worth making your own items. Not only is table linen quite expensive, but at times it is also hard to find what you need in a size to fit your table. Table linen is all very simple to make, even circular shapes are not hard to construct.

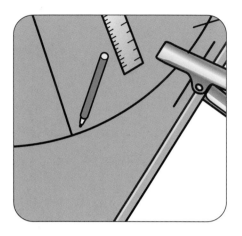

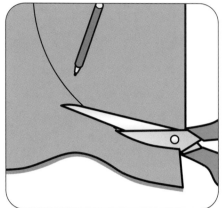

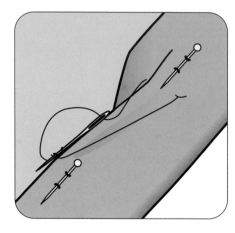

1 ▲ **Short circular tablecloth**
Measure the table and cut a square of fabric the diameter of the table, plus twice the drop, plus hems. Fold the square in half then in half again the other way and pin the edges. Cut a piece of string the length of one quadrant side and mark a quarter circle.

2 Cut along the marked line through all four layers of fabric, then unpin and open out the circle. Even up any jagged edges, then machine stitch 3 mm (⅛ in) in from the raw edge all around on the right side.

3 Press the fabric under along the stitching line, then machine stitch again all around, 3 mm (⅛ in) in from the edge of the fold. Press under along the new stitching line, so the raw edge on the wrong side is now enclosed. On the right side, topstitch as close as possible to the edge of the hem all around.

4 This simple circular tablecloth can be made any length you require by adjusting the length of the drop. You can also add trims to the hemmed edge for a different look, or a contrast border.

Laundering considerations

Tablecloths will need to be laundered regularly, so use fabric that is easy to wash and iron. Dry-clean only fabrics will not be suitable, except perhaps for dress cloths on a table that is only for show. Make sure the trims you choose can be washed, as well.

Check any purchased trims for colourfastness, particularly if they are a contrast with the cloth. Otherwise hours of work can be ruined in the first wash.

Matching patterns

If you want to join printed fabric it is important that you match the pattern across the seam as closely as possible.

1 Trim the edge of one piece to be joined and press 12 mm (½ in) to the wrong side along the trimmed edge. Lay the second piece of fabric flat with right side up and match the folded edge of the first piece to the pattern. Pin in place along the folded edge.

2 Moving the pins as you work, fold the fabric to work on the wrong side and stitch the seam from the wrong side, using the folded edge as a guide. Press the seam open. When you look at the right side, the seam should be almost invisible.

Lace insert border cloth

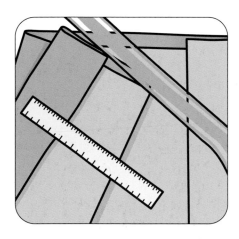

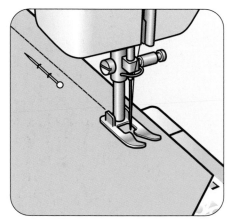

1 Cut the main piece the width of the table plus the drop, minus the lace and outer border width. Estimate the length in the same way. Cut four strips of lace the length of the edge of the main piece, plus twice the width of the lace. Cut four border strips twice the required border depth and the length of the very outside edge of the cloth.

2 Pin and stitch a length of lace to one edge of the main piece, right sides together, leaving the ends unstitched for the moment. Work one side at a time, centring the strip of lace on the edge each time.

3 Turn the lace out and press flat. Make a neat mitre in the corner of each strip of lace, or join the end of each strip by overlapping the next, as shown here.

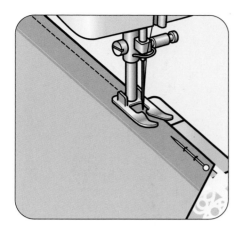

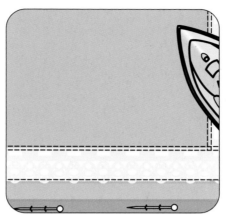

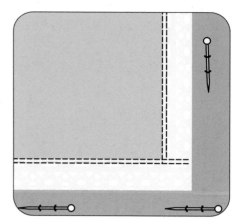

4 With right sides together, pin the border strips to the outside edge of the lace all round, leaving overlaps on all the corners as you did on the lace.

5 Press under the raw edge of a border strip and fold it back to cover the raw edge of the lace on the reverse of the cloth. Pin in place. At the corner, fold under the short end of the border level with the outer edge of the lace. Press under the short edge of the next border level with the outer edge of the first, then press under the long raw edge and fold back to cover the edge of the lace as before.

6 Repeat on all sides, pinning the border into position as you work and working each corner as described in step 5. On the last corner, fold under the edge of the first strip and tuck it inside the fold of the last strip before pinning.

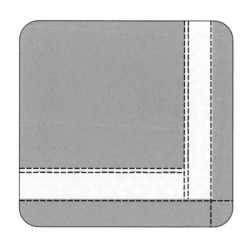

7 Topstitch around all sides of the tablecloth along the fold at the lace edge, making a neat square at each of the corners, as shown here. The overlap method works best for most lace designs, but for some a mitred join will be better.

Turning the corner

To mitre the lace strips, first centre the design on each side of the tablecloth. Cut the strips of lace so they overlap by at least the width of the strip at each corner. Add the strips as described in step 2 of Lace insert border tablecloth opposite. At the corner, fold the tablecloth diagonally through the centre of the corner, with right sides together. Stitch the ends of the lace together at the corner along a line that is a continuation of the diagonal fold you just made. When the fold is opened out, the lace strips will be neatly mitred.

home furnishings

Scalloped-edged cloth

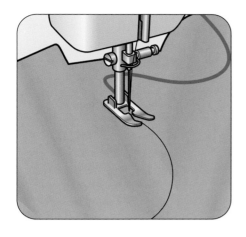
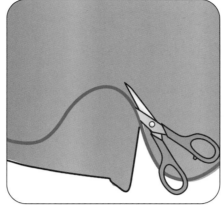

1 Work out the size to fit a perfect number of scallops along each edge, and cut a template for the scallop. Mark the scallops around the edge of your tablecloth. Following the marked line, satin stitch through one layer of fabric.

2 Using a pair of small, very sharp scissors, trim away the excess fabric outside the stitching line. Cut as close as possible to the stitching, but be very careful not to cut through it.

3 The satin stitching stops the edge from fraying and finishes it off in a decorative way. It can be worked in matching or contrasting thread, and any shape can be repeated along the edge of the cloth.

Tips for making and decorating tablecloths

Matching or contrasting bias binding is a neat way to edge any kind of tablecloth. Use purchased bias binding, or make your own as described on pages 44–45.

A lace border adds a pretty touch to a plain cloth. Use a fairly coarse lace design, as the finer ones will almost certainly be too delicate for frequent laundering.

To add a shaped border, see instructions above. Just work out a perfect number of repeats of the shape around the edge and make your own template for any shape you wish.

An inset border in a contrasting fabric is also very smart on a tablecloth. It can be positioned near the hem, or much further in so that it borders the edge of the top.

Purchased braids and trims are a quick way of adding colour or a new look. Bobbles and fringes can add a three-dimensional quality—but make sure they can be safely laundered.

For an even simpler decorative solution, try layering different colours, sizes and even shapes of tablecloth over one another.

home furnishings

Napkins

Small items like napkins have to be the easiest sewing projects in the world. You are only working with simple shapes and with small pieces of fabric. Extra napkins are always useful—and if you make a long version to match it can be used as a runner down the centre of the table. Reversible napkins give you a choice of table colour schemes.

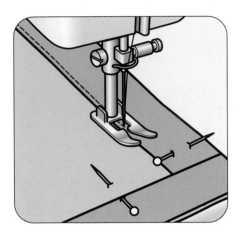

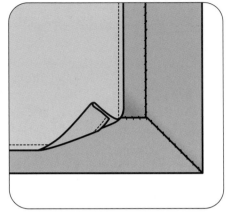

Napkin tips

Napkins are washed every time they are used, so pick a good quality washable fabric.

Don't use fabric that is too shiny or non-absorbent. Keep it simple—no fancy trims or embellishments.

1 ▲ Plain napkin
Cut a square of fabric to the size of the napkin, plus hems on all sides. Fold and pin a narrow double hem all round the square. Stitch the hem, but at the corner stop with the needle down. Lift the presser foot, pivot the fabric, lower the foot, and start stitching again.

2 Both plain and mitred edges are a neat finish for napkins. You can also add a deep border in a matching or contrasting fabric, but in general try to keep things simple as the napkins need to be functional. Instructions for making a mitred napkin are given below.

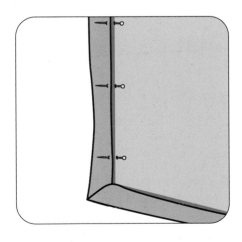

◄ Mitred napkin
Measure, mark, and cut the fabric as for the plain napkin, but allow a 12 mm (½ in) wide strip of extra fabric all round for a deep double hem. Fold one corner diagonally in half through the corner, wrong sides together. With the two raw edges aligned, measure 12 mm (½ in) in from the point along the raw edges and stitch across the corner at a right angle from this mark. Trim off the point near the stitching. Repeat on the other three corners. Turn the mitres you have just made to the right side, easing out each corner into a neat right angle. Fold and press along the napkin edges all around. Turn under a narrow hem along the raw edges, pin in position, and stitch from the right side.

Placemats and runners

On tables with polished surfaces, placemats and a runner are often a more attractive option than a cloth. If you make your own you can make mats and napkins to match or coordinate.

The simplest mat is just two pieces of fabric with or without wadding in the middle, but even this can be of two different fabrics so it is reversible.

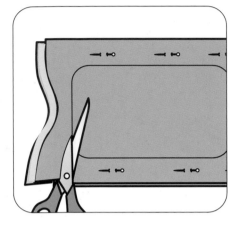

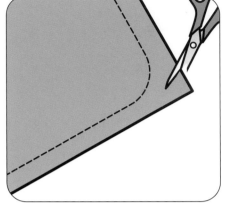

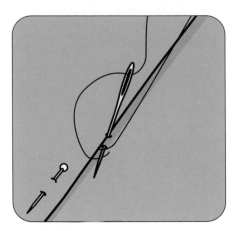

1 ▲ **Reversible placemat or runner**
Cut two pieces of coordinating fabric the same size. With right sides facing, pin together and mark the finished size of the mat on one piece. Trim 15 mm (⅝ in) from the marked line.

2 Stitch along the line you just marked, leaving a gap of around 10 cm (4 in) to turn the mat through. Clip corners and trim seams.

3 Turn the mat right side out through the gap left. Press around the edges, pulling them out completely. Slipstitch the gap closed.

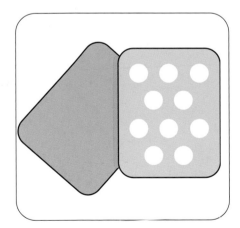

4 Repeat to make as many placemats as you need; extras are always useful! The runner is just a long placemat made to the length required.

Quilting placemats or runners

To add wadding or batting to a reversible placemat or runner, cut a piece a little smaller than the mat and tack to the wrong side of one piece of fabric before pinning the two pieces together in step 1. If the placemat has wadding, you can also quilt a design to add an attractive three-dimensional effect.

Self-bound placemat or runner

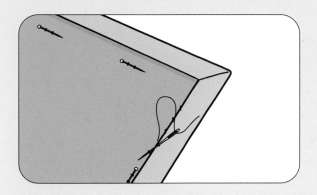

1. Cut fabric for the top and a piece of wadding the size required. Cut the backing 5 cm (2 in) bigger all around. Tack top and batting together, then place the backing behind, right side out. Turn the edge of the backing to the front and pin a hem.

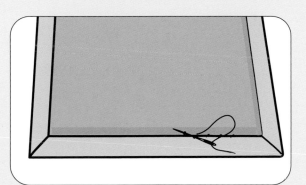

2. Mitre each of the corners and pin in place. Topstitch along all four edges, working close to the edge of the inner fold and removing the pins as you work. The turned edge of the backing piece forms a neat contrast border on the front.

slipcovers

As long as you have basic sewing skills, a reasonable amount of space in which to work, and are methodical and patient, making slipcovers is straightforward and will certainly save you a great deal of money. Slipcovers for sofas and chairs work on exactly the same principle, but if they are a simple shape you may not need a toile, and if there is already a cover you may be able to remove it to use as a template.

Sofa slipcover

Sofas are perhaps the most complicated-looking pieces of furniture in your home, so making a cover may seem a daunting task. However, work in strict order, checking and fitting as you go, and you will achieve a successful result.

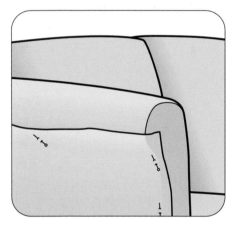

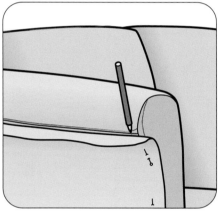

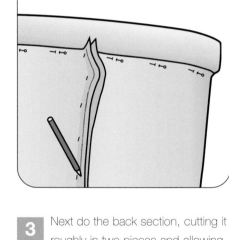

1 ▲ **Making a toile**
Measure the sofa all round, allowing for an opening in the back so the slipcover can fit tightly but be removed easily. Cut one outside arm section roughly from calico (muslin), leaving a good deal of extra around the edges. Using large dressmakers' pins, smooth the cut piece on the outside arm of the sofa and pin around it, positioning it as closely as possible to the surface.

2 Mark the seamline around the pinned piece. The marks do not have to be at all neat, but they must be clear. Cut and pin another piece for the other side.

3 Next do the back section, cutting it roughly in two pieces and allowing for an overlap in the centre. Pin the first half in place, turning back and pinning the central fold. Repeat for the other back piece. Mark seamlines.

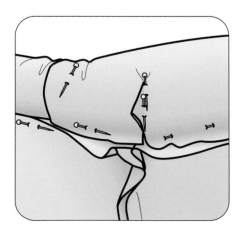

4 Roughly cut one inside arm edge, allowing extra fabric to tuck in and to shape at the corners. Pin in place as before, cutting a dart where necessary to shape around the corner. Work on the join between the corner and outside arm piece until they fit snugly.

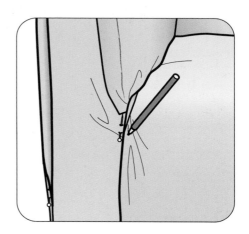

5 Smooth along the inside arm, tucking it into the corner of the back. Mark seamlines clearly, especially the one inside the tuck. Clip into the seam allowance at the top inside corner to ease tension and mark the corner. Repeat steps 4 and 5 on the other arm.

6 Next work on the inside back piece. Pin it in place as for the other sections and smooth and tuck in along the line where it meets the seat. Mark all the seamlines, pushing the pen right into the join and any tight corners.

7 Cut the seat and front skirt as one complete section. Smooth it into position starting from where it meets the back section and moving towards the front. Tuck it into the corners and around the sides.

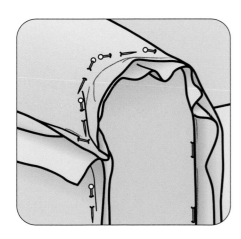

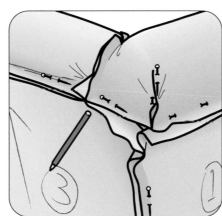

8 Cut the front arm gusset roughly. Pin it to the inside and outside arm sections from the top of the curve working downward. Pin down along the long edges to the inside and outside arm sections and to the skirt. Repeat for the other side.

9 Mark each section with numbers or letters so they can be clearly identified, and draw arrows so you can tell which side is up.

10 Unpin all the sections. Lie them flat and go over all the seamline markings with a ruler, straightening them up.

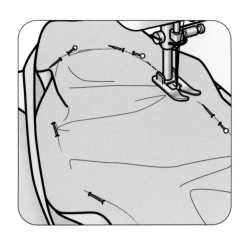

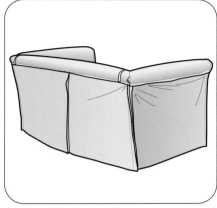

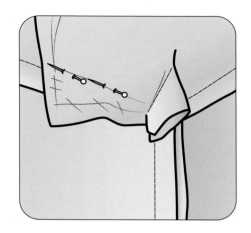

1 ▲ **Checking the fit**
Working in the same order as you did for the pinning and using a very loose machine tack, stitch all the pieces together along the marked seamlines. The stitching must be easy to remove and adjust as required.

2 Put the tacked cover on the sofa, wrong side out. Drape over the arms first, then work over the rest of sofa, smoothing the fabric into place.

3 Check over the cover. Wherever the fit is not perfect, remark the seams drawing dashes through the old marks. Re-pin along the new seamline, then remove the cover and unpick where necessary. Tack again along the new seamline.

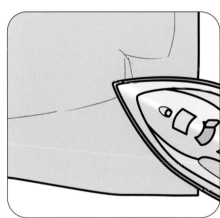

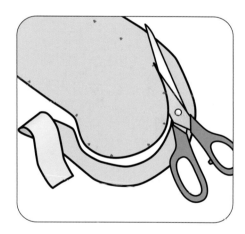

4 Repeat steps 2 and 3 until the cover fits perfectly over the entire sofa. When you are totally satisfied with the fit, draw the hemline in.

5 Remove the cover and make sure all the correct seamlines can be identified and are visible. Unpick all the tacking and press each piece flat with a dry iron.

6 Trim each section carefully along the seamline. When cutting out the final cover, remember to add the seam allowance all around each piece.

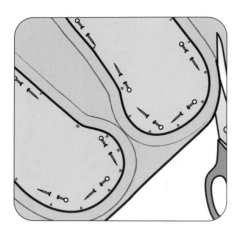

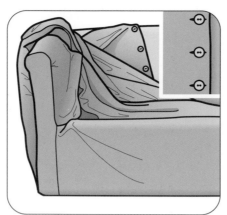

Slipcover tips

The secret to a well-fitting slipcover is to make a toile from inexpensive fabric that can be cut and stitched to alter it until everything looks right. You can then take it apart and use it as a pattern for the main fabric.

Use a hardwearing and washable fabric, as this type of seating will be subject to considerable wear and may need to be washed regularly.

1 ▲ **Finishing the slipcover**
Use the pieces of the toile to cut out all the shapes of the final slipcover. Make sure all the pieces are right side up and that you have allowed for left and right hand sections. Match fabric patterns, if necessary. Mark around each piece, allowing a generous 12 mm (½ in) seam allowance all around. Transfer all identifying marks. Cut out the pieces, then stitch them together in the same order as for the fabric toile.

2 Put the finished cover on the sofa, working from front to back. Check the fit, then mark and handstitch the hem all round the bottom. Add buttons and buttonholes at the centre back seam, or insert a zipper. Replace the cover on the sofa.

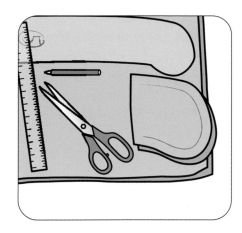

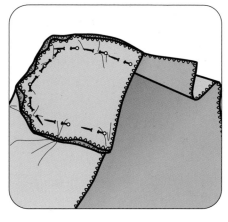

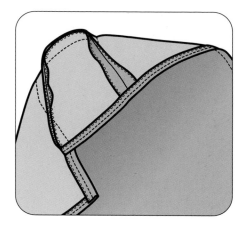

1 ▲ Making arm covers
Cut two rectangles of fabric the size and shape of the inside arm of the sofa. Cut two front arm gusset tops from the fabric, using only the top part of the front arm gusset pattern made previously. Don't forget to add seam allowances all around.

2 Zigzag stitch along the raw edges. Pin and tack one front arm gusset top, right sides together, to one rectangle, beginning from the straight edge of the rectangle. Repeat to make a piece the mirror image of the first for the other side.

3 Turn and pin a narrow hem along all raw edges to neaten them and pin the seam on each short edge. Tack in position if you prefer. Starting at the long front corner, stitch a single hem all round. Turn the corners neatly. Repeat for the other cover. Armcovers will protect the arms of the sofa from the worst wear and spills.

Slipcover facings

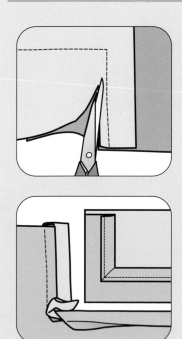

Facings on slipcovers will not only finish the edges, but also carry fastenings securely.

1. Mark the seamline on the main fabric. Cut a piece of facing fabric larger than the area to cut away. Pin and stitch along the seamlines, right sides together. Clip away the excess and clip corners.

2. Turn the facing to the wrong side of the fabric to enclose the raw edges. Pin and topstitch. The stitching appears on the right side, the facing on the wrong side.

home furnishings

care and repair

Many items are so inexpensive to replace these days that it may not seem worth repairing them. However, everyone has a few treasured or expensive items that are worth repairing to extend their life. Here are some simple techniques, plus information on laundry, stain removal, and general care.

repairs

Mending small rips or holes prevents problems from getting worse and helps items have a longer shelf life. With a little care it is often quite possible to make repairs that will hardly show when the item is used.

Holes and tears

Small holes and tears can be repaired with darning or stitching, while larger ones may require a patch of some kind.

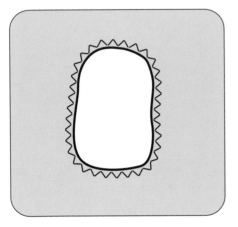
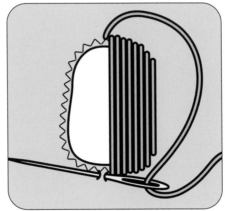
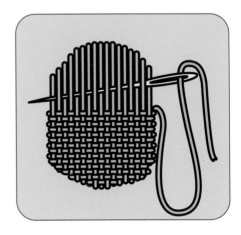

1 ▲ **Darning a hole**
Trim around the hole to remove any loose threads and neaten the edges. Run a narrow line of zigzag stitch around the hole very near the opening to stabilize the edges.

2 Use a thread that matches the colour and weight of the fabric as closely as possible. Work long vertical stitches close together from top to bottom, until you have covered the hole completely.

3 Now work across the hole, weaving the thread up and down through the vertical threads. Keep each row as close as possible to the previous one, and start and end each row with a small stitch through the edge of the hole to secure.

Tips for patching and darning

If you work neatly when darning and use the correct yarn, the darn can be practically invisible.

If you need to patch a ready-made item, you may be able to cut a patch of the same fabric from an inside hem or another inconspicuous place.

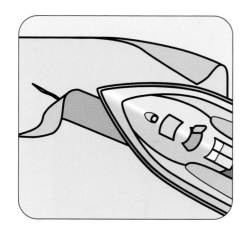

1 ▲ **Repairing a tear**
Cut a strip of iron-on mending tape slightly longer and wider than the tear. Working on the wrong side, press the tape to affix it over the tear, making sure the torn edges are as close together as possible.

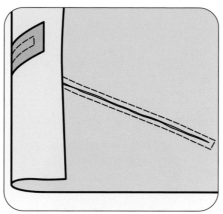

2 On the right side, use matching thread in the machine and run a line of straight stitch along each side of the tear and across each end to hold the mending tape in place. Snip off any loose threads to neaten.

Repair tips

Check over items before you put them away—if they need repair do it straight away before the damage gets worse.

Whenever possible, mend by machine as it is quicker and stronger than hand mending.

If you shorten a garment, keep the fabric you cut off as it may be useful as a patch later.

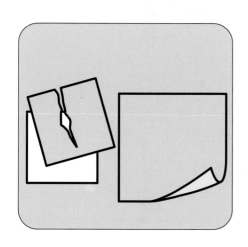

1 ▲ **Patching a hole**
Cut away the edges of the hole to make a neat square or rectangle. Cut another piece of the same fabric around 6 mm (¼ in) larger than the hole. On patterned fabric, make sure the patch matches the pattern exactly.

2 Place the patch right side up under the hole. Stitch around the hole just inside the edge of the patch in matching thread. On the right side, clip halfway towards the stitching at each corner.

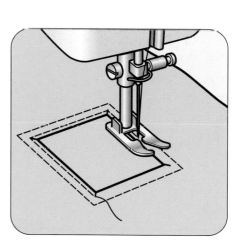

3 Fold the raw edges of the hole under by around 3 mm (⅛ in) on all four sides. Edge stitch along the fold around all sides in matching thread. The finished patch should blend perfectly.

care and repair

Ready-made patches

A wide variety of different ready-made patches can be purchased, either in plain fabric or with a design. Since they are designed to be applied to the right side, they should be regarded as decorative.

▲ **Leather patch**—These are usually oval in shape and may have stitching holes punched around the edge. They can be stitched by hand or machine and are usually used to reinforce elbows and knees on jackets or trousers.

▲ **Iron-on or stitch-on appliqué patch**—Available in a range of fabrics, colours, and designs, these are not only used for repairs but to add a decorative element as well. Remember to follow the manufacturer's instructions.

▲ **Woven patches**—These patches are available in both iron-on backing and stitch-on forms. They can be plain or decorative, and should be applied according to the manufacturer's instructions.

Seams and stitching

A seam or other stitching that has come undone can be repaired in no time at all. Use thread to match the original for a barely-there repair.

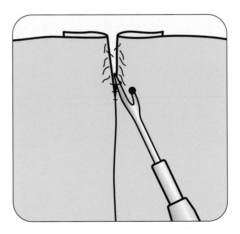

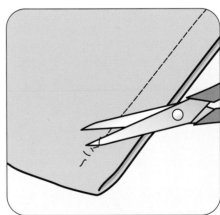

Ripping seams

You may need to undo a few stitches to more easily access the area in need of repair. This can be done with a seam ripper or with small, sharp scissors.

▲ **Seam ripper**—Hold the seam open slightly at one end and use the curved blade of the seam ripper to slice through the stitches.

▲ **Scissors**—Place the item on a flat surface and use the tip of the blades to snip through a couple of stitches on the right side of the fabric. Gently pull out the loose threads.

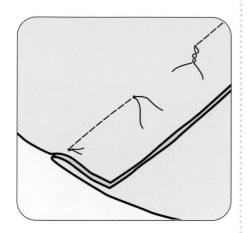

1 ▲ **Repairing a seam**
Working from the wrong side, pull the broken threads through to the wrong side. Tighten the threads so the remaining stitching is pulled back into place, then knot the threads together close to the fabric's surface at each end of the damaged section.

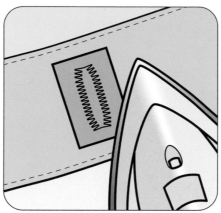

1 ▲ **Repairing buttonholes**
Cut a patch of iron-on mending tape large enough to cover the entire buttonhole area, and iron in position on the wrong side.

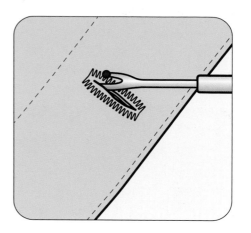

2 Working on the right side, stitch a new buttonhole over the old. Carefully cut through the mending tape with sharp scissors or a seam ripper to open the buttonhole.

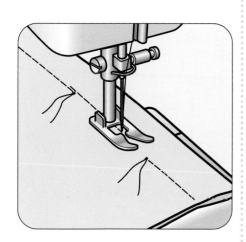

2 Stitch the damaged section of stitching on the machine, matching the thread colour to the original as closely as possible.

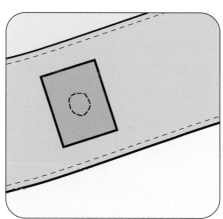

1 ▲ **Repairing button bands**
Cut a patch of iron-on mending tape large enough to cover the entire damaged area, and iron in position on the wrong side.

2 On the right side, stitch the button back in place over the mending tape. The button itself will hide the hole beneath.

care and repair

laundering

Regular cleaning or laundering of items will not only keep them smelling fresh but also prolong their lives. Follow the instructions for laundering on the item or for the type of fabric used. Keep in mind that you have the best chance of stain removal success if you deal with accidents as soon as they happen.

Fabric care symbols

Following the manufacturers' recommendations about the care and laundering of fabrics ensures that you will enjoy them for years to come. This universal pictograph system of care symbols is used as a simple guide in many countries.

Washing

Normal cycle at 60°C (140°F) normal spin

Normal cycle at 40°C (100°F) normal spin

Normal cycle at 30°C (85°F) or gentle cycle, normal rinse, normal spin

Handwash only

Dry clean only

Do not dry clean

Tumble dry at low heat

Tumble dry at high heat

Do not tumble dry

Bleaching

Diluted cold chlorine bleach may be used

Do not use chlorine bleach

Any solvent except Trichlorethlene

Ironing

High cotton/linen 200°C (400°F)

Warm polyester blends/wool 150°C (300°F)

Low synthetics/silks 110°C (200°F)

Do not iron

Stain removal chart

The treatments shown below apply only to washable fabrics. Stains on non-washable and delicate fabrics should be handled by a professional drycleaner. Find the stain in the left hand column, then follow the treatment numbers in ascending order. If one number is repeated, you can select the most convenient method.

Key
- Cold water
- Warm water
- Hot water

STAIN	Soak	Rinse	Wash	Blot	Harden by rubbing with an ice cube	Scrape	Pretreat with appropriate chemical	Bleach (whites only)	Lemon	Salt	Press	
Adhesive and glue	4		4		1	2	3					
Alcohol			1									1 part white wine vinegar to 3 parts water if stain persists
Blood	1						2					
Chewing gum			1		1	2	3					
Chocolate		1					2					
Cosmetics							1					
Eggs							1					Treat basically as grease
Grass							1	2				Use enzyme (biological) washing powder
Grease and oil			2				1					
Ink			2				1					Washing may set the stain
Mildew			2					1	1	1		Mix lemon juice with salt and sun-dry
Milk			1									
Paint: water-based		1	2									
Paint: oil-based			3	1			2					
Perspiration	1		2									Soak affected area in water with a spoonful of borax added
Rust			3						1	2		Mix lemon juice with salt and hold over steaming water
Scorch marks			1						2	2		
Shoe polish						1	2					
Tea and coffee	1						2					
Wax			3	1						2		
Wine and fruit-juice	1		4	2			3			1		

NB: If no temperature symbol is given, follow the washing instructions for the garment

care and repair

glossary

abutted seam – a seam used to join non-woven interfacings. The two edges are butted together over a narrow band of lightweight fabric underlay, and a line of wide zigzag machine stitching down the join holds the two pieces together. A single line of straight stitching can also be added at each side for extra security.

actual measurement/size – the final dimensions of the finished garment given in a pattern, which may vary from the given "to fit" measurement.

anchor – to fix the end of a piece of yarn or thread, or to attach a piece of fabric at one point, so it will not pull away from the main piece. Some stitchers begin sewing with a few small running stitches to anchor the thread; others prefer to knot the end so it will not pull through the fabric.

appliqué – a decorative technique in which a shape or motif is cut from one fabric and applied to another. It is technique often used in quiltmaking but also to decorate garments and household furnishings.

awl – a small, sharp, pointed tool used in sewing to punch holes for eyelets, or to make belt holes in leather. A metal punch may also be used instead.

balance lines – lines marked on paper pattern pieces indicating where the lengthwise and crosswise grains of the fabric should fall at key parts of the figure to ensure a good fit. If the pattern pieces are adjusted to fit individual measurements, the relative positions of the balance lines should be retained if the garment is to fit as it should.

beading – adding beads to the surface of fabric by stitching them in place. In sewing, beads can be threaded onto the needle as they are needed.

bias strip or binding – a strip of fabric cut on a 45° diagonal to the straight grain of a fabric and used to bind edges, particularly curved ones. It stretches easily so should be handled with care.

blend – a yarn or fabric that is a mixture of two materials, such as polyester/cotton. The mix can be in equal amounts, such as 50 percent mohair/50 percent wool, or unequal amounts, such as 50 percent merino wool/33 percent microfibre/12 percent cashmere. The exact composition of a yarn is given on the ball band, while for fabric it is usually given on the end of the bolt.

block – to outline the principal sections of a loose cover for an upholstery project on paper or fabric, before the cover is cut in the final fabric. Pattern pieces of a garment are also sometimes blocked before cutting from patterned fabric to ensure that the design will match across the seams perfectly.

bolt – an amount of fabric wound onto a round tube or a flattened oval cardboard form. The fabric is usually folded lengthwise with the right sides together. The amount in a bolt depends on the type of fabric and the manufacturer. Wholesale fabric stores often sell fabric by the bolt, rather than by cut length.

boning – narrow strips of plastic or metal inserted into a casing of fabric and used to stiffen sections of a closely fitted garment to prevent slipping or rolling—the bodice of a strapless dress, for instance. The name comes from the fact that the strips were originally made of whalebone.

butting – bringing two edges together so they touch but do not overlap.

canopy – fabric draped or hung over a frame attached to the head of a four-poster bed, or a decorative fabric treatment above a headboard.

casing – a hem or tuck through which ribbon, tape, or elastic can be threaded, or the opening across the top of a curtain through which a curtain rod can be threaded.

catch – to attach one piece of fabric to another, generally with a few tiny backstitches made by hand. For instance, a facing could be attached to a seam allowance.

centre line – a vertical line marking the centre of a pattern piece. It is marked on the relevant pieces—usually only the back and the front—and should be transferred to the fabric with an erasable marker, tailor's chalk, or a couple of tailor's tacks.

clip – to cut a short distance into a seam allowance or selvedge with the point of the scissors. It is used in areas such as curved seams and square corners to remove excess fabric, allowing the seams to lie flat when pressed.

colourway – the range or combination of colours that a style or design is available in.

composition – the percentage of each material that a yarn or fabric is made from. With yarn and thread this is given on the band or wrapper, while with fabric it is generally on the end of the bolt. It is important to know the composition so that you care for the finished item properly when it needs cleaning or pressing.

conditioner – a substance to run the thread through before sewing to make it easier to pull through the fabric and less likely to tangle or knot. Traditionally beeswax or paraffin wax was used, but now many needlecrafters use Thread Heaven®, which is specifically designed for this purpose.

count – the number of warp and weft threads in an inch of fabric. It is used to indicate the fineness or coarseness of a fabric.

cutting guide/layout – diagram given in a paper pattern that shows you how to lay out the pattern pieces on different widths of fabric. It also indicates—usually by shading—which pieces, if any, need to be placed printed side down on the fabric for cutting. Some pieces may need to be placed with one edge to a fold and this will also be indicated on the layout as well as on the paper pattern.

cutting line –the outermost solid line on a paper pattern, which indicates where you cut the piece out. Some people cut through the centre of this line, others cut just to the outside of it. It doesn't really matter which you choose as long as it is consistent.

dart – used to mould the fabric of a garment to the curves of the body. They can be straight for a loose fit or curved for a tighter fit, and they usually start at the seam line and taper to nothing at the tip. Double-pointed darts are used on dresses, jackets, and fitted shirts; they are a diamond shape with the widest point at the waist tapering to a point at the bust or shoulder blade and hips. They should be sewn as two darts back to back, working from the centre to the point on each one.

drape – a fabric's ability to fall into folds; if it falls gracefully it is said to drape well or have good drape.

directional stitching – stitching the seams in the correct direction of the grain so the fabric will not stretch as it is being sewn.

distressing – creating decorative textural effects in fabric by fraying the edges, melting areas of synthetic fabric, or pulling the weave apart.

dress form/shape – a sized or adjustable body shape on a stand that is used to fit garments during construction. It may be made from many materials, but it should have a surface that will accept pins.

ease allowance – the amount added to body measurements to make garments comfortable and to allow for movement.

edge stitching – to stitch close to a finished edge, seam, or fold, either as a decorative feature or to stop a piece of fabric, such as a facing, rolling round to the front.

eyelet – small round hole in fabric created with an awl or a punch that may be hand stitched or lined with a metal ring that grips the fabric on the reverse. Hand-stitched eyelets are edged with overcast stitching or blanket stitch to stop the edges fraying. Eyelets are used for decorative effect, for lacing and in belts.

facing – a shaped piece of fabric stitched onto the seam line of the main garment piece and turned inside to cover the raw edges and create a finished edge.

feed dogs – the "teeth" under the plate on the sewing machine that move the fabric along as it is stitched.

fly front zipper – a type of zipper application traditionally used on men's wear but now often used in women's attire. One half of the opening is stitched close to the zipper teeth; the other half is a flap that overlaps the opening and typically is stitched in a parallel line to the opening, curving round under the zipper at the end.

frill – a gathered or pleated border also known as a ruffle.

fusible interfacing – a non-woven fabric with a heat-activated glue on one side that can be ironed on, usually permanently. It is used to stiffen fabrics.

gathering – a method of controlling fullness by running a double line of large stitches through a fabric, fastening the threads at one end, and pulling on the other end to reduce the fabric to a smaller length.

gimp – narrow, flat braid or rounded cord of fabric used for trimming.

grain – the direction of the threads making up a woven fabric. Each piece has two: lengthwise (warp) and widthwise or crosswise (weft).

gusset – small, shaped piece of fabric set into a slash or a seam for added width and ease. In garments it may be found at the underarm, when sleeves and bodice are cut in one piece, or in the crotch of briefs or knickers.

hook & loop tape – a type of fastening that comes in two parts; one half has tiny loops and the other tiny hooks so when pressed together they cling to each other. It is often used in children's clothing and shoes, and for items that need to be unfastened quickly. In the UK and the US it is known as Velcro®.

interfacing – this is an extra layer of fabric to provide support and shape in some areas of a garment such as collars, waistband, and opening edges. Interfacing is usually a non-woven fabric and can either be sewn in or fused to the back of the main fabric. Fusible interfacing is quicker and easier to use, but is not suitable

for sheer or very heavily textured fabrics, or for those requiring a cool iron. If you choose to use fusible interfacing, follow the manufacturer's instructions carefully for the best result.

interlining – a fabric placed between the lining and the main fabric. It is used in heavyweight garments, such as coats, to give added warmth or bulk.

knit fabric or jersey – this type of fabric is made up of interlocking loops of yarn, rather than woven threads, giving it the ability to stretch in any direction. It is a good choice for fitted garments.

lap/overlap – to extend or fold one piece of fabric or a garment section over another.

lapel – the section of a coat, jacket, or blouse that is turned back between the top button and the collar.

lengthwise fold – a fold down the length of a piece of fabric. Fabric on a bolt is generally folded lengthwise with the right sides together.

mercerized – a finish for cotton that adds strength and lustre, and makes the fibres more receptive to dyes.

metal or metallic thread/yarn – thread or yarn made of pure metal, this term is at times also applied to synthetic threads with the appearance of metal. Metallic-effect thread/yarn is a synthetic thread or yarn with the appearance of metal. Metallized thread/yarn is made with a thin layer of real metal over a nylon or polyester core for strength and flexibility.

mitre – a diagonal join between two strips of fabric meeting at a square corner.

mounting - Layer of fabric used to support a garment and stitched directly into the seams.

nap – the projecting threads on fabric such as velvet, cord, or faux fur that create a "furry" surface that looks lighter or darker depending on which way the thread ends lie. When making garments in fabric with a nap, the pattern pieces must be carefully laid out so the nap will run in the same direction when the garment is worn. Always stitch in the direction of the nap.

neaten – to finish off by pulling loose threads to the wrong side and tying or stitching them in before cutting off. Seam edges can be neatened and prevented from fraying by binding, pinking, or zigzag stitching.

notches – V-shaped marks on the cutting line of a pattern indicating matching points on a seam. Notches on separate pattern pieces are matched up when seamed together. Notches should be marked when cutting out, usually by cutting round them so they protrude. Some people cut them in, out of the seam allowance instead—but this is not a good idea, particularly if the fabric is liable to fray.

notions – small sewing items, such as thread, needles, pins, zips, buttons, and bias binding. Also known as haberdashery.

one-way designs—designs based on motifs with a distinct top and bottom. They run in only one direction and look different if the fabric is turned upside down. When laying out pattern pieces on one-way fabric, use the layout for napped fabric to be sure that the design will run the same way visually on the finished garment.

openweave – fabric that is loosely woven, creating gaps between the threads. An extreme example would be netting, but linen and aida are also openweaves.

overlap/overwrap – the part of a garment or other item that extends over another.

pattern repeat – most patterns are made up of one or more components that repeat along the length and/or width. The length of a pattern repeat is determined by measuring from a set point on a motif to the matching point on the next. In a half drop repeat, alternate rows of motifs are repeated half a repeat down, creating secondary diagonals. In a full drop repeat, the rows are all repeated with the motifs in line both down and across.

pile – raised threads or loops on the surface of a fabric. Pile may also have a nap.

pintuck – a narrow, stitched tuck in fabric. Several are often made in close parallel rows to give a decorative look to a garment. Some blouses are made with pintucking on the bodice for a more tailored look.

pivot – to lift the presser foot and turn the fabric on the machine needle without lifting the needle from the fabric. Used when stitching square corners.

placket – a finished overlapping opening, often leading to a pocket, a concealed zip or other fastener, or in the sleeve at the cuff. The term also covers the flap of fabric often found behind such an opening.

pleat – even folds in fabric to add fullness, usually at the hem and often partly stitched down just below the waist. The different types used in dressmaking are: accordion, fine and narrow, usually made by machine; box, two knife pleats that turn away from each other; Dior or kick, short pleat at the hemline of a skirt with a layer of fabric under the opening; inverted, two knife pleats that turn towards each other; knife, series of pleats of the same width and in the same direction; release, partly stitched at the top or bottom of a lining to give ease of movement; sunray, wider at the bottom than at the top, usually machine made.

preshrunk fabric – fabric that has been shrunk before cutting so its dimensions will not decrease further when laundered or dry cleaned. Many fabrics are preshrunk by the manufacturer.

presser foot – part of the sewing machine that holds the fabric in place against the feed dogs as it is being stitched.

raw edge – a cut edge of fabric that has not been finished off in any way.

reinforcing – strengthening an area that will be subjected to strain by making extra rows of stitching or adding an underlay or patch of fabric.

revers – turned back fabric creating shaped lapels on a jacket, coat, or blouse. They can be wide or narrow.

rickrack – a decorative, zigzag-shaped braid. If it is applied at the edge it creates an attractive scalloped border.

right side – the right side is the side that will be seen when the garment is worn. In printed fabrics the pattern will be clearer and brighter on the right side, but the difference is not always so obvious. The term is usually abbreviated as RS.

rouleau – a narrow tube of fabric stitched into the edge seam of a garment as a loop. It fastens over a button to close an opening.

running under – a method of securing the end of a thread before stitching by running the needle under a few threads of the fabric on the wrong side before bringing it through to the front surface.

seam allowance – amount of fabric allowed for seams when joining two pieces of fabric together. Paper patterns usually have a seam allowance of 15mm (⅝ in) between the cutting line and the seamline.

seed beads – tiny round beads, available in both glass and plastic and in a wide range of colours and sizes. They are usually sold by weight and used for jewellery and stitched beading

selvedge – this is the finished edge along either side of the length of fabric. These edges will not fray, but it is usually better to avoid incorporating them into a garment as they are more tightly woven and can pucker when the fabric is laundered.

shank – the stem between the back of a button and the surface of the fabric. It can be part of the button or made of thread when the button is stitched on. The shank allows room for the layers of fabric on the buttonhole side when the button is done up.

shawl collar – a long, sweeping collar that folds right down the front of a garment, with one side overlapping the other.

sheer – fabric that is semi-transparent. Sheers is also a general term used in the UK for semi-transparent curtains, known as voiles in the US.

shirring – gathering with three or more parallel rows of stitching to control fullness. Shirring elastic can be put on the bobbin of a sewing machine to gather large areas of fabric, allowing it to fit closely around the body.

sizing – a finish applied to fabric to add body and stiffness. It can be removed by laundering.

sloper – a basic pattern from which other designs can be developed. It has no style of its own, but is fitted—with a minimum ease allowance—and can be used to figure out where standard patterns need to be adjusted for fit.

slub – an uneven thread or yarn with thick and thin sections, either accidentally or by design. When woven the fabric will have random nubs running throughout the weave. With some fabrics, such as slubbed silk, this is an essential character of the fabric.

snaps – a small round fastening, one side of which has a little knob and the other a sprung hole. Snaps are usually of metal, but can also be plastic. In the UK they are called press studs or poppers.

straight of grain – threads running lengthwise, or parallel, to the selvedges, are on the straight of grain. Threads running widthwise, or from selvedge to selvedge, are on the cross grain.

swatch – a small piece of fabric used as a colour sample.

tacking – a technique to temporarily hold layers of fabric together for fitting or to stop them slipping as seams are stitched. The US term is basting.

tuck – stitched fold of fabric, either as a decorative feature or to hold extra fabric in place until it is needed. For example, to allow for a garment to be lengthened as a child grows. See also pintuck.

underlap/underwrap – edge of a garment that extends under another edge. See also overlap/overwrap.

underlining – a lining used to add body to a garment without concealing and finishing seams.

vent – a lapped opening, usually in the hem at the back of a tailored jacket but sometimes in other areas of the garment.

wrong side – the side of a fabric that will not be seen when the garment is worn. In printed fabrics the pattern will be fainter and duller on the wrong side, but the difference is not always so obvious. The term is usually abbreviated as WS.

yoke – part of a garment that fits over the shoulders. It may be a separate piece of fabric to which the main part of the garment is attached, often in gathers or pleats.

about the author

Marie Clayton has been sewing since she was a child. After a course in dressmaking and fabric technology, she worked as a designer and eventually became an editor and writer for various craft books. She has authored *The Needlecrafter's Companion* and *Make Your Own Clothes*.

Ultimate Sewing Bible is a comprehensive sewing reference for beginner and seasoned sewing enthusiasts. Certain challenges are often faced when learning to sew. As a novice, you must acquire a basic understanding and the necessary tools and equipment to embark on the journey. As an expert, you become aware of the principles behind each technique and your boundaries are limited only by your imagination.

Each chapter brims with essential techniques which are accompanied by clear and concise instructions and easy-to-follow step-by-step illustrations. From basic techniques to advanced tailoring to care and repair, this indispensable reference is chock-full of information needed for sewers of all skill levels.

This comprehensive guide is jam-packed with easy-to-follow techniques and over 1000 illustrations to guide sewing enthusiasts through every aspect of the craft. It'll be the one-stop resource that you turn to time and time again.

suppliers

canada

Fabricland
www.fabricland.ca

Michaels
www.michaels.com

united states

Jo-Ann
www.joann.com

M&J Trimming
www.mjtrim.com

Michaels
www.michaels.com

united kingdom

HobbyCraft
www.hobbycraft.co.uk

John Lewis
www.johnlewis.com

acknowledgements

With special thanks to Maggi McCormick-Gordon, some of whose work formed the starting point for this book. I would like to thank everyone at Collins & Brown for commissioning this book and for their constant support, particularly Michelle Lo and Katie Hudson. Thanks to Kuo Kang Chen and Barking Dog Art for the excellent illustrations and to Louise Leffler for the stylish design. And finally, with love to William and Emily without whom this book would have been written a lot faster.

index

abutted seams 247
accent colours and fabrics 141, 143, 199
adjustment line, in patterns 60
altering patterns 65–8
appliqué 147, 203, 242, 247
appliqué foot 18
arrowhead tacks 35
Austrian blinds 190
awls 247

backstitch 27, 37
balance lines 247
bar tacks 34
base fabrics 142
basting 13, 27, 38
bay windows 152, 163
beads and beading 33, 247, 251
bed linen 157, 219–21
belt loops 85, 86–7
bias, working on the 20, 83, 104, 127, 128, 158, 159
bias binding 42, 44–5, 101, 227, 247
blanket stitch 29
blind hemming 28, 100
blinds 151–3, 163, 189–97
block 247
bobbins 16
bobbles 227
bodices 65, 66–7, 126
bodkins 13
body measurements 58–9
body shapes 64
bolster cushions 154, 212
boning 126, 247
borders 44, 46–8, 213, 214, 227
bows 132–3
box cushions 154, 210–11
box pleats 75
    box-pleat headings 167, 170
    box-pleated valance 185
braids 146, 227
burlap see hessian
butting 248
button bands 243
buttonhole foot 18

buttonhole stitch 29
buttonholes 108, 110–15, 243
buttons 32, 108, 111–12, 130, 147, 203, 207

café curtains 173, 179–81
calico 142, 232
canopies 248
canvas 140
care and repair 238–43
casings 87–8, 167, 168, 191, 248
catch, attaching fabrics 248
centre line, of patterns 60, 248
chain stitch 29
chain-stitch thread 37
chairs: cushions 155, 209
    slipcovers 155
chalk 10, 63
checked fabric 61, 74, 138, 143, 144
chenille 141
chiffon 56, 99
chintz 144
circles, cutting 160
clamps 15
clipped seams 43, 51, 248
closures 69, 108–15
collars 69, 76–8, 121–2, 251
colours: colourfastness of trims 133, 222
    colourway 248
    home furnishings 137, 138, 143, 147, 177
conditioner, for thread 248
cording 49, 207
cording blinds 190–1
corduroy 140
corners: clipping 43
    mitred 225, 228
    stitching 40
cotton fabric 54, 128, 140, 143, 144, 145, 177
couching stitch 36
count, fabric 248
crewelwork 141
cross stitch 29

crotch depth, increasing 68
crow's foot tacks 35
cuffs 69, 81–4, 95
curtain tracts 148
curtains 36–7, 142, 145, 162–88
    café curtains 179–81
    curtain supports and supplies 167–8
    headings 167–73, 180, 183
    lining and interlining 174–8
    measuring for 148–52
curves: clipping 43
    curved borders 46
    curved hems 96
    cutting 160
    sewing 38, 63, 71
cushions 154, 198–212
cutting equipment 12
cutting fabric 15, 62
cutting guide/layout 248
cutting lines 60, 248
cutting mats 12

damask 141, 145
darning 240
darning foot 18
darts 60, 69, 73, 248
decorative stitches 29–31
denim 55
differential feed 19
Dior bow 133
directional stitching 248
distressing 248
doors, French 151, 162
double topstitched seam 39
drape 248
dress forms 15, 248
dressmaker's carbon 10
dressmaker's chalk 10
dressmaker's shears 12
dressmaking 52–115, 116–33
drop, of curtains 149, 150, 189
dupion 56, 141
duvet covers 218

ease allowance 248
easing curves 71
edges 38
    finishing off 44–50, 248, 249, 250
    straightening fabric edges 160
elastic waistbands 85, 87–8
embellishments 32–3, 130–3, 146–7, 187
    bed linen 214
    cushions 203, 207–8
embroidery 29–35, 147
embroidery foot 18
embroidery scissors 12
equipment 10–19
evening wear 126–33
eyelets 167, 248
    eyelet blinds 152

fabric 20–3
    buying tips 21
    curtains and blinds 149, 150, 189
    cutting 15, 62, 158–61
    double-sided fabric 144
    dressing furniture 153
    dressmaking 54–7, 128
    fabric care symbols 244
    flaws 160
    home furnishings 138–45
    knitted 20, 21, 39, 40, 55, 249
    laundering 55, 142, 244–5
    marking up 10
    mounting and lining fabric 119
    non-woven fabric 21
    patterned 23, 61, 138–9, 143–5, 224
    pre-shrinking 159, 250
    pressing 14, 51, 59, 73
    printed 138, 139, 144, 145
    storage 16
    widths 21
    woven fabric 20
facings 69, 249

collars and necklines 70–2, 122, 127, 128
  hems 100
  slipcover 237
fasteners 69, 108–15
feather stitch 30
feed dogs 18, 249
felt 21
finials 166
flat fell seams 39, 41
flat seam 39
fleece fabric 55
flexible curves 11
floral patterns 61
fly-front zippers 108–9, 249
foldline 60
fraying, prevention of 28, 71, 79, 161
French doors 151, 162
French knots 30
French pleats 167, 171–2
French seams 41, 215
frills 50, 249
fringes 146, 208, 227
fur fabric 57
furnishings 134–237
furniture 136–7, 153–7
fusible interfacing 249

gabardine fabric 55
gathering 249, 251
  gathered headings 167, 168
  gathered valances 186
gathering stitch 38
gimp braid 146, 249
goblet pleats 167, 172
grain, of fabric 20, 158, 159, 249
grain line 60
gusset 249

haberdashery 250
hand-stitching 13, 26–37
  hems 95
headboard covers 157
headings, curtain 167–73, 179, 180, 183
heart-shaped cushion covers 205
hemming foot 18, 100, 103
hems 27–8, 69, 94–104, 106

hand-sewn 95
  jacket hems 125
  pressing 51
herringbone stitch 27, 30
herringbone weave 143
hessian 140, 143
holdbacks 187, 188
holes, repairing 240–2
home furnishings 134–237
  bed linen 157, 213–21
  blinds 189–97
  chairs and sofas 154–5
  curtains and blinds 148–52, 162–88
  cushions and pillows 198–212
  fabrics 138–45, 158–61
  furniture 153–7
  slipcovers 232–7
  styles 136–47
  table linens 156, 222–31
  trims and embellishments 146–7
hook and bar fasteners 115
hook and eye fasteners 115
hook and loop tape (Velcro®) 115, 249
hooks: curtain hooks 166, 169, 173
  headings 167, 173
housewife pillowcase 217

interfacing 21, 69, 118, 119, 249
  collars 121
  one-piece facings 70
  separate facing 71
  V-neckline facing 71–2
interlining 174–8, 249
intersecting seams 40
inverted pleat blinds 190
ironing boards 14
irons 14

jackets 105–6, 118–25
jersey knit fabric 55, 249

kick pleats 106
knife pleats 75
knitted fabric 20, 21, 39, 40, 55, 249
knotting 26

lace 21, 214, 224–5
lamé fabric 57
lap 249
lapels 119, 249
lapped seams 40
laundering 55, 133, 244–5
  bed linen 219
  home furnishings 142
  table linen 222, 228
lazy daisy stitch 29
lengthwise fold 249
lighting 16, 17
linen fabric 54, 140, 143, 145
linings 69, 142
  curtains 174–8
  jackets 105–6, 118–20
  skirts 105
  waistcoats 107
locking-in stitch 36
loops, handsewn 34
Lurex® 57

machine stitching 37–41
  hems 98–104
Mandarin collars 78
marker pens 10, 63
marking equipment 10
marking from patterns 63
measurements: actual measurements 247
  blinds 151–3, 189, 190
  body measurements 58–9
  curtains 148–52, 183
  furniture 153–7
measuring equipment 11
mending tape 243
mercerized, cotton 249
metallic threads 249
mirrors 15, 33
mitres: mitred binding 47–8
  mitred corners 225, 228, 249
  mitred hems 98
moleskin 141
motifs 139
mounting, fabric 118–20, 249
mounting boards 197

nap, of fabric 14, 23, 61, 140, 249

napkins 228–9
necklines 70–2, 128–9
needle threaders 13
needles 13, 17, 19, 26, 39
net 21
neutral colours 143
non-woven fabric 21
notches 60, 62, 250
notions 250

one-way designs 250
openweave fabric 250
organza 56, 120
overcasting 28
overlap 249, 250
overlockers 19, 40
oversewing 28
overstitching 28

padded plaits 188
panel blinds 190
patch pockets 69, 88–9, 90, 94
patching 240–2
pattern repeats 23, 138, 153, 160, 250
patterned fabrics 60, 61, 138–9, 143–5, 161, 224
patterns, paper 58–68, 72
  altering 65–8
pelmets 150, 184–6
pencil pleat headings 167, 169
pens, marker 10, 63
pile, of fabric 23, 61, 140, 250
pillowcases 214, 215–17
pillows 198–212
pincushions 13
pinking shears 12
pinning patterns 62
pins 13, 56
pintuck foot 18
pintucks 250
piping 18, 49, 127, 202
  bed linen 214
  cushions 210–11
placemats 230–1
plackets 69, 82–4, 250
plaid 61, 144
pleats 35, 69, 74, 79, 250
  box pleats 75, 167, 170, 185
  curtain headings 169–72

French pleats 167, 171–2

goblet pleats 167, 172

headings 167

inverted pleat blinds 190

kick pleats 106

knife pleats 75

pencil pleat headings 167, 169

pockets 35, 69, 88–94

points, turning out 77

popper snaps 115, 251

preshrunk fabric 250

press studs 251

presser blocks 15

presser foot 18, 250

pressing 14, 51, 73

pull cords 196

quilter's rule 12

quilting foot 18

quilting placemats 230

raglan sleeves 80–1

raw edges 19, 38, 39, 41, 250

reinforcing fabric 250

repairing items 238–43

revers 250

rickrack 250

right side of fabric 250

rings, curtain 166

roller blinds 153, 190, 192–3

Roman blinds 152, 190, 191, 194–7

rope trims 146

roses, ribbon 130

rotary cutters 12

rouleau 250

ruffed cuffs 81–2

ruffles 48, 50, 128–9, 209, 216, 249

runners, table 230–1

running under, thread 250

sample boards 137

sateen 142

satin fabric 56

satin stitch 31, 227

scalloped headings 179, 180

scissors 12, 43, 242

seam allowances 10, 42, 62, 127, 251

seam gauge, adjustable 11

seam rippers 12, 242

seams 37, 39–43, 242–3, 247

French seams 215

pressing 51

seam finishes 42

shoulder seams 120, 122

seed beads 251

seersucker fabric 54

selvedges 20, 149, 251

sequins 32, 57, 130

sergers 19

set squares 11

sewing machines 17–18

see also machine stitching

shanks, button 32, 111, 251

shawl collar 251

sheer fabric 183, 251

sheets 213–14

shirring 251

shirt collars 77

shoulder seams 120, 122

silk 56, 120, 128, 141, 145

single topstitched seam 39

sizing, fabric finish 251

skirts 65, 68, 105, 106, 127

slant hemming 28

sleeveboards 14

sleeves 65, 68, 69, 79–81, 123–4

slipcovers 155, 232–7

slipstitch 27, 106

slipstitch hemming 28

sloper pattern 251

slub 251

snaps 115, 251

sofas 154, 155, 232–7

square cushions 204–5

stabbing stitch 36

stain removal 245

staystitching 38

stem stitch 31

stitches and stitching 26–38

satin stitch 227

slipstitch 106

stitch length 19, 37, 38, 127

stitching silk 56

straight stitch 37

topstitching 96, 99

storage 16

straight of grain 251

straight stitch 37

striped fabric 61, 74, 128, 138, 139, 145

styles, home furnishings 136–47

supports, curtains 149, 165, 166

swags 186

swatches 251

symbols: fabric care 244

pattern 60

T-squares 11

tabbed headings 180, 183

table linen 222–31

napkins 228

placemats and runners 230–1

tablecloths 156, 222–7

tables 15, 156

tacking 13, 27, 38, 96, 251

tacks: handsewn tacks 34–5

tailor's tacks 28, 63

taffeta 145

tailoring 116–33

tailor's chalk 63

tailor's ham 14

tailor's tacks 28, 63

tape measures 11, 148

tapes, heading 167

tapestry 144

tapestry inserts 208

tassels 146, 203

tears, repairing 240–2

templates: curtains 179, 187

making 203, 206, 209

textured fabrics 140–1, 143

thermal lining 142

thimbles 13

thread conditioner 248

thread loop 34

threads 13, 16

anchoring 247, 250

contrasting colour 27, 29

finishing off 28

matching with fabric 21, 55

metallic 249

sergers 19

tension 18

threading a needle 26

tips 26

throws 144, 154

ticking 142

ties: curtain tiebacks 149, 187–8

cushions 205, 209

tied curtain headings 180

toiles 72, 155, 232, 236

topstitching 76, 96, 99

topstitched seams 39

tracing wheel 10, 63

tracks, curtain 165, 169

triangle headings 180

trims 146–7, 214, 222, 227

trousers 65

tube lining 177

tucks 69, 74, 251

tufts 147

tweed 55

underlap/underwrap 251

underlining 251

valances 150

bed linen 157, 219–21

curtains and blinds 184–6, 196

Velcro® 115, 249

velvet 140, 141, 145, 161

vents 251

voile 56, 120, 143

waistbands 69, 85–8

waistcoats, lining 107

widths, curtain 189

windows, dressing 148–53, 162–97

wool fabric 55, 128, 144

working practice 16

woven fabric 20, 161

wrong side of fabric 251

yardstick 11

yoke 251

zigzag stitch 38, 40

zipper foot 18

zippers 108–10, 199–201, 211, 249

photo credits

Camera Press/Avantages/Fair Lady 182;
MCI/T.Dhellemmes/C.Vannier/C.Soulayrol 217;
Picture Press 201, 223, 246; Schoner Wohnen 198, 226, 229;
/VISI 22, 181, 220; Woman's Value 137

Getty Images/Dorling Kindersley 195; Dorling Kindersley/Andy
Crawford, Steve Gorton 52; Image Source Pink 2; Neo
Vision/Shinya Sasaki 4; Stockbyte 7, 159

istockphoto
210, 212, 231, 235, 236
Michael Wicks
2, 4, 5, 8, 10-14, 19-21, 23, 24, 33, 50, 54-57, 61, 63, 64, 72,
78, 101, 102, 111, 114, 125, 131, 132, 134, 138-140, 142,
143, 144-147,161, 165, 166, 173, 178, 193, 238

| PAVILION |

Whatever the craft, we have the book for you – just
head straight to Pavilion's crafty headquarters.

Pavilioncraft.co.uk is the one-stop destination for all our
fabulous craft books. Sign up for our regular newsletters
and follow us on social media to receive updates on
new books, competitions and interviews with our
bestselling authors.

We look forward to meeting you!

www.pavilioncraft.co.uk

Also in this series:

978-1-91023-177-7

978-1-84340-563-4

978-1-84340-450-7

978-1-84340-672-3

978-1-90939-718-7

978-1-90844-901-6

978-1-84340-574-0

978-1-90939-797-2

978-1-90939-798-9

Published in the United Kingdom in 2016 by
Collins & Brown
1 Gower Street
London
WC1E 6HD

An imprint of Pavilion Books Company Ltd

Copyright © Collins & Brown 2008
Text copyright © Marie Clayton

Distributed in the United States and Canada by Sterling Publishing Co., Inc.
1166 Avenue of the Americas, New York, NY 10036

The moral right of the author has been asserted.

ISBN 9781910231760

A CIP catalogue for this book is available from the British Library.

10 9 8 7 6 5 4 3 2 1

Reproduction by Rival Colour Ltd
Printed in Singapore

This book can be ordered direct from the publisher at www.pavilionbooks.com